MW00628377

Greece & Rome

NEW SURVEYS IN THE CLASSICS No. 46

GREEK RELIGION
Second Edition

BY
JAN N. BREMMER

Published for the Classical Association
CAMBRIDGE UNIVERSITY PRESS
2021

Shaftesbury Road, Cambridge CB2 8EA, United Kingdom

One Liberty Plaza, 20th Floor, New York, NY 10006, USA

477 Williamstown Road, Port Melbourne, VIC 3207, Australia

314–321, 3rd Floor, Plot 3, Splendor Forum, Jasola District Centre, New Delhi – 110025, India

103 Penang Road, #05–06/07, Visioncrest Commercial, Singapore 238467

Cambridge University Press is part of Cambridge University Press & Assessment, a department of the University of Cambridge.

We share the University's mission to contribute to society through the pursuit of education, learning and research at the highest international levels of excellence.

www.cambridge.org
Information on this title: www.cambridge.org/9781009048798

A catalogue record for this publication is available from the British Library

ISBN   978-1-009-04879-8   Paperback

In Memory Of

MARIUS DANIËL BREMMER
(1933–1992)

CONTENTS

PREFACE TO THE FIRST EDITION

Students of Greek religion are fortunate in having at their disposal the best recent study of a 'dead' religion: Walter Burkert's *Greek Religion* (Oxford: Blackwell, 1985). Since the English edition is not essentially different from the German original of 1977, my survey will concentrate on developments since approximately that date. Although Burkert's handbook will be quoted only incidentally, its influence is pervasive, and is always to be presupposed. In the survey I shall offer a synthesis of new insights, join in some important debates, and offer various extended analyses as possible methodological models.

In the notes I quote only the most recent literature. Many of these studies are not the work of Anglo-Saxon scholars: the most important modern contributions have come from Switzerland and France; in third position, *ex aequo*, England and the Netherlands; the United States enters as fourth, with Italy as a potential runner-up. To quote only English publications would thus give a completely wrong impression.

Although it has not always been explicitly mentioned in this context, every country has its own culture which naturally influences the image of Greek religion that it produces. These images may range from a more romantic approach (the Germans), via a more philosophical (the French), to a more common-sensical (the English). The present survey, written by a Dutchman, is deliberately eclectic, but other students of Greek religion will surely unmask this pretension.

The turmoil of Dutch universities at this present time does not offer very favourable conditions for research, and I would not have succeeded in finishing this survey in time without the help of family and friends. Annemiek Boonstra energetically assisted me in a number of ways. My wife Christine and Matthijs den Besten helpfully commented on the first version. Professor Herman Brijder, Director of the Allard Pierson Museum (Amsterdam), kindly advised me in the choice of pictures and generously put the photographs at my disposal. Finally, Ian McAuslan was patient to a fault and skilfully edited the text at the last possible moment. I am, however, indebted most to Barbara Boudewijnse and André Lardinois, who, from their respective anthropological and classical expertise, weeded out mistakes and forced me to clarify or rethink numerous points. If this survey in some ways contributes to a better understanding of Greek religion, it is largely due to their careful reading and stimulating discussions.

I have always enjoyed oral and written exchanges of opinion on Greek religion with friends and colleagues, old and new. It is therefore appropriate to thank Claude Bérard, W. Burkert, Richard Buxton, Claude Calame, Susan Cole, Ken Dowden (who kindly corrected the penultimate version of the first and last chapters), Chris Faraone, Nick Fisher, Fritz Graf (who discussed Orphism with me), Albert Henrichs, Jean-Marc Moret, Dirk Obbink (who discussed the gods with me), Robert Parker, Christiane Sourvinou-Inwood, H. S. Versnel, and Pierre Vidal-Naquet. The best way, of course, of starting the study of Greek religion would be to read the works of all these scholars.

Finally, I dedicate this modest book to the memory of my uncle Marius, who advised me to study Classics and was always there as a friend to talk to, not least in matters of religion. His untimely death was a great loss to his family and to all who were privileged to know him.

Jan N. Bremmer
Groningen, June 1994

PREFACE TO THE SECOND EDITION

In 1995, Richard Hamilton concluded an appreciative review of the first edition (1994) with the words; 'Let us hope B(remmer) is willing to give us an update in a decade' (*BMCR* 1995.06.02). Alas, time went too fast to fulfil this wish, as the reprint (1999) only contained a few pages with addenda, but it gives me much pleasure that I am able to release a second edition after a quarter of a century. I had been updating the notes to some extent in the German (1996), Italian (2002), Dutch (2004), Spanish (2006), and French (2012) translations, but for the second edition I have wholly revised the notes and adapted the main text to take stock of new insights regarding the problems treated in the first edition, and also to add reflections on recent developments in the field, such as the discussions about the notion of belief, the nature and authority of *polis* religion, and the importance of mythography.

The first edition profited from the input of many colleagues. It is therefore sad to see that quite a few important scholars of Greek religion have passed away in the intervening years.[1] Fortunately, we now have several collections of their articles at our disposal, which will make research into the study of Greek religion much easier than it used to be.[2] It also means, however, that we are in a kind of transitional stage in which interests have been shifting away from myth and ritual to cognitive approaches and to hitherto somewhat neglected aspects, such as magic, theology, local religion, or the place of animals in Greek religion.

I have been very fortunate that I could discuss the whole of the present edition with my friends Bob Fowler and Julia Kindt, who alerted me to oversights, obscure formulations, and new topics, while several individual chapters were commented upon by Anja Klöckner, Norbert Oettinger, and Katja Sporn. I am most grateful for the care and attention they have all given to my text, as well as to Phil Horky and John Taylor for soliciting the new edition and the latter also for reading my final draft so carefully. Finally, Hester Higton's meticulous

---

[1] I remember with gratitude Walter Burkert (1931–2015), Marcel Detienne (1935–2019), Albert Henrichs (1942–2017), Michael Jameson (1924–2004), Christiane Sourvinou-Inwood (1945–2007), Pierre Vidal-Naquet (1930–2006), and Jean-Pierre Vernant (1914–2007).

[2] See Vernant 2007; Burkert 2001–11; Jameson 2014; Henrichs 2019.

copy-editing greatly improved my text. I do not expect to complete a
third edition, but I do hope that the present book will long remain a
reliable guide to the fascinating world of Greek religion and mythology.

Jan N. Bremmer
Groningen, November 2020

LIST OF ABBREVIATIONS

APM	Allard Pierson Museum, Amsterdam
BNJ	*Brill's New Jacoby* (Leiden: Brill, 2007–)
CGRN	Carbon, J.-M., S. Peels, and V. Pirenne-Delforge (eds.), *A Collection of Greek Ritual Norms* (Liège, 2015–), http://cgrn.ulg.ac.be/
Der neue Pauly	*Der neue Pauly. Enzyklopädie der Antike* (Stuttgart: Metzler Verlag, 1996–2003)
FGrH	F. Jacoby, *Die Fragmente der griechischen Historiker* (Berlin and Leiden: Brill, 1923–58)
IC	*Inscriptiones Creticae*
IG	*Inscriptiones Graecae*
LIMC	*Lexicon Iconographicum Mythologiae Classicae* (Zurich and Düsseldorf: Artemis, 1981–2009)
RAC	*Reallexikon für Antike und Christentum* (Stuttgart: Hiersemann Verlag, 1950–)
SEG	*Supplementum Epigraphicum Graecum*

For texts and fragments I have used the most recent standard editions. Translations are my own, unless indicated otherwise.

LIST OF ILLUSTRATIONS

All APM photographs are from Allard Pierson, University of Amsterdam, Open Access. I am most grateful to Geralda Jurriaans-Helle for her help in procuring the photos at the time of the COVID-19 lockdown.

I. INTRODUCTION: GENERAL CHARACTERISTICS

Was there ever such a thing as 'Greek religion'? It may be an odd question to start this Survey with, but it should be absolutely clear from the start that Greek religion as a monolithic entity never existed. When archaic Greece emerged from the Dark Ages around 800 BC, religious unity and diversity had evolved together with the unity and diversity of the Greek world as a whole, as it came into existence with the emergence of the *polis*. Every city had its own pantheon in which some gods were more important than others and some gods not even worshipped at all. Every city also had its own mythology, its own religious calendar, and its own festivals (Chapter IV, §3). No Greek city, then, was a religious clone.[1] Yet the various city-religions overlapped sufficiently to warrant the continued use of the term 'Greek religion'. The family resemblance (to borrow Wittgenstein's famous term) of these 'religions' was strengthened by poets such as Homer and Hesiod (see below), who from the eighth century onwards produced a kind of religious highest common factor by inventing, combining, and systematizing individual traditions, which they then spread via performances at aristocratic courts or local and Panhellenic festivals (below, §3).[2]

Greek religion received its characteristic forms in the thousand or so big and small cities, the *poleis*, which spread Greek culture from modern-day Spain to the Black Sea.[3] The independence of these cities gradually diminished through the development of larger powers, such as Sparta and Athens, and they eventually had to cede their sovereignty to Philip and his Macedonians. These developments brought about rapid changes in the structure of Greek religion (Chapter VII). In this Survey, we will concentrate on the religious practices and beliefs during the 'glory that was Greece', namely the archaic and classical periods. Given its pre-eminence in the sources, Athens will often be our most important example, but I intend to show also something of the diversity of Greek religious culture.

[1] As was first argued, in an exemplary investigation of Aphrodite in Locri Epizephyrii, in Sourvinou-Inwood 1991: 147–88. Excellent local and regional studies are: Graf 1985; Jost 1985; Parker 1996, 2005; Sporn 2002; Polinskaya 2013; Mili 2015; Pilz 2020.

[2] Kowalzig 2007.

[3] See M. Hansen and Nielsen 2004.

Before we start looking in more detail at the different aspects, it may be helpful to sketch its main qualities in broad outlines. Greek religion was 'embedded'; it was public and communal rather than private and individual, and it had no strict division between sacred and profane (below, §1). It was also polytheistic and 'interconnected'; it served to maintain order and produce meaning; it was mainly concerned with the here and now, and passed down by word of mouth rather than through written texts (below, §2). Finally, it was male-dominated (Chapter VI) and lacked a religious establishment (below, §3).

I would like to conclude this brief introduction with two more observations. First, religious historians often present a relatively static picture of the archaic and classical age, as if during this period religion remained more or less unchanged until the Hellenistic period. Admittedly, it is not easy to keep a proper balance between a synchronic system and diachronic developments. Yet a modern history should at least try to stick to a minimal diachronic perspective. Second, the table of contents of this book may suggest to the reader that the following chapters are all independent subjects, which have little to do with one another. Nothing is further from the truth. Gods and sanctuaries, myths and rituals, beliefs and practices, sculptures and vase-paintings[4] – since they are mutually supportive, they should ideally all be treated together in one close-knit treatise.[5] Such a treatment is hardly possible in this brief compass, but it will be one of our challenges to show the interdependent nature of Greek religion.

1. Embeddedness

Most Western countries have gradually separated church and state, at least on an ideological level, but this is not the case everywhere, as shown by societies such as Iran and Saudi Arabia. In ancient Greece, too, religion was totally embedded in society – no sphere of life lacked a religious aspect.[6] Birth, maturity, and death, war and peace, agriculture, commerce, and politics – all these events and activities were

---

[4] See T. Smith 2021.

[5] Bruit Zaidman and Schmitt Pantel 1992: 158.

[6] The terminology derives from the economist Karl Polanyi (1886–1964); see Gemici 2008. It was applied to Greece in Parker 1986: 265, unconvincingly rejected by Nongbri 2008. See also Kindt 2012: 16–19.

accompanied by religious rituals or subject to religious rules; even making love was named after the goddess of love, *aphrodisiazein*.
Sanctuaries dominated the skylines, statues of gods stood on the cor-
ners of the streets, and the smell of sacrifice was never far away.[7]
Indeed, religion was such an integrated part of Greek life that the
Greeks lacked a separate word for 'religion' in the modern sense,
which emerged only during the Enlightenment.[8] When Herodotus
wants to describe religions of the neighbouring peoples of Greece, he
uses the term 'to worship the gods', *sebesthai tous theous*, and when he
wants to describe the Greek nation, he speaks of 'the common blood,
the common language and the common sanctuaries and sacrifices'
(8.144.2). In other words, for Herodotus the problem of describing foreign religions could be reduced to the question 'Which [other] gods do
they worship and how?'[9] In such an environment, atheism was simply
unthinkable. The term *atheos* did not originate before the fifth century
and even then indicated only a lack of relations with the gods.[10]

Embeddedness went together with the virtual absence of personal
religion, since in classical Greece the notion of a private sphere was
still in an early stage of development. There could be individual cult
acts, such as sacrifice, the dedication of an ex-voto (Chapter III, §3),
or a silent prayer (Chapter IV, §2), but cult was mostly a public, communal activity. Worship outside the basic groups of family, *deme* (com-
mune), tribe, and city hardly attained respectability before the
weakening of the *polis* at the end of the fifth century, and remained
long vulnerable: witness Demosthenes' famous attack on Aeschines,
or Theophrastus' *Superstitious Man*.[11] This public character also meant
that religion was strongly tied up with social and political conditions.
As life in Greece was dominated by free males, they could (and did)
seriously restrict religious opportunities for women (Chapter VI, §1),
metics,[12] and slaves, whose religious position was modest, except for
those festivals where the social order was temporarily suspended and
they could enjoy themselves (Chapter IV, §3).[13] The role of politics is

[7] Attention to the role of the senses in Greek religion has become more important in recent
times. For smell, see Mehl 2018.
[8] See Bremmer 1998; Feil 1986–2012.
[9] Harrison 2002; Burkert 2001–11: vol. 7.
[10] Bremmer 2007, 2015.
[11] G. Martin 2009: 104–15 (Aeschines); Kindt 2015.
[12] Wijma 2014.
[13] Fischer 2017.

visible, for example, in the struggle for religious authority in Sparta. There, in their competition for power with the kings, the highest magistrates had created alternative modes of consulting the gods in order to be independent of the seers, who were controlled by the kings.[14] It is also illustrated by Athens: when the city became more democratic, it created priesthoods that were additional to those controlled by the aristocrats; when it became more imperialistic, it started to extend the cult of its most important goddess, Athena, in other cities.[15]

Embeddedness also influenced the conceptualization of the sacred. In modern Western society, the sacred is limited to a direct connection with the supernatural and is sharply separated from the profane, but the situation was rather different in Greece. Here a variety of words existed to express our notion of the sacred. The most important term in this respect is *hieros*, which is everything that has to do with sanctuaries and the gods; for example, to sacrifice is *hiereisthai* and a priest is a *hiereus*. In short, *hieros* is 'as it were the shadow cast by divinity',[16] but it does not mean 'taboo', a quality often associated by anthropologists with the sacred; the more dangerous and unapproachable side of the sacred is expressed by the verbs *hagizo, enagizo,* and *kathagizo*.[17] In addition to *hieros*, the Greeks used *hagnos*, which could be applied to both humans and gods: regarding the gods and important social institutions, such as supplication and the oath, it denotes their awesomeness, but in the case of humans it refers to their ritual purity. The two notions are not easily combined, and in the late archaic age, when the gap between the human and the divine became enlarged,[18] a new word, *hagios*, was introduced, which is first attested for altars (Simonides fr. 519.9) and applies especially to temples, rites, and mysteries.[19]

Another key term in this area is *hosios*. It had a wide range with a basic meaning of 'what humans do to please the gods and to give them the *timê* [honour] they deserve, and whatever action or attitude the speaker can convince others that it belongs to that category'.[20]

---

[14] Jacoby on *FGrH* 596 F 46; Bremmer 1993.

[15] On priesthoods, see Lambert 2010; Horster and Klöckner 2012. On Athens/Athena, see Smarczyk 1990, to be read with Tuplin 1999; Parker 1994; Jameson 2014: 232–69.

[16] So, strikingly, Burkert 1985: 269; see also Parker 1983: 151f.

[17] Parker 1983: 328–31; Parker 2011: 148f.

[18] For this process, which is in need of further analysis, see Bremmer 2019e: 89–93, 106.

[19] For the vocabulary of the sacred, see Parker 1983: 147–50; Motte 1986; Nuchelmans 1989; Rudhardt 1992: 231–52.

[20] Peels 2016: 255f.

For example, *hosios* can denote purity because pollution is offensive to the gods, but also the proper bonds between guests and hosts, parents and children, and proper dealings with suppliants and the dead.[21] More strongly, it also includes the notion of 'justice', as is illustrated by a funerary epigram of a certain Sosikrates, who died 'not in a *hosios* way but through an unjust death' (*SEG* 38.440). From the fifth century onwards, the Athenians often used the combination *hiera kai hosia* to indicate two types of prime importance to society: the right ritual behaviour and the correct treatment of fellow humans. Even if the latter was not 'sacred', it was still felt to be parallel to and co-ordinate with the other sphere.[22] The same goes, in a way, for important institutions of society, such as the symposium or political offices, which were marked with a certain sanctity by the wearing of garlands. So, in Greece, the sacred 'appears as the intensely venerable rather than the absolutely other'.[23]

2. Polytheism, piety, and pollution

Unlike Christianity and Islam, Greek religion was polytheistic. This is not just a difference in quantity. In polytheism, the pantheon constitutes a kind of system, where gods may complement one another or may be in mutual opposition (Chapter II, §3). Did every Greek worship all the gods of their pantheon? We do not know, but it is unlikely. Wealthy Athens had dozens of sanctuaries, whereas excavators have found only few temples in small Priene on the west coast of modern Turkey. In some cases, worshippers may have tried to remedy the lack of sanctuary of a specific deity by dedicating a figurine of one god in the sanctuary of another, but on the whole inhabitants of rich urban centres must have had many more possibilities for worship than the ordinary person in the country or in small *poleis*.[24]

Unlike God or Allah, polytheistic gods only cover a limited sphere of life. Their importance, as for example expressed in sacrifice (Chapter IV, §2), depends on their specific realm. As only the totality of the gods was believed to cover the whole of life, ranging from orderly

[21] Peels 2016: 27–67.
[22] See the discussion of recent scholarship on *hiera kai hosia* in Peels 2016: 225–30.
[23] So Parker 1983: 153 (also for garlands).
[24] Alroth 1989: 64–105, reviewed in van Straten 1992.

Apollo to bloodthirsty Ares, piety never meant devotion to only one god, although the closeness of a shrine may have fostered a special relationship with a god or hero (Chapter III, §2). It was only in Hellenistic times that faith in one god, *pistis*, became possible (Chapter VII, §3); only after the birth of Judaism and Christianity do we find conversions.[25] In fact, religious single-mindedness was definitely dangerous, as Euripides showed in his *Hippolytus* (428 BC), where the protagonist comes to a sad end through worshipping Artemis but refusing Aphrodite.[26] Consequently, piety did not yet include loving a god. As Aristotle (*Mag. Mor.* 1208b30) bluntly states: 'it would be absurd if someone were to say that he loves Zeus'.[27]

Proper Greek piety, *eusebeia*, on the other hand, was connected with a root **seb-* ('retreat in awe'), but in the classical period the element of reverence had come to the fore and even extended to loving parents, patriotism, and keeping to the ancestral customs: as Isocrates observed: 'piety consists not in lavish expenditures but in changing nothing of what our ancestors have handed down' (7.30). In fact, *eusebês* ('pious'), came very close to *hosios*, although more focusing on the abuse of temples, altars, and images of divinities.[28] That abuse was considered to be *asebeia*, which also included holding the wrong ideas about the gods.[29] Even though the evidence for many Athenian trials for impiety against famous philosophers is late,[30] Socrates was executed on the charge of innovation in regard to the gods, not for, say, religious theft.[31] Religious tolerance was not the greatest of Greek virtues.

Whereas the Christian world-view increasingly separated God from this world, the gods of the Greeks were not transcendent but directly involved in natural and social processes. Myths related divine visits on earth, and in Homer's *Iliad* gods even participated in the fighting before Troy.[32] Gods also intervened in the human world in cases of moral transgressions: the myth of Oedipus relates the fatal consequences of incest, and the Spartans believed that their murder of

---

[25] For *pistis*, see Bontempi 2013. On conversion, see Bøgh 2014; Bremmer 2016.

[26] Gladigow 2005: 138–48.

[27] For a discussion of the notion 'loving god (God)', which ranges from classical times to the early Christian period, see Söding1992.

[28] See the illuminating analysis, based on a statistical comparison, in Peels 2016: 68–106.

[29] Vicente Sánchez 2015; Eidinow 2016: 48–62; Naiden 2016.

[30] For the full evidence, see Filonik 2013 and 2016.

[31] For the much-discussed case of Socrates, see, most recently, Karavas 2018; Bremmer 2020c: 1016–20.

[32] On visits, see Flückiger-Guggenheim 1984.

helot suppliants in a sanctuary of Poseidon had caused the catastrophic earthquake of 464 BC.[33] It is for such connections between the human and divine spheres that the Greek world-view has been called 'interconnected', in contrast to the Christian 'separative' cosmology.[34]

An important consequence of overstepping or breaking existing cosmological, social, and political boundaries was the incurring of pollution. The vocabulary of pollution and purity, together with its concomitant practices, was most frequently used in Greek religion to indicate proper boundaries or categories not to be mixed. Natural pollutions are to a certain extent understandable, with the messiness accompanying birth and the smells arising from a decaying body. But we would not so readily use the vocabulary of pollution for the violation of temples, divine statues, and sacred equipment, which infringes the domain of the gods, or for murder, which infringes social relations, as does killing suppliants, while madness and other diseases infringe the wholeness of the physical person. On the other hand, incest and cannibalism were seen as monstrous, polluting crimes, which confuse the boundaries between humans and animals. Males who confused gender roles by assuming the passive role in homosexual acts and women who transgressed boundaries of respectability by prostituting themselves were also considered to be polluted. The latter, though, were not seen as contagious or dangerous and the committers of these sexual activities did not need to purify themselves. The employment of this particular vocabulary with the corresponding rites of purification can, in one way, be seen as an important Greek means of dealing with maintaining religious and social norms and values in times when the legal process was still underdeveloped.[35]

In addition to removing disorder, Greek religion gave meaning and explanation to life. Dreams, waywardness of behaviour, unforeseen events such as shipwrecks, plagues, and earthquakes – all could be traced to particular gods and in this way were given a recognizable and clear place in Greek world-view; if necessary, there were even anonymous and unknown gods to take the blame.[36] On the other hand, not everything became clear through the mediation of religion,

---

[33] For Oedipus, see Bremmer 1990a. For the Spartans, see Hdt. 1.128; also Parker 1983: 184. In general, see Speyer 1989: 254–63.

[34] Oudemans and Lardinois 1987.

[35] Parker 1983, unconvincingly criticized in Osborne 2011: 158–84; Petrovic and Petrovic 2016; Carbon and Peels 2018.

[36] Van der Horst 1994: 165–202; Henrichs 2019: 299–334.

and some divine actions remained inexplicable. Tragedians explored these actions, but their juxtaposition of the human and the divine in such plays as Aeschylus' *Agamemnon* or Euripides' *Bacchae* shows something of the bafflement evoked, on occasion, by the gods' reactions.[37]

Most Greek religion, though, was directed at this life not the hereafter. In Homeric times, death was still more or less the end of life, although most people believed in a journey to the underworld as their final destination.[38] In the course of the archaic age, life after death became an issue for reflection. Aristocratic circles (probably the more intellectual among them) began to think about their personal fate and crave for an existence prolonged beyond their allotted lifespan. Salvation through leading a model life or through initiation into mysteries gradually gained in popularity (Chapter VII, §1), but belief in a life after death never flourished to the extent it did in the Christian Middle Ages. There, if anywhere in Greek religion, it seems that opinions differed widely.[39]

Such a variety of opinion is hardly surprising in a society that was oral rather than literate. Books did not play a role in Greek religion except for a few groups outside mainstream Greek religion, such as the Orphics (Chapter VII, §2), and children were religiously socialized by attending and practising rituals.[40] This meant that religious ritual played a much larger role in Greek life than in modern society. We should not deduce from this that the Greeks had no beliefs, but in classical times a Greek would never say 'I believe': the modern term 'belief', with its propositional content, is the fruit of a very long development which we should not retroject on classical Greece or, for that matter, early Christianity.[41] Together with the absence of a holy book went the absence of a creed and, consequently, of heresy, but not of a certain amount of theology, which has recently started to receive attention, although usually neglected in previous studies of Greek religion.[42] Religious authority was widely fragmented because priests were

---

[37] Gould 2001: 203–34; Buxton 2013: 161–72 (bafflement).

[38] Nesselrath 2020.

[39] For the development of beliefs and attitudes regarding death, see Sourvinou-Inwood 1995; Scholl 2007; E. Giudice 2015; Schlatter 2018; Mackin Roberts 2020.

[40] For books, see Parker 2011: 16–20. For children, see Prescendi 2010; Auffarth 2012.

[41] *Contra* Versnel 2011: 539–59 and see also Harrison 2015; Bremmer 2020e. For early Christianity, see T. Morgan 2015; Frey *et al.* 2017.

[42] Eidinow *et al.* 2016, to be read with Bonnet 2017.

rarely professionals, and there was no Greek equivalent to Christian ministers, Jewish rabbis, or Islamic mullahs (Chapter III, §1). Most citizens could sacrifice by themselves; indeed, Herodotus was amazed that the Persians had to call upon a magus to perform their sacrifices (1.132).

3. Religious specialists

It was mainly outside their own homes, though, that the Greeks could meet certain religious specialists, in particular poets, priests, and seers. Originally, poets were undoubtedly the main religious 'inventors' and 'reproducers'. Even if he exaggerated slightly by implicitly suggesting that there was only the barest of religion before Homer and Hesiod, Herodotus was not far wrong when he stated that these poets defined the theogony, gave the gods their epithets, assigned their functions, and described their forms (2.53.2). Poets could exert this influence because they were supported by the aristocrats, who controlled life through their religious, political, social, and cultural hegemony.[43] Poets also enlarged their religious capital by claiming to be in close contact with the gods. Not only did they manage to make the Greeks believe, if not unconditionally, in the divine guarantee by the Muses of the information they supplied, but they also claimed a privileged knowledge about the gods which was denied to normal humans, as for instance when Homer tells us that an owl is called *chalkis* by the gods but *kumindis* by humans (*Il.* 14.290–1).[44]

Poets also regularly 'invented' religious traditions, if necessary by borrowing from neighbouring peoples. It was only realized in the 1950s that the myth of Kronos' castration of his father, Ouranos, derived from the Near East: the slow but steady decipherment of ever more clay tablets has now shown that this myth ultimately derived from the Hurrians, having passed through Hittite and Phoenician intermediaries.[45] Only a few decades ago, it also became clear that the division of the world between Zeus, Poseidon, and Hades through the throwing of lots, as described in the *Iliad* (15.187–93), derives from

---

[43] See Bremer 1991; Weber 1992.

[44] For the idea of a separate language of the gods, which goes back to Indo-European times, see M. West 2007: 160–2; Willi 2009: 247–9; this volume, Chapter II, §1.

[45] See, most recently, Rutherford 2018.

the Akkadian epic *Atrahasis*. And when Hera, in a speech to deceive
Zeus, says that she will go to Okeanos, 'origin of the gods', and
Tethys, the 'mother' (*Il.* 14.201), she mentions a couple derived
from the parental couple Apsu and Tiamat of the Babylonian creation
epic *Enuma Elish*.[46]

Priests and priestesses (Chapter VI, §1) conducted larger rituals and
supervised sanctuaries (Chapter III, §1), but never developed into a
class of their own because of the lack of an institutional framework.
Consequently, they were unable to monopolize access to the divine
or to develop esoteric systems, as happened with the Brahmans in
India or the Druids among the Celts. On the whole, priesthoods had
no great influence except for those of certain important sanctuaries,
such as the Eumolpides and Kerykes in Eleusis (Chapter VII, §1)
and the Branchidai at Apollo's oracle at Didyma (Chapter III, §3).
Despite their modest status, priests must have played an important
role in the transmission of local rituals and myths, and Hellanicus
(*FGrH* 4 F 74–84), one of the earliest historians, used priestesses of
Hera in Argos as his most trustworthy chronological source.

In the case of problems or inexplicable events, it was a male seer
(although more recently several female seers have emerged [Chapter
VI, §1]) who could bring help. In the archaic age, seers were still aristocrats, who participated in every aspect of aristocratic life, including
the battlefield. But, despite their expertise, their words were not defini-
tive. People were free to accept or reject their advice, and epic and tragedy supply various examples of seers whose word was wrongly
neglected, such as that of Teiresias in Sophocles' *Oedipus Rex*, which
must have contributed to the status of the seers.[47]

Despite this support from tragedy, the position of poets and seers
gradually declined in the later classical age through various developments, such as the rise of literacy, increasing knowledge of the world,
and growing self-reliance. Even though tragedians still held an important position in the adaptation and formation of religious traditions in
the fifth century, they now had to share their one-time monopoly
with historians and philosophers. After the fifth century the former

---

[46] See Burkert 1992: 89–93 and 2004: 30–1. See also Currie 2016: 204; Yakubovich 2017: 365
(with further linguistic arguments); this volume, Appendix.

[47] Flower 2008; S. Johnston 2008: 109–43; Naerebout and Beerden 2012; Trampedach 2015;
Foster 2018; Bremmer 2019e: 147–64; Van Hove 2019. For a comparison with the ancient Near
East, see Beerden 2013; Nissinen 2017.

took over to a large extent the task of preserving religious traditions, and the latter became the main 'theologians'. Moreover, at the end of the archaic period the most important religious authority had become the *polis*, which now mediated and articulated most religious discourse and controlled much of the cultic activity. This control has led to the expression *polis* religion,[48] but we should beware of overstressing such control. There were always certain areas, such as magic, mysteries, mythography, and oracles, where that control was less than complete, and more or less space for individual agency remained available;[49] individual households may also have differed in their religious practices.[50] In addition, it should be noted that there is a certain Athenocentric bias in the approach, which neglects the innovations in, for example, southern Italy, or the freedom in colonial outposts or even in the periphery of Attica itself.[51] As there was no creed or divine revelation, the *polis*, when challenged, appealed to the traditional nature of rites, *ta nomizomena*, and customs, *ta patria* (Chapter IV, §1). Such a stress on tradition could lead to rigidity, but possible tensions between conservatism and innovation were resolved by introducing new cults rather than abandoning old ones.[52]

---

[48] Sourvinou-Inwood 2000.

[49] See especially Rüpke 2011; Kindt 2012: 12–35; Bremmer 2019e: 125–46. But see also the spirited defence of Parker 2018b.

[50] See Boedeker 2008; Faraone 2008.

[51] On outposts, see Demetriou 2017; Bremmer 2019e: xii; Lemos and Tsingarida 2019. On the periphery, see Scholl 2018.

[52] On accepting new gods, see Garland 1992; Auffarth 1995; Parker 2011: 273–7.

II. GODS

Rather surprisingly, gods have not been at the centre of modern discussions of Greek religion until very recently. Although they usually appear relatively late in twentieth-century histories of Greek religion,[1] the situation has changed dramatically in the last decade or so.[2] And rightly so, given the importance of the gods within Greek religion. There are several questions worth asking: what is a god? What did the Greeks see as important differences between themselves and the gods, and between gods and heroes? Which factors helped to define the identity of individual gods (§1)? How should we study the pantheon (§2)? What did the Greeks consider to be the sphere of influence of individual gods? What was the nature of the divine hierarchy? And, last but not least, were the gods persons or powers – or both (§3)?

1. God, gods, and heroes

At an early stage of their history, the Greeks replaced the Indo-European word *deiwos* (Latin *deus*) with *theos*, cognates of which have been recognized in Armenian and Phrygian. The new term semantically developed from 'to put, to place' to 'what has been characterized by what has been put/built in a sacred place, by the divine, by the sacred'.[3] Sometimes, however, the Greeks used a different term. Whenever the presence of the divine remained vague enough not to be pinned upon one of the major deities, or when the Greeks felt that a god intervened for a short period directly and concretely in their lives, they spoke of *daimôn*, which acquired its unfavourable meaning mainly in later time.[4]

---

[1] See Nilsson 1967: 383–603; Burkert 1985: 119–89; Bruit Zaidman and Schmitt Pantel 1992: 176–214; Rudhardt 1992: 55–111.

[2] Grassinger, de Oliveira Pinto, and Scholl 2008; Bremmer and Erskine 2010; Versnel 2011; Clauss, Cuypers, and Kahane 2016; Pironti and Bonnet 2017; Gagné and Herrero de Jáuregui 2019. From the older literature, Sissa and Detienne 2000 (first published 1989) remains valuable. Historiographical surveys: Konaris 2016; Henrichs 2019: 255–98. Note also the lemmata for the different gods in van den Toorn, Becking, and van der Horst 1999; *Der neue Pauly*; and *LIMC*.

[3] De Meyer 2016.

[4] De Jong 2004: 158, 239–40; Bremmer 2019a. For major deities, note the exceptions of *Il.* 3.420 and *Od.* 3.166.

Greek gods resembled and differed from the Christian God in important aspects.[5] Like Him, they had agency and were mostly invisible, anthropomorphic, and immortal,[6] but they seem to have had their own language,[7] and were not loving (Chapter I, §2), almighty, or omnipresent; moreover, they were 'envious and disorderly' (Hdt. 1.32.1), their presence could be uncanny, sometimes horrific, and, occasionally at least, they were frivolously amoral.[8] In particular, the divine sense of justice in Homer is problematic, but we reach a better understanding when we consider the relationships between gods and mortals as analogous to those between princes and commoners. Although gods did uphold the rules of justice, their obligations to kin and friends had priority. This attitude reflects the absence in Homeric society of a developed legal system, and it is only natural that in a more regulated period such a lack of a divine sense of justice came to be questioned.[9] Divine uncanniness comes to the fore in tragedy, as for example in Euripides' *Hippolytus*, where Poseidon despatches a bull from the sea in order to kill Hippolytus. This darkness of divinity is typical of tragedy, but its prominence in this particular genre should not lead us to make it the starting point of generalizations: approaching the gods from their role in comedy would lead to completely different results.[10] Rather, it is typical of Greek religion that it combined this polarization and radicalization of experiencing the divine.

The gods' frivolous behaviour accentuates mortal plodding and is typical of their outspoken anthropomorphism, which is Homer's greatest contribution to Greek religion.[11] Even Greek onomastics shows its success: names indicating the gift of a specific deity, like Athenodorus or Apollodorus, appear only after Homer.[12] However, the resemblance between gods and humans is only relative. As the appearance of Demeter in her *Homeric Hymn* (275–80) illustrates, divine epiphanies show the gods as tall, beautiful, sweet-smelling,

---

[5] For how to define a (Greek) god, see Thomassen 2016; Henrichs 2019: 361–82. Good observations on the nature of the Greek gods also in Jost 1992: 1–34; Parker 2011: 64–102.

[6] Baratz 2015.

[7] Bader 1989; M. West 2007: 160–2; Willi 2009: 247–9; Viti 2017.

[8] Griffin 1980: 144–204 (the gods' serious side); Burkert 2001–11: ii.96–118.

[9] See van Wees 1992: 142–9, but, in contrast, Lloyd-Jones 1983; Parker 2011: 4, 34f.

[10] On tragedy, see Mikalson 1991: 17–68; Parker 1997. Comedy is insufficiently considered by Gould 2001: 203–34.

[11] Burkert 2001–11: i.80–94.

[12] For such names, see Parker 2000c.

awe-inspiring – in short, as 'superpersons'.[13] Precisely because of divine anthropomorphism, it was necessary to stress the immortal–mortal boundary. In several Greek myths, gods are being tested: Ariadne challenging Athena's weaving skill or Marsyas questioning Apollo's flute-playing genius. The stories invariably end badly for mortals, as do love affairs with gods: Semele was burned to ashes, when she begged Zeus to appear in full glory. The message of these myths is clear: the gap between gods and humans is unbridgeable,[14] as Pindar noted: 'for the one race is nothing, whereas the bronze heaven remains a secure abode forever' (*Nem.* 6.3–4, trans. Race 1997).

The success of Homeric anthropomorphism should not make us forget that the gods were also regularly associated with animals. Whereas Christian theologians thought long and wrote much about the body of God,[15] it is not so easy to discover what the Greeks thought about the body of their divinities,[16] let alone about their theriomorphism. However, we should not forget that some Greek gods were closely connected with animals or even (partially) identified with these, such as Pan with his goat's legs or Dionysos appearing as a bull. In a way, the theriomorphic body of these divinities puts them in opposition to the anthropomorphic ones and is a signifier of their alterity, which is confirmed and supported by the non-standard rituals connected with them.[17] An older layer of Greek religion even imagined gods in the shapes of stones or trees.[18] Yet such representations continued to coexist with the anthropomorphic shapes well into late antiquity. Surely, all Greek divinities were different, but some were clearly more different than others.

Anthropomorphism made the gods vulnerable to criticism,[19] which Xenophanes (*c.* 500 BC) was the first to state publicly. Subsequent generations of intellectuals took these criticisms seriously and tried to counter them through the strategies of allegory and rationalization.[20] Others would be more daring, and Herodotus' allusion (2.53.1) to

---

[13] Platt 2011; Petridou 2015; Henrichs 2019: 427–64. Note that Vernant 1994: 41 speaks of a 'superbody'.

[14] On tests, see Weiler 1974: 37–128. For affairs, see Piccaluga 1974: 9–35.

[15] Markschies 2019.

[16] Cf. Vernant 1991: 27–49; Osborne 2011: 185–215 (on 'godsbodies').

[17] For this under-explored aspect of the gods, see Aston 2011; Kindt 2019; Bremmer 2020d.

[18] See Gaifman 2012, 2017: 335–52.

[19] See Wifstrand Schiebe 2020.

[20] For Xenophanes, see Trépanier 2010: 276–81; Versnel 2011: 244–66; Tor 2017. For subsequent generations, see Feeney 1991: 5–33.

Protagoras' famous statement 'Concerning the gods I am unable to discover whether they exist or not, or what they are like in form' (B4 Diels/
Kranz) shows to what extent fifth-century intellectuals were already
questioning the traditional picture of the gods (Chapter VII, §3).

If the gods differed from humans, they also differed from another
category of supernatural beings: the heroes, who occupied a kind of
intermediate position between gods and humans. Although the origin
of this supernatural category is still unclear, hero cult as such developed
relatively late, not before the middle of the sixth century BC, and should
not be retrojected into earlier centuries. In that period we have tomb
cults, cults of ancestors, and cults of founders of cities, but it is only
from the late archaic age onwards that we start to have hero cults in
the technical sense of the word. Before that time, the term 'hero' simply
does not occur in a religious sense.[21]

In the end, 'hero' seems to have become a kind of lowest common
denominator for mythological grandees like Heracles, faded divinities
like Helen (Chapter V, §2; Chapter VI, §1), mythological culture heroes
like Prometheus, and important historical figures like Brasidas, a
Spartan general who was killed in action in 422 BC (Chapter VII, §3).
Usually, heroes were benevolent and played an important role in guard-
ing oaths and protecting cities, but they could also be malicious and
send all kinds of diseases. In a fragment published only in 1967, the
chorus of Aristophanes' *Heroes* says: 'we are the guardians of good
things and ill; we watch out for the unjust, for robbers and footpads,
and send them diseases – spleen, coughs, dropsy, catarrh, scab, gout,
madness, lichens, swellings, ague, fever. That's what we give to
thieves.'[22] Even though gods and heroes regularly overlapped in function, and heroes were sometimes called 'gods', the heroes' radius was
usually more limited and their cult concentrated on a tomb. Yet the
boundaries between gods and heroes were often fluid, and conceptions
of the hero varied widely in the Greek world.[23]

What established the identity of an individual god? The question is
not easy to answer, as local manifestations of gods could vary widely
even within a single city. Yet a number of factors contributed to a

---

[21] Bremmer 2019e: 85–93, accepted by Gordon 2013, unpersuasively contested by Parker
2011: 287–92.

[22] Ar. fr. 322, translated and commented upon by Parker 1983: 243f.

[23] Kearns 1989; Larson 1995; Lyons 1997; Hägg 1999; Pirenne-Delforge and Suárez de la
Torre 2000; Ekroth 2002; Hägg and Alroth 2005; Jones 2010. Brelich 1956 is still valuable.

recognizable core. Most important was the name of the divinity, although its meaning was usually, like that of heroes, opaque: their awesomeness forbade a straightforward approach.[24] The name was often further specified by an epithet denoting function or origin, like Hermes Agoraios, 'Of the market', or Demeter Eleusinia, 'From Eleusis' (Chapter VII, §1). The significance of these divine epithets is not always clear, and recent research has only partially succeeded in satisfactorily explaining their sense and function. Robert Parker notes two main functions: to distinguish the worship of the same god in different places, such as Athena Polias and Athena Nike in Athens, and to stress a particular power or function of a divinity. It remains unclear, though, if the ordinary Greek saw these epithets as referring, eventually, to one god, or simply considered, say, Artemis Agrotera as a goddess different from Artemis Lochia. Or was the same name sufficient in evoking a kind of general picture of a divinity?[25]

However that may be, a divinity's name was given substance by myth (Chapter V), which related his or her family and deeds. Family ties were means of establishing connections or indicating related functions among divinities: we cannot separate Leto's motherhood of Apollo and Artemis from the connection of all three divinities with initiation.[26] Deeds helped to define and reflect on divine functions. The *Homeric Hymns*, for example, show Hermes as thief, Aphrodite as seductress, and Demeter as founder of the Eleusinian Mysteries. The *Hymns* also relate divine appearances: Dionysos looked 'like a young man on the brink of adolescence' and Apollo like a 'vigorous youth on the brink of manhood'. Art equally reflected on and contributed to the mental image that the Greeks made of their gods. Vases and mirrors frequently display gods with fixed attributes: Poseidon with a trident, Athena with an owl (Figure 1), Zeus with a thunderbolt, Aphrodite with doves (Figure 2).[27] These attributes must have helped to identify individual gods, just as in dreams gods appeared in a shape familiar from the

---

[24] Graf 1996a; Parker 2017a: 1–9 (a wide-ranging review).

[25] Most recently, see Graf 2010: 67–74; García Ramón 2013; Hornblower 2014; Marcos Macedo 2017; Parker 2017a and 2017b: 9–31. For a new database, see Bonnet and Lebreton 2019.

[26] Bremmer 1990b: 263; on Leto's connection with initiation in Chios, see Graf 1985: 60f.

[27] On Poseidon, see Bérard 1983: 15–20. On Athena, see Shapiro 1994a; Kreuzer 2010a and 2010b. On Zeus, see Arafat 1990: 166 (who notes that Zeus's thunderbolt is almost completely absent from the later fifth century onwards); Marcos Macedo 2017. On doves, see Robert 1990: 159–83.

Figure 1. Athena with her owl. Attic black-figure lekythos, Athena Painter, *c.* 490 BC.

(often local) painted and sculptured representations.[28] A final determining factor was cult. The place in the calendar, prominent or not
(Chapter IV, §3); the location of a sanctuary, be it in town or country
(Chapter III, §2); the nature of the sacrificial victim, normal or 'abnormal' (Chapter IV, §2); the mode of ritual, supportive of or undermining
the social order (Chapter IV, §3): all these elements contributed to a
specific perception of individual gods and helped to reinforce their
image for their worshippers.

[28] See van Straten 1976: 14–16.

Figure 2. Greek bronze mirror with Aphrodite and doves, *c.* 470 BC. In Greece, doves were a typical lovers' gift.

2. The pantheon

Before we discuss individual gods, we must first look at the Greek pantheon as a whole. The main gods were a group of twelve who resided on Mount Olympos. The number goes back at least to about 600 BC, when Alcaeus uses the expression 'one of the twelve' (fr. 349e Voigt/ Liberman) in his poem about the entry of Dionysos into Olympos with the help of Hephaistos. This shows that around 600 BC the idea of a Dodekatheon was already prevalent on Lesbos, an island where Hittite influence is in evidence. The latter suggests the role of the twelve gods in Hittite religion via the twelve Titans, who were almost certainly derived from the Hittites.[29] However, it was not until the

---

[29] Near Eastern influence seems more likely than that of the twelve months, *contra* Parker 2011: 71. For possible ties between Hittite and Greek religion, see Rutherford 2020.

late sixth century that the younger Pisistratus dedicated an altar to the Twelve Gods in the Athenian agora (*c.* 520 BC: Thuc. 6.54.6). The reduction to a main group of twelve gods coincides with the rise of the category of heroes and the distinction of a god from his or her statue (Chapter III, §1). For reasons still unclear, it seems that the pantheon was rationalized to some extent in the later sixth century.[30]

How do we find order in the ragbag of Greek gods which, in addition to the major ones, comprised many minor divinities, such as Pan and the Nymphs (Chapter VII, §3), but also rivers and the winds?[31] A popular approach has long been to distinguish between Olympian and Chthonian gods (that is, those of the earth and of the underworld). This view originated during the Romantic period and was already prevalent in the early 1800s. Following a notice in Porphyry's *The Grotto of the Nymphs* (6), Olympians were claimed to have temples and high, square altars for food sacrifices, whereas Chthonians and heroes had only low, circular altars for burnt offerings (Chapter III, §1). In fact, modern archaeology has proved that this distinction has no general validity for the classical period. Even though some gods have connections with the dead and the underworld, there is no clear-cut distinction to be made on these grounds in the Greek pantheon.[32]

More recently, Jean-Pierre Vernant (1914–2007) and his school have stressed that the pantheon is a system whose structures we should study instead of concentrating on divinities as individuals.[33] Which gods are paired and which are opposed to each other? What is the precise mode of intervention? What logic governs their being? In addition to these questions, we should try to search for the, often hidden, hierarchies within the pantheon. Here new possibilities have been opened up by a study of divine representations. A fine example is a black-figured cauldron of the painter Sophilos (*c.* 580 BC) with the wedding procession of Thetis and Peleus moving towards the house of Peleus: we see Hestia and Demeter, Chariclo and Leto, Dionysos, Hebe, Cheiron, Themis, and three Nymphs; Hera and Zeus on a cart followed by three females (the accompanying inscription has been lost); Amphitrite and Poseidon on a cart followed by three Charites; Aphrodite and Ares on a cart

---

[30] See Georgoudi 2001: 346–54; Dowden 2007; Rutherford 2010; Bremmer 2019e: 9 (Alcaeus). The Near Eastern evidence has been overlooked by Versnel 2011: 507–15. For local panthea, see Pirenne-Delforge 1998.

[31] Bremmer 2019d; Eidinow 2019.

[32] Parker 2011: 80–4, 283–6.

[33] For a balanced assessment of the structuralist approach, see also Parker 2011: 84–97.

followed by five Muses; Apollo and Hermes on a cart followed by three
Muses; Athena and Artemis on a cart followed by three Moirai,
Okeanos, and two Eileithyiai (Chapter III, §2). The procession is concluded by Hephaistos on the back of a donkey; naturally, Hades had no
place in this festive happening. The images show not only the pairing of
certain gods but also a clear hierarchy: some gods go by cart, others on
foot. Following this approach, I will now discuss the major gods and
conclude by analysing the structures and hierarchies within the Greek
pantheon, and the problem of whether the Greek gods were persons
or powers – or perhaps both.[34]

3. Gods orderly and disorderly

The main divinity of the Greek pantheon was Zeus, whose development from a weather god worshipped on mountaintops to the supreme
god shows influences from Anatolia, which was also the source of the
succession myths relating his coming to power (see Appendix).
However, Zeus never reached the same position in Greece as Jupiter
Capitolinus in Rome: his festivals were not important, and only a few
cities named months after him. Instead, he became the protector of
the social and moral order.[35] Zeus's first wife was probably Dione,
whose name is attested in Linear B, but who 'survived' only in outlying
Dodona and, as Diwia, in faraway Pamphylia;[36] by Mycenaean times
she had already been replaced by Hera, whose name may mean
'Mistress'. Hera was the goddess who 'holds the keys of marriage'
(Ar. *Thesm.* 973), and in this function her cult was Panhellenic but
not prominent.[37] On Samos, she received votives in the shape of
ships, and it is typical of the plasticity of Greek polytheism that the
importance of the sea for Samos could add this local aspect to her
cult.[38]

If Zeus was the 'chief' of the pantheon, Athena and Apollo had the
greatest number of main *polis* sanctuaries (Chapter III, §2). Athena's
temple is attested on many *acropoleis* throughout the Greek world; her

---

[34] Vernant 1974: 103–20; Bruit Zaidman and Schmitt Pantel 1992: 183–6; Laurens and
Lissarrague 1990 (Sophilos).
[35] In general, see Arafat 1990; Dowden 2006; Kreutz 2007.
[36] Bremmer 2019e: 34.
[37] De la Genière 1997; García Ramón 2016; Pirenne-Delforge and Pironti 2016.
[38] Baumbach 2004; Casadio 2004; Frielinghaus 2017.

statuette, the Palladium, functioned as a *polis* talisman, and she frequently received the epithet Polias or Poliouchos. As a city goddess
she also watched over the new generation. In Athens, youths were integrated into the *phratries* (the primary civic community for most people,
with hereditary membership and usually fixed locality[39]) during her and
Zeus's Apatouria festival, and during the Arrhephoria young girls, the
Arrhephoroi, ended their participation in weaving the new peplos for
the Panathenaea (Chapter IV, §2) via a secret ritual that confronted
them with sexuality, thus preparing them for adult life (Chapter VI,
§1). Although this initiatory function was not entirely absent elsewhere,
it was prominent in Athena's special city: one more testimony to the
fluidity of Greek polytheism.[40]

Athena's protecting function was reflected in her armed appearance,
which was probably influenced by the popular armed goddesses of the
Orient. In war, Athena especially functioned as an adviser to warriors –
witness her close relationship with Achilles and Odysseus in Homer.
She displayed the same intelligence as Athena Ergane, the supervisor
of spinning and weaving, two of the main tasks of Greek women:
many sanctuaries of Athena contain dedications of distaffs and loom
weights. However, Athena's intelligence connected her not only with
women's crafts but also with artisans (and thus with Hephaistos),
with carpenters in building the Argo and the Trojan Horse, and with
knights in mastering horses. In all these cases Athena represents civilization and cleverness against nature and brute force.[41]

The name of Apollo, the other central *polis* god, has been thought to
derive from the yearly Doric assembly, the *apellai*, where the youths
were incorporated into the community of the adults. Yet the etymology
remains disputed (and was so even in antiquity),[42] and we can hardly
say more than that the god possibly derives from Anatolia, where his
mother, Leto, and sister, Artemis, also originated.[43] In any case,
Apollo is clearly situated between adolescence and adulthood. It is
this aspect which made him not only the supervisor of initiatory rites,

[39] Humphreys 2018: ii.569–625.
[40] On talismans, see Faraone 1992. For Polias/Poliouchos, see Graf 1985: 44, 181–2, 209
(archives). On Athena and initiation, see Calame 1997: 128–34; Graf 2000a; Parker 2005: 458–
61 (Apatouria). For Athena in Athens, see Meyer 2017.
[41] For Athena Ergane, see Graf 1985: 211–12; Villing 1998. On intelligence against force, see
the seminal discussion in Detienne and Vernant 1978: 187–213.
[42] Hunter and Laemmle 2020.
[43] Oettinger 2015.

but also the centre of political institutions of the *polis*, especially when worshipped with the epithets Delphinios and Lykeios. From this function it also becomes understandable why Apollo was closely connected with music and dance, given that Greek youths had to be able to sing and dance, and it explains why he was the god of Greek colonization: the position of groups of colonists often resembled that of the initiands outside civilization. The incorporation of ephebes also meant a fresh start for society. Apollo embodies this aspect of renewal by being closely associated with purification, which often separates the new from the old, culture from nature, and the pure from the impure. This 'purificatory' aspect perhaps explains his 'divinatory' function as god of seers and 'owner' of the Delphic oracle: just as he separated the pure from the impure, so he separated the certain from the uncertain in the present, past, and future – even though his utterances often remained, to humans, opaque.[44]

Apollo's sister, Artemis, goes back to an age in which hunting was still of prime importance, witness her title 'Mistress of the Animals' (*Il.* 21.470) and the corresponding iconography. Ethnology shows that such ladies/lords of the animals were often initiatory gods, and this may explain why Artemis supervised the transition of girls into womanhood and in some cities even boys' initiation. The initiatory role is reflected in myth, which often pictures Artemis and her nymphs hunting in the wild.[45] According to Vernant, Artemis manages 'the necessary passages between savagery and civilization…strictly maintaining the boundaries at the very moment they have been crossed'.[46] Indeed, she represents the incursion of disorder in festivals of reversal (Chapter IV, §3), and she marks the boundaries of normality by receiving sacrifices before and after battle.

Like Apollo, Artemis played a role in the life of the state in her manifestations as Phosphoros ('Light-bringer') and Soteira ('Saviour'). 'Light' often means 'life' or 'salvation' in Greek, and many a legend related the intervention of Artemis in a difficult situation for the community: a beam of light showed Thrasybulus and his band the way in their successful attempt at restoring democracy in Athens in 403 BC,

---

[44] On Apollo and initiation, see Graf 1985: 56–7 (Delphinios), 220–7 (Lykeios); Versnel 1993: 289–334; Jameson 2014: 41–61 (Lykeios). On music, see Sarti 1992. In general, see Graf 2009.

[45] On Artemis and initiation, see Graf 1985: 52 (boys), 237–8 (girls), 243–9 (disorder/order), 414–15 (boys); Dowden 1989; Calame 1997 (≈ Calame 2019); Viscardi 2015. On boundaries see Vernant 1991: 195–206.

[46] Vernant 1991: 204.

and the Byzantines were saved from Philip II and his tunnel-digging Macedonians through clouds of fire sent by Artemis Phosphoros. As with 'purificatory' Apollo, this 'saving' aspect can be understood from Artemis' initiatory role, which saved the community from extinction through the access of new members.[47]

If Zeus, Athena, and Apollo especially stood in the centre of the *polis*, the position of some other gods was more 'off centre'. Poseidon was connected with the sea, horses, and men's associations. Homer pictures him as driving his chariot over the waves, while the monsters of the deep play beneath him: 'they know their lord' (*Il.* 13.28). Poseidon also controlled the power of the earth: earthquakes were ascribed to his anger, and many cities, especially on the earthquake-prone western coast of Turkey, worshipped him as Asphaleios ('Immovable'). In addition to ruling the powers of nature, the god was widely associated with horse racing and breeding, as his epithet Hippios illustrates. Finally, Poseidon was the ancestor of various tribes, such as the Boeotians and Aeolians, the god of alliances of cities, such as the pan-Ionic league, and the supervisor of boys' maturation. Not surprisingly, women were forbidden entry into some of the sanctuaries of this macho god. In short, Poseidon is the god of chaos in nature and brute force in men and animals.[48]

Various myths describe Poseidon's defeat by other gods, in particular Apollo and Athena, as is well illustrated by a famous Athenian myth. When Athena and Poseidon struggled for supremacy over Attica, he brought forth a salt sea, traces of which were said to be visible on the Acropolis, whereas she planted the first olive tree: in the ensuing trial, Athena prevailed. In Delphi, it was related that Apollo had obtained the city from Poseidon in exchange for the oracle of Taenarum; according to another version, Poseidon had ceded Delphi to Apollo in return for Kalaureia. The message of these myths is clear. Even though his power was inescapable, there was no place for Poseidon in the ordered society of the Greek city-state or its most famous oracle.[49]

In many places Poseidon was closely connected with Demeter. According to Arcadian myth, he even turned himself into a stallion

---

[47] Graf 1985: 228–43 (Phosphoros, Soteira); Vernant 1985; Cole 2004: 178–230.
[48] Mylonopoulos 2003; Doyen 2011; Bremmer 2019e: 21–7.
[49] For Poseidon and Athena, see Rambach 2011; Jubier-Galinier 2012; Meyer 2017: 377–415. For Poseidon and Apollo, see Mylonopoulos 2003: 404f.

when Demeter fled from him in the shape of a mare, thus begetting the first horse – a type of myth with clear Indo-European parallels.[50] The nature of the association is obscure but strongly suggests that Demeter was perceived as a goddess whose relationship to the social order was problematic. This impression is confirmed by the extramural location of many of her sanctuaries (Chapter III, §2) and the fact that her favourite sacrificial victim was the 'abnormal' pig (Chapter IV, §2). More positively, the *Homeric Hymn to Demeter* movingly relates how Demeter searched for her kidnapped daughter, Persephone – her motherliness is an important difference from Hera[51] – and on her return instituted the Eleusinian Mysteries (Chapter VII, §1); later times, drawing on Demeter's connection with fertility (Chapter VI, §3), added the gift of agriculture. In various places the goddess was even closely associated with political power – witness her cult among the ruling Sicilian family of the Deinomenids and the royal family of Ephesus.[52] Demeter's festival, the Thesmophoria, was the great women's festival, when men were excluded from sex and sometimes, if only symbolically, from power (Chapter VI, §3). It is surely this aspect of the goddess, not her agricultural function, which made her position 'eccentric' in the male-dominated social and religious order.

Finally, Dionysos, the god most discussed in modern times,[53] as his elusive nature well fitted both the Romantics and our own postmodern times. It was long thought that he was a latecomer among the gods until a Linear B tablet from Cretan Khania firmly established his presence in the Mycenaean pantheon.[54] Vernant and his school paid much attention to Dionysos, defining him as the Other who is at the same time male and female, young and old, near and far, and so forth, but the polar opposites on which this view is based are mostly neither attested very early nor always persuasive: the effeminate Dionysos seems to have a background in initiation, when boys were temporarily dressed as girls (Chapter IV, §3).[55]

---

[50] Burkert 1979: 127–8; Doniger O'Flaherty 1980: 166–212 (interesting parallels, improbable interpretations).

[51] The differences between the two goddesses are well analysed in Klöckner 2008.

[52] Farnell 1907: 68–75. Also Hdt. 7.153 (Deinomenids); Strabo 14.1.3 (Ephesus); and her epithet 'Patroie' in Thasos (*SEG* 29.766).

[53] Historiography: Henrichs 1984a, 1993, and 2013.

[54] See Bernabé 2013.

[55] For the lateness of the polarities, see Henrichs 1984a: 235 n. 85. On Vernant, see Henrichs 1993: 31–9. On Dionysos as effeminate, see Bremmer 1999c; Jameson 2014: 62–80.

Methodologically, this approach also takes the wrong turn, because our point of departure should be the god's festivals. These are the oldest testimonies to his sphere of action and speak a clear language: although they abounded with merrymaking, the festivals also displayed characteristics of a break-up of the social order, such as the split of society into its two gender halves during the widespread Agrionia; the equality of slaves during the Anthesteria (Chapter IV, §3); or the prominence of the phallus during the Dionysia. Perhaps the performance of plays at the god's festivals would be another example of a temporary dissolution of the normal order.[56] At times, this 'anti-order' aspect could make these festivals unpleasantly ambiguous: on Chios, armed forces occupied the streets leading to the agora, where, presumably, the sacrifice for Dionysos took place during the Dionysia. In a few neighbouring islands, the 'dangerous' side of Dionysos also came to the fore in some of his epithets: on Chios he was called Omadios ('Raw'), on Lesbos Omestes ('Eater of raw meat'), and on Tenedos Anthroporrhaistes ('Destroyer of man'). Myth stressed this negative side by letting Dionysos arrive from a barbarous country, Thrace, as it did with Ares, another problematic god (Chapter IV, §3).[57]

Similar ambiguities came to the fore among the satyrs and maenads, Dionysos' mythical followers. Satyric drama and vases often show us the happy side of the Dionysiac world through the satyrs: buffoonery, drinking, and all kinds of sexual activities (Figures 3 and 4). Yet some of the last, such as masturbating and coupling with animals, were definitely not socially acceptable, although the god himself was also sometimes associated with the mule, a very randy animal (Figure 5).[58] And tragedy and vase-paintings showed his female followers, the maenads, both resting in serene peace and committing the most gruesome murders in their ecstasy (Chapter VI, §3), as Euripides' *Bacchae* well illustrates; in fact, Dionysos frequently received the epithet Bakchos (or one of its variants), the Greek term par excellence for ecstasy and madness.[59]

Dionysos' divine relationships similarly display this tension between order and 'anti-order'. He was sometimes, understandably, connected

---

[56] For Dionysos and Attic dramatic festivals, see Wilson 2018.

[57] On the Agrionia, see Bremmer 2019e: 37–41. On 'dangerous' Dionysos, see Graf 1985: 74–96; also *POxy.* 53.3711 (local explanation of the epithet Omestes).

[58] Carpenter 1986; Lissarrague 1990; Hedreen 1992; Schlesier and Schwarzmaier 2008; Heinemann 2016.

[59] Jiménez San Cristóbal 2009; Santamaria 2013.

Figure 3. Dionysos with *cantharus* and satyr with erect member. One side of Attic black-figure eye-cup, *c.* 530 BC.

to Aphrodite: in antiquity, too, wine and love went together. He was also connected with Artemis and it fits in with her marking of the boundaries of normality (see above) that she more than once supervised the restoration of order after Dionysiac disorder, as when she cured the madness of Proitos' daughters (Chapter VI, §2). It is rather surprising that he was even associated with Apollo, most clearly in Delphi where Dionysos 'ruled' three months in the winter and Apollo the rest of the year. Yet this relationship perhaps sums up best Dionysos' position in Greek society: society cannot live without a temporary relaxation of the social order, but order has to be restored.[60]

If I had more space, I would also have analysed Hermes (but see below), Hephaistos, Aphrodite, and Ares (Chapter IV, §3), personifications like Eirene ('Peace') (Chapter VII, §3) and Thanatos ('Death'),[61]

---

[60] For Aphrodite, see Dodds 1960: 123. For Artemis, see Graf 1985: 242f. For Apollo, see Burkert 1983: 123–5; Calame 2018: 364–9. For Dionysos in general, see especially Henrichs 1982; Versnel 1990: 96–205; Schlesier 2011; Bernabé *et al.* 2013.

[61] For Hermes, see Jaillard 2007; Versnel 2011: 309–77. For Hephaistos, see Bremmer 2019e: 47–60. On Aphrodite, see Pirenne-Delforge 1994; Pironti 2007; this volume, Chapter IV, §3. For Ares, see Wathelet 1992; Nicgorski 2004. On personifications, see Shapiro 1993; Stafford 2000; Borg 2002. For Thanatos, see E. Giudice 2015: 35–56.

Figure 4. Satyrs treading grapes, while a monkey sits under the table. Attic black-figure oinochoe, Gela Painter, *c.* 500–490 BC.

or even a very small god, despite his oversized member, such as Priapus.[62] However, the discussion so far is sufficient to draw some conclusions: first, Vernant and his school were clearly right to draw attention to connections and relationships of similarity and difference between gods. It is important to see that both Athena and Poseidon are connected with horses in rather different ways, that Apollo and Athena always defeat Poseidon, that Apollo and Dionysos are opposites but both still necessary for the city. On the other hand, these connections do not replace a study of the sphere of action of the individual gods. Athena and Apollo are both more than the sum of their connections: the Greek pantheon was not the product of an ancient logician.

Second, when we now return to Sophilos' vase, we see that those at the centre of the social order went by cart: Zeus, Athena, Apollo, and Artemis. Considering the disruptive effects of male power and sex, it may surprise that they were joined by Poseidon, Ares, and Aphrodite, but male force always remained necessary for the survival of the *polis,*

[62] See Parker 2020.

Figure 5. Dionysos on a mule with his panther. Attic red-figure krater, Flying Angel Painter, *c.* 570 BC.

while sexual pleasure was necessary for its reproduction.[63] However, the location of Poseidon's sanctuaries (Chapter III, §2) and the deviant nature of the sacrificial victims of Ares and Aphrodite (Chapter IV, §2) show that these last three gods clearly were considered to be more at the margin of the social order.[64] On the other hand, the great gods who went on foot, Demeter and Dionysos, are those with festivals in which the normal social order was temporarily dissolved, whether by the dominance of women or by the prominence of wine

[63] For this ambiguous character of some Greek gods, see also Oudemans and Lardinois 1987: 95f.

[64] Versnel 2011: 145 n. 433 misrepresents my argument here.

and the phallus. Since both gods are (virtually) absent in Homer and both are *the* gods of Greek mystery cults (Chapter VII, §§1–2), both were evidently seen as different and occupying an 'eccentric' position in the pantheon. The position of gods on other Attic vases confirms this picture:[65] a central place for Zeus and Apollo but an eccentric position for Ares, Hermes (the god of thieves, merchants, and ephebes – in short, of socially marginal groups), Poseidon, and Dionysos.[66] Evidently, a divinity's relationship to the social order was an important consideration for the Greeks in the (conscious or unconscious) construction of their pantheon.

Yet we cannot speak of a Greek divine hierarchy without two important qualifications. The picture I have sketched is, perhaps inevitably, too static. The pantheon was not a fixed entity but was subject to constant negotiation and repositioning. Worshippers of Pan and the Nymphs gained much in prominence in the course of the classical period (Chapter VII, §3), and in 340/339 BC a Delphic hymn to Dionysos proclaimed that the god should be worshipped the whole year round – not only during the winter as had been usual.[67] The picture also insufficiently takes into account the fact that each city had its own pantheon, in which particular gods could be more prominent than in other cities. For example, Demeter was especially popular in Sicily and she, naturally, was the most important divinity in Eleusis (Chapter VII, §1), whereas on Chios Dionysos enjoyed a particular popularity – reputedly, the first settler of the island was his son Oinopion.[68] In short, the picture is basically a Panhellenic model, from which we should not automatically extrapolate to individual cities and moments in time.

Third and finally, whereas Burkert approached the Greek gods as persons, Vernant and other francophone scholars prefer to see them as powers.[69] Indeed, to a certain extent Greek gods did personify specific powers and qualities. This appears clearly from the oppositions between gods (above, §2): when Poseidon and Aphrodite are contrasted

[65] However, we should always beware of claiming a straightforward relationship between the nature of gods and their representations. From the late fifth century onwards, both Aphrodite and Asclepius became very popular, but the goddess figures on many vases, whereas the god does not. In addition, the popularity of Aphrodite seems to be more a question of fashion, whereas that of Asclepius is one of religion (Chapter VII, §3).

[66] Arafat 1990: 177–8 (Zeus); Laurens and Lissarrague 1990; Bruneau 1984: 491 (Ares). For Hermes, see Siebert 1990; Durand 1992; Miguel 1992.

[67] Käppel 1992: 206–84; Furley and Bremer 2001: i.121–8, ii.52–84.

[68] Graf 1985: 74–97, 125f.

[69] See Pirenne-Delforge and Scheid 2017.

in ritual (Chapter IV, §3), the opposition can hardly be separated from their respective embodiments of 'brute power' and 'love'. Similarly, when Athena defeats Poseidon, many a Greek would not have failed to notice that 'intelligence' defeats 'brute power'. The distinction I have posited between 'orderly' and 'disorderly' gods in the Greek pantheon would, if correct, be an additional illustration of this side of the Greek gods. Moreover, the growing allegorization and euhemerization of the Greek gods in the course of the fifth century (Chapter VII) could hardly have taken off without this quality. On the other hand, art, cult, and literature incessantly impressed upon the Greeks the personal aspect of their gods. 'Power' and 'person' are two sides of the Greek gods which could both come to the fore at different times and in different contexts. Poets stressed the personal side, whereas philosophers started to promote the 'power' aspect of the divinities. The two approaches coexisted for a long time and the tension between them reflects an essential quality of the ancient Greek gods.[70]

---

[70] Similarly Parker 2011: 94f.

III. SANCTUARIES

The way in which Greek places of worship feature in the current popular imagination is much influenced by the remnants of a few surviving temples, such as Athena's Parthenon or Poseidon's temple at Sounion. Yet these aesthetically pleasing but ruined and empty buildings give little insight into their former functions or furnishings.[1] Moreover, a (perhaps unconscious) comparison with modern religious buildings, such as churches, mosques, and synagogues, might lead us to think of an ancient sanctuary as normally consisting of just the temple – which would be a real mistake.[2] So let us first look at sanctuaries proper (§1), then their locations (§2), and, finally, their secular and religious functions (§3).[3]

1. Buildings, statues, and personnel

In our oldest literary source, Homer, sanctuaries with a temple, statue, and priest(ess) are already well established. Hector's mother, Hecuba, went to the temple of Athena on the Acropolis of Troy, where the priestess Theano opened the doors, put Hecuba's valuable gift of an embroidered robe on the knees of Athena's statue, and pronounced a prayer (*Il.* 6.286–311), and Zeus went to Cretan Ida, the site of 'his *temenos* and...altar' (*Il.* 8.48). As archaeology has shown, this combination of *temenos* (a piece of land set aside for gods or heroes) and altar was already emerging in the Dark Age,[4] but it was not until the eighth century that the first temples appeared on the scene, gradually being distanced from the dwellings of rulers;[5] this late arrival of the temple precluded a standard form, and some temples always remained roofless.[6]

---

[1] For a good introduction, see Miles 2016.

[2] Note the interesting observations of Naerebout 2005 and Steuernagel 2009.

[3] Older bibliography: Østby 1993; Burkert 2001–11: vi.177–207; Brulé 2012. Recent informative collections: Mazarakis Ainian 2017; Partida and Schmidt-Dounas 2019. Note that Parker 2011: xi–xii pays virtually no attention to sanctuaries.

[4] For the development of Greek sanctuaries from the Mycenaean period until the early Iron Age, see the instructive survey in Eder 2019.

[5] Fehr 1996; Burkert 2001–11: vi.196-207; Mazarakis Ainian 2016. For the vocabulary of sanctuaries, see Casevitz 1984; García Ramón 2007.

[6] Hellmann 1993.

Typical features of a sanctuary were water (for ritual use), a tree or grove, and a stone (to mark the place as special),[7] but only the altar was indispensable.[8] Sanctuaries differed greatly in size and complexity, ranging from large supra-local ones, such as Delphi and Olympia, via urban sanctuaries, to very simple rural shrines and caves;[9] in fact, even some larger sanctuaries never acquired a temple.[10] There was no sharp distinction between gods and heroes in these respects. Admittedly, a sanctuary of heroes (*herôon*) was normally smaller than that of major divinities or often wholly absent, but some *herôa* were large enough to allow the squatting of Attic refugees during the Peloponnesian War (Thuc. 2.17.1).[11]

The Greeks had a rich vocabulary for what we nowadays call a 'cult image',[12] depending on the size, nature, and material of the images, as well as on the literary genre in which they were mentioned.[13] The earliest statues were probably of wood: a sitting one, such as Athena's in Troy, was normal for goddesses in archaic Greece, whereas male gods preferred the more manly attitude of standing (Figure 6).[14] Other divinities, however, could have aniconic statues: Apollo Agyieus regularly appears on coins as a conic column, and the famous image of Eros in Thespiae was only a rough stone.[15] Such statues coexisted with the more 'normal' figurative ones, which were much more decorated and colourful than the surviving examples suggest,[16] but in the course of the classical age aniconism started to sometimes evoke a certain 'abnormality' of the statue.[17] And indeed, strange statues of Artemis and Hera, but also of Dionysos, were regularly associated with festivals of reversal (Chapter IV, §3); sometimes these statues were considered so dangerous that they were tied up and only released

[7] On water, see Cole 1988; Trinkl 2009. On trees, see Burkert 1985: 29–30. For sacred groves, see Birge 1982; Scheid 1993; Bonnechere 2007. On stones, see Dowden 1989: 138–40.

[8] On altars, see Etienne 1992; Ekroth 2001, 2009; Hellmann 2006: 122–44.

[9] Genovese 1999; Baumer 2004; Sporn 2013b; Laferrière 2019.

[10] Sourvinou-Inwood 1993: 8, 16 n. 60 (e.g. no temple in the Miletan Delphinion before the Romans).

[11] Kearns 1992: 65–8; Pariente 1992: 204–16; Boehringer 2001.

[12] Bremmer 2019e: 101–3.

[13] There has been much recent interest in this area: Scheer 2000; Bettinetti 2001; Graf 2001; Steiner 2001; Linant de Bellefonds *et al.* 2004; Mylonopoulos 2010; Collard 2016; Hölscher 2017; Bremmer 2019e: 104–13.

[14] Jung 1982; see also Graf 1985: 44f.

[15] Fehrentz 1993 (Apollo Agyieus); Graf 2006 (Eros). In general, see Gaifman 2012; Lang 2016; Hölscher 2017: 224–38.

[16] See Brinkman and Scholl 2010.

[17] Bremmer 2019e: 108–11.

Figure 6. Gilded bronze statue of Apollo in temple with adjacent picture of the god himself with his lyre. Fragment of south Italian (Taranto) red-figure calyx krater, *c.* 390 BC.

once a year.[18] Heroes also had a statue and were often portrayed in armour, as many were believed to have been great warriors,[19] unlike, of course, healing heroes such as Asclepius. And, unlike images of Jesus or Mary in Christian churches, cult images were often shielded from the worshipers by a barrier, thus highlighting the distance between mortals and immortals.[20]

As with cult images, the Greeks also had a wide-ranging vocabulary for those officiating in sanctuaries, whom we usually range under the umbrella term 'priest'; in addition, the terms used even varied from city to city.[21] In fact, the modern term covers a motley of functions, such as ritual experts, sacrificers, preservers of sacrificial knowledge, representatives of divinities, mediators between mortals and immortals – albeit not all of them all of the time.[22] Unlike their Roman Catholic

[18] Graf 1985: 81–96 (fundamental); Icard-Gianolio 2004; Eich 2011: 371–99; Boschung 2015; Hölscher 2017: 148–71.

[19] Ar. fr. 240; *Adespota* fr. 948 Kassel/Austin; van Straten 1974: 187–9.

[20] Mattern 2007; Mylonopoulos 2011.

[21] For priests and priestesses, see Pirenne-Delforge and Georgoudi 2005; Dignas and Trampedach 2008; Parker 2011: 48–57; this volume, Chapter 1, §3 and Chapter VI.

[22] For the difficulties in defining the priesthood and differentiating it from a magistracy, see Bremmer 2012; Henrichs 2019: 177–92.

counterparts, Greek priests could inherit their function and, unlike priesthoods in all modern mainstream religions, priesthoods could be bought in Asia Minor and the islands off its coast.[23] Priests distinguished themselves through their white or purple clothing, and on vases they are pictured with sacrificial knives, whereas priestesses are often pictured with metal keys, some of which have been excavated.[24] In fact, temples were usually closed to worshippers and only opened on fixed or festive days.

Male priests usually served for gods, and priestesses (Chapter VI, §2) for goddesses, but, as with sacrificial victims (Chapter IV, §2), there was no iron rule: Athena regularly had a priest. Priests performed sacrifices and guarded the treasures of the sanctuary. In larger sanctuaries special personnel did the more menial jobs, such as preventing birds from fouling statues, whereas in smaller, rural sanctuaries priests were not always present and worshippers themselves could sacrifice after having called for the priest in vain.[25] Rather strikingly, male and female adolescents sometimes occupied a priestly function in initiatory cults. This shows how different Greek priests could be from ours. The occasional appearance in the outfit of their divinities is another illustration of this difference; on Attic vases Athena's priestess is sometimes difficult to distinguish from the goddess. Was this identification perhaps a priestly strategy to increase status because Greek priests were always subject to the authority of the people and never managed to develop into a ruling class, as they did in India or ancient Israel?[26]

In the end, though, it was the altar, not the temple or the statue, which was the real centre of a sanctuary, even though the temple itself may have been more important in rituals than is suggested by the literary tradition.[27] Several authors, who are all later than the fourth century BC, distinguish between a divine (bômos) and heroic (eschara) altar, the first being rectangular, monumental, and with a projecting step or stepped base, whereas the latter would be low, hollow, circular, and standing directly on the ground. As with the distinction between

---

[23] Parker 2011: 43 (inheritance), 49, 235–6 (priesthoods for sale).

[24] Mantis 1990: 28–65 (keys), 82–96 (iconography of priests), 114–15 (catalogue of preserved keys); Karatas 2019.

[25] Graf 1985: 40 (calling), 214 (Athena's priest). On bird fouling, see Eur. *Ion* 106–9; Maxmin 1975 (metal 'umbrellas' to protect statues); Danner 1993.

[26] On adolescents, see Bremmer 1999c: 189–90; Cole 2004: 132; Leventis 2019: 72–4. On identification with the gods, see Bérard 1989; Pirenne-Delforge 2010.

[27] Sporn 2015.

Olympian and Chthonic gods (Chapter II, §2), reality was more diverse, and various heroes had a divine altar.[28]

2. Locations

Major sanctuaries outside the walls or situated at remote places played important roles in political federations and the birth of the *polis*. Delphi and Olympia developed in an especially spectacular way in the ninth and eighth centuries because here the aristocracies of the surrounding areas could meet and compete in games and conspicuous offerings, thus fostering a feeling of common Greek identity. Other sanctuaries away from major cities developed into centres of political federations, such as Poseidon's at Boeotian Onchestos and on the isle of Kalaureia, off Troizen. Finally, sanctuaries could mark the borders of a city's territory, such as those of Hera Lacinia and Apollo Aleos, respectively south and north of Croton in south Italy. They could even be used to strengthen ties with border areas, as the Peisistratids did by connecting Athens with the outlying sanctuaries of Brauron and Eleutherae. In short, the location of the sanctuary contributed to determining its social and political roles.

But why were some divine sanctuaries located in the *polis* and others not?[29] Some scattered settlements had kept their most important cults at the original places before constituting *poleis* and federations.[30] Yet there is also a more interesting aspect to location. If a sanctuary important for the religious life of the community is not situated in the heart of that community or at such a distance that citizens have to leave their familiar surroundings in order to worship, it is also possible that these cults are in some ways in opposition to those which occupied a more central location. As cults co-determine the character of gods (Chapter II, §1), an extramural cult may therefore point to an 'eccentric' or less central divinity.[31] Is this supposition true?

In the heart of the city we naturally find Zeus and Athena, who as *polis* gods par excellence had sanctuaries in the agora and on the acropolis,

---

[28] Ekroth 2001, 2002: 23–74, 2009.

[29] On locations of sanctuaries in Magna Graecia, see Edlund 1987; Pugliese Carratelli 1988: 149–58. On Greece and the Aegean, see Schachter 1994; Osborne and Alcock 1994; Cole 2004: 21.

[30] For the supra-local sanctuaries, see Freitag and Haake 2019.

[31] As is persuasively argued by Graf 1982: 166.

respectively, although Zeus's origin as weather god remained visible in his sanctuaries on mountaintops.[32] Apollo and Demeter were more ambivalent cases. Apollo's sanctuary was often located in the agora, as in Peloponnesian Argos, Cretan Dreros, and Crimean Olbia, but he was also worshipped away from the centre at the seaside, especially with the epithet Delphinios, or in the 'suburbs', as in the Athenian Lykeion. The differing locations probably reflect his own ambivalent position between adolescence and adulthood (Chapter II, §3).[33] When inside the city, Demeter's sanctuaries were nearly always away from inhabited areas and the agora, as in Corinth and Priene, except for Athens, where the Eleusinion was in the agora. As a general rule, they were situated in front of or somewhat outside the city, often on the slope of a hill, which fits Demeter's 'eccentricity' (Chapter II, §3).[34] Finally, sanctuaries of the birth goddess Eileithyia could be found near the city gate, except in Sparta (Paus. 3.14.6): there was no place in the heart of the city for a goddess closely connected with pollution.[35]

Outside the *polis* we usually find sanctuaries of Poseidon,[36] Dionysos,[37] Hera, and Artemis. The Heraion was about 6–10 kilometres away from the city centre in Argos, Croton, and Paestum, and on Samos; on Paros it was situated in a hilly area. Hera's sanctuaries were connected with initiation and festivals of reversal; moreover, the rituals were often performed by women but concluded by men. Clearly, the Homeric picture of the quarrelsome wife of Zeus overlaid a much older, more complex cult.[38] Artemis' sanctuaries could also be found in mountainous regions, but their distinctive feature was the closeness of rivers and swampy places – witness her epithet Limnatis

[32] For Athena, see Burkert 1985: 140; Graf 1985: 44. For Zeus, see Graf 1985: 182, 197, 202–3 (mountains); Parker 1996: 29–33; van den Eijnde 2010–11; Romano 2019. On mountains in general, see Langdon 2000; Accorinti 2010; Sporn 2013a.

[33] Graf 1979a (near the sea or in the agora) and 1985: 222 (Apollo Lykeios in the agora); Jameson 2014: 41–61 (Apollo Lykeios outside the walls in Athens).

[34] Cole 2000 (fundamental). See also Işik 2000: 230; Tantillo 2015. Locations of Demeter's sanctuary on an acropolis (Thebes, Mytilene, Lepreon) may derive from the goddess's connection with political power (Chapter II, §3).

[35] See Paus. 2.5.4 (Corinth), 2.18.3 (Argos; see also Piérart 1982), 2.35.11 (Hermione).

[36] Poseidon's sanctuaries are often near the sea but also in the mountains: see Bremmer 2019e: 26.

[37] There were no temples of Dionysos in classical times, but the name of his sanctuary in Athens, *en limnais* ('in the marshes'), suggests locations outside the city, as does the fact that on vases Dionysos' sanctuary is often a cave (see Bérard 1976).

[38] Corso 1984 (Paros); Lattanzi 1991: 67–71 (Croton); Hägg 1992: 14–16 (Argos); Junker 1993 (Paestum); Walter, Clemente, and Niemeier 2019 (Samos). In general, see Graf 1982: 166–71.

('of the marshes'). This 'watery' environment was typical of Artemis, and the second-century rhetor Maximus of Tyre noted that 'fountains of water, hollow thickets and flowery meadows are sacred to Artemis' (8.1). Given Greece's aridity, these areas connected with Artemis must have been conspicuous for their moist, luxuriant lushness. As places of eternal spring they were particularly suited to girls in the full bloom of youth – a striking confirmation of Artemis' initiatory function.[39]

The location of hero shrines does not seem to have been very different from temples, although the former were usually simpler than the latter. They could be sited on prominent hills, in the midst of mountains (such as the *temenos* of Telephos on the Arcadian Mount Parthenion), or near springs (like the one at Attica where Makaria was worshipped). Heroes (never heroines) who had founded a city were often buried in the agora and clearly closely connected with the life of the *polis*;[40] in some cities, as in Athens and Thebes, there was even a secret heroic grave on which the safety of the city depended.[41] Some heroes' shrines were situated near the city gates because they were the most vulnerable parts of the city, which therefore needed support from supernatural warriors: Apollo was also often invoked as defender of the gates.[42]

Our analysis of the location of sanctuaries, then, has confirmed our discussion of the gods and heroes: those connected most with the political and social order also occupied central places in the Greek *poleis*. For a complete picture of Greek gods and heroes, the location of their sanctuaries cannot be neglected.

Finally, familiarity breeds contempt, as the proverb says, but does it also promote intimacy? In other words, was it religiously important to live close to a sanctuary? For the Greeks, of all the good relationships between humans, that between neighbours was considered to be best. It would hardly be surprising, therefore, if they also developed a special relationship with those gods and heroes whose shrines and sanctuaries were in their neighbourhood or even adjacent to their houses. In fact, many examples in ancient literature show that 'a hero whose shrine

[39] Cole 2004: 179–97.
[40] Leschhorn 1984; Malkin 1987: 189–240; Hornblower 1991–2009: i.20f.
[41] Malkin 2009; Bremmer 2019e: 215–17 (secret graves).
[42] On hero sanctuaries, see Kearns 1992; Ekroth 2007: 108–11. For Apollo, see Graf 1985: 173–6; von Mangoldt 2013.

was near an individual house might be "domesticated" and receive regular greetings and offerings from his mortal neighbours; in return, the hero was expected to influence the fortunes of "his" family'. If, indeed, our literary evidence mainly concerns heroes, this does not mean that the closeness of a divine shrine was considered to be insignificant. On the contrary: many Greek parents gave their children names that were expressive of the fact that a god was their neighbour (*geitôn*), such as Athanogiton (Athena), Damatrogiton (Demeter), Diogeiton (Zeus), Pythogeiton (Apollo), or just Theogeiton, 'God's neighbour'. One may even wonder whether these names were not suggestive of a more personal devotion to a specific god.[43]

3. Social, economic, and religious functions

Greek sanctuaries functioned in a much more varied way in society than modern churches or mosques do, as some examples of their social, economic, and political roles may illustrate.[44] Excavations as well as epigraphic and literary testimonia show that many sanctuaries contained temporary and permanent buildings which were used for dining; in some cases, as in Corinth, the cooking pots and drinking cups could still be recovered. In coastal or island sanctuaries, there is evidence for abundant consumption of fish. The small Greek houses offered little possibilities for larger groups to convene and a sanctuary was a secure place to meet, since it was divine property.[45] That is also why slaves, criminals, and political victims frequently sought refuge in temples through the ritual of supplication. As today, the number of suppliants could be considerable: Herodotus mentions the presence of 300 boys in a Samian sanctuary of Artemis (3.48). Not surprisingly, some sanctuaries had to set aside large tracts of land on which to house these 'permanent pilgrims'.[46]

Like many medieval Christian churches, major sanctuaries owned large estates to pay for their upkeep, personnel, and construction of new buildings, though the precise nature of their property remains a subject of debate, and the relationship of *polis* and sanctuary in this

---

[43] Rusten 1983 (quotation from 296). On onomastics, see Robert 1989: 261; Parker 2000c.
[44] These aspects are under-researched, but see Ghinatti 1983.
[45] Leypold 2008; Bentz and Bumke 2013; Mylona 2015.
[46] Christensen 1984; Sinn 2000.

respect is often rather complicated.[47] Yet these estates also had a wider economic function. The land was leased and on Delos, for instance, we hear of farms, trees, barley, and vineyards.[48] And like the medieval Church – witness the dissolution of the monasteries by Henry VIII – rich estates stimulated greed. Many a sanctuary issued a sacred law to prohibit the grazing of its meadows and the cutting of its trees.[49] The land could even be so valuable that various wars were fought over the uncultivated land of the Cirrhaean plain below Delphi; comparable wars took place in Crete well up to the end of the second century BC.[50]

Temples also functioned as reserve banks. According to Thucydides (6.20.4), in the debate before the second Athenian expedition to Sicily (415 BC) Nicias warned the Athenians that the Sicilians had not only considerable private means but also great wealth in the sanctuary of Selinus, where, as in other temples, objects of precious metal were safeguarded by countersigning them with names of gods. Indeed, the inventories of Greek sanctuaries, in which temple officials recorded the treasures and dedications (see below) of the temples at the end of their service, demonstrate the sanctuaries' considerable wealth, the lure of which some people clearly could not resist.[51] Inventories also show that in times of need cities and their inhabitants happily borrowed from their gods but were not always as forthcoming in paying back. The gods were lenient creditors.[52]

In addition to their economic function, temples played a role in political life. The first written laws in Greece were deposited in a sanctuary or actually inscribed on the more visible walls of the major temple of the city, such as the famous laws of Cretan Gortyn on the walls of the sanctuary of Apollo Pythios. Indeed, it was usually a sanctuary of Apollo that contained the laws, decrees, and treaties of a city, although the Athenians used the sanctuary of the Mother of the Gods, the Metroon, as their city archive. At least initially, the choice of a temple

---

[47] Horster 2004; Papazarkadas 2011; Rousset 2013 (with thanks to Edward Harris); Patera 2016.

[48] Brunet 1990; Dillon 1997; Mylonopoulos 2008; Horster 2010.

[49] On trees, see Jordan and Perlin 1984; Henrichs 2019: 503–27.

[50] Parker 1983: 160–6; Chaniotis 1988.

[51] For Selinus, see *SEG* 34.970. It was not until the fourth century that these treasures, which the inviolability of sanctuaries had always protected, became the object of looting: see Parker 1983: 170–6; Pritchett 1991: 160–8; Trampedach 2005. On stealing from temples, see Kosmetatou 2003.

[52] On temples as banks, see Ampolo 1989–90; Chankowski 2005, 2011; Migeotte 2006.

for 'publication' and preservation must have suggested inviolability and
a binding character. When the Ephesian philosopher Heraclitus (*c.* 500
BC) deposited his work in the temple of Artemis (Diog. Laert. 9.6), his
gesture may have been a continuance of this tradition.[53]

But what about worship? Did all sanctuaries fulfil the same functions? That was not the case. Some of them were specialized, such as
those for mysteries and healing cults (Chapter VII, §§1–2) or those
that provided oracles. Divination has to uphold a certain amount of
objectivity to remain credible and, consequently, major oracular shrines
were situated at a fair distance from the territories of influential
city-states: Homer knew of the wealth of Delphi (*Il.* 9.404–5) and faraway Dodona with 'the Helloi, your interpreters, with unwashed feet,
sleepers on the ground' (16.234–5, trans. Janko 1992); Olympia, too,
started as an oracular shrine before giving us the Olympic Games.[54]
But some oracles were nearer home, such as those of Amphiaraos in
Oropos, not far from Athens, Trophonios, not very far from Thebes,
Didyma near Miletos, and Klaros on the edge of the territories of
Notion and Colophon.[55] There is a certain difference between these faraway and near-to-home oracles. The former flourished especially in the
archaic period and were consulted in such matters as colonization and
land distribution, the great problems in the period of Greek state formation. The latter were more often consulted in matters of potential
civic troubles. But in all cases ancient oracles assisted in making choices
and setting the seal on collective decisions, rather than in predicting the
future.[56] The crystal ball is a recent invention.

The main purpose of most sanctuaries, however, was to enable worshippers to sacrifice (Chapter IV, §2) and to make votive offerings,
through which they could also express personal devotion.[57] Whenever
the Greeks wanted to thank the gods and/or tried to obtain a favour,
they could dedicate a votive offering, which would be a more lasting testimony than a sacrifice. Even though the extremes in value (poor painted
wooden panels and rich gold and silver objects) have all but disappeared,

[53] Thomas 1989: 38–40 (the Metroon); Hölkeskamp 1992: 99–102; Hawke 2011.

[54] For Dodona, see, most recently, Parker 2016; Chaniotis 2017; and, in general, Piccinini
2017. On Delphi, see C. Morgan 1990; Scott 2015. On Olympia, see Sinn 1991. For oracular
shrines in general, see Friese 2010.

[55] For the Amphiaraion, see Roesch 1984. For the Trophoneion, see Bonnechere 2003. For
Didyma and Klaros, see Oesterheld 2008.

[56] Parker 2000a.

[57] Rask 2016.

just as the textiles that were once dedicated,[58] many inscriptions and votive reliefs have been preserved which allow us a unique glimpse into Greek religious practice. Through them we see who thought of the gods and why, where, and what offerings were thought suitable.[59]

Thanks to the possibility of using very cheap material, all sections of society could make votive offerings, even though, of course, not only poor people dedicated modest votives.[60] Men, women, families – the gods were most hospitable. Sometimes, foreigners too made dedications to Greek gods. Herodotus mentions the many votives in gold and silver that Croesus offered (1.50–2, 90),[61] but he was not the only one to do so. In archaic times especially, many traders, in particular Phoenicians but also the occasional Etruscan, Lydian, and Egyptian, enriched Greek sanctuaries.[62]

The 'why' of offerings is sometimes explained by the 'what' (and vice versa). After a victory, part of the booty could be consecrated, or soldiers dedicated their own weapons.[63] As here was a story to tell,[64] local sanctuaries thus served as a kind of museum, helping to keep collective memories alive, and, in a way, as *lieux de mémoire*.[65] A girl could dedicate her toys to Artemis on the eve of her wedding and a boy his statue (one of the famous *kouroi*) to Apollo on the occasion of his initiation, even if these were sometimes extremely small (Figure 7).[66] Healing gods received replicas of the limbs they had cured and so their sanctuaries were filled with arms and legs, vulvae and penises.[67] In other cases, worshippers dedicated figurines of divinities in their specific sanctuaries but also in those of other gods; once again, the gods were most hospitable.[68]

[58] Brøns 2016.
[59] Van Straten 1981, 2000; Osborne 2004; Parker 2004; Duplouy 2006: 185–249; Greco and Ferrara 2008; Prêtre 2009; Papasavvas and Fourrier 2012; Lindström and Pilz 2013. For painted votives, see Nowicka 1990. For formulas of votive inscriptions, see Lazzarini 1989–90.
[60] Salapata 2018.
[61] Nenci 1993; Bassi 2014.
[62] On Phoenicians, see Kilian-Dirlmeier 1985, to be read with the qualifications of Mylonopoulos 2008; on Etruscans, see A. Johnston 1993; on Lydians, see Kerschner 2006; on Egyptians, see Bumke 2007; in general, see Kaplan 2006.
[63] Baitinger 2011; Frielinghaus 2011; Jim 2014: 176–202; Graells i Fabregat and Longo 2018; J. Schröder 2020: 24–101.
[64] For this aspect of sanctuaries, see Eidinow 2020.
[65] See Scheer 1996; Shaya 2006; Haake and Jung 2011.
[66] *Anth. Graeca* 6.280 (girl); Martini 1990.
[67] See Forsén 1996; Oberhelman 2014; Schörner 2015; Petridou 2016; Draycott and Graham 2017; Hughes 2017; Graham 2020.
[68] Alroth 1989, 1989–90.

Figure 7. A kouros could be small: this one from eastern Greece, *c.* 580 BC, is only 28 cm high.

Finally, there were costly gifts whose purpose was clearly not only to please gods but also to impress humans, such as those by Croesus; the gift of golden tripods to Delphi by Sicilian tyrants at the beginning of the fifth century was in the same vein.[69] Several states even had treasure houses, which were specially prominent at Delos, Delphi, and Olympia and served to store the valuable dedications of their citizens, but also to glorify the relevant *poleis*.[70] And people dedicated curiosities. In the Heraion of Samos, a jaw of a crocodile, teeth of a hippopotamus, antlers of an antelope, and eggs of an ostrich have been found. In the same sanctuary even living curiosities, peacocks, walked about.[71] In

[69] Krumeich 1991.
[70] Nering 2015.
[71] Boessneck and von den Driesch 1981, 1993; Ekroth 2018a. In general, see Tassignon 2005. On peacocks, see Antiphanes, fr. 173; Menodotus *FGrH* 541 F 2.

other words, some major sanctuaries must have looked like a kind of 'curiosity shop' or museum.[72] And what about the inside of popular temples?[73] An inventory of the Athenian temple of Asclepius describes in great detail where the dedications were located: a gold crown, iron finger-ring, and gold chain 'at the ridge beam', and a woman's face and ten silver reliefs 'on the left as one enters. First rafter'. The inventory thus allows us to reconstruct the whole interior of the temple, which 'must have closely resembled not the bare rooms of our drawings but the most jumbled and crowded antique store or museum storeroom that most of us can imagine'.[74]

Finally, dedications have a history, too. In the course of the archaic age, striking changes took place in the major Greek sanctuaries. A good example is the dedication of bronze jewellery in Olympia. An older investigation, the results of which still seem to reflect the chronological development, even if the precise numbers are out of date, noted only 49 finds from the period *c.* 1050–750 BC, but 948 finds from *c.* 750–450 and, again, only 77 finds from *c.* 450–150. These changes, which can be paralleled in other objects such as weapons, are not easy to explain.[75] They probably reflect the changing status of the aristocracy at the end of the archaic age, but other factors may also have played a role. The absence of informative texts prevents a clearer view in this respect.[76]

---

[72] Shaya 2005; Tanner 2006: 205–36.
[73] D. Harris 1995; Paliompeis 1996; Krumeich 2008: 73–7; Sporn 2014.
[74] Aleshire 1989: 177–248 (inventory), 1991: 41–6 (quotation at 46).
[75] See Frielinghaus 2010, 2013.
[76] On the changes, see Snodgrass 1989–90; Barringer 2010: 170–1.

IV. RITUAL

When Herodotus describes the religion of non-Greek people, he mainly concentrates on their ritual. Consequently, it seems a reasonable conclusion that he, and presumably also his fellow Greeks, understood the significance of religion largely in ritual terms.[1] Although recent scholarship has paid much attention to belief (Chapter I), there can be little doubt that ritual constitutes the heart of ancient Greek religion. Accordingly, Burkert began his analysis of classical Greek religion with a chapter called 'Ritual and Sanctuary'.[2] However, as the content of the term is not self-evident, I will start this chapter with some introductory observations on the use of the term and on the possibilities for studying ancient ritual (§1). Subsequently I will analyse important ritual acts, such as prayer, procession, and, in particular, sacrifice (§2). I conclude with a discussion of various larger ritual complexes (§3).

1. What is ritual?

Considering the importance attached to ritual by Herodotus, it is perhaps surprising to notice that the Greeks did not have an all-embracing category called 'ritual'.[3] They were not alone in this. We find the same phenomenon in, for example, Japanese and Turkish religions. Apparently, when ritual is the core of a religion, it need not be distinguished as a discrete class of religious phenomena.[4] The Greeks approached ritual acts and processes from at least three different angles. First, they called many of their ritual activities *ta nomizomena* ('what is customary'; see Chapter I, §3); modern scholarship of ritual similarly stresses the importance for rites to look traditional, even if they are recent constructions or innovations.[5] Second, they often named rituals after their central, most prominent part: the Athenian festival Anthesteria was often called Choes from its most striking day (see §3), and the *sphagia*, a type of sacrifice which was not followed by a banquet, was named after its most

---

[1] Thus, persuasively Gould 2001: 359–77.

[2] Burkert 1985: 54–118, but more problem-oriented in Burkert 1979: 35–58. Bruit Zaidman and Schmitt Pantel 1992 also begin with ritual, but Rudhardt 1992 with the vocabulary of the sacred, Jost 1992 with the gods, and Parker 2011 with the absence of authoritative sacred texts.

[3] As observed by Calame 1991: 196–203.

[4] See the fascinating study of Stausberg *et al.* 2006.

[5] For a good introduction to modern theories, see Stephenson 2019.

salient act, the 'piercing of the throat'.[6] Third, many elaborate rituals were called *heortai*, a term associated with good food, good company, and good entertainment, as appears from a statement by the philosopher Democritus: 'a life without *heortai* is like a road without inns' (B230 Diels/Kranz).[7] The term is usually translated as 'festival', but our modern equivalent hardly covers the variety of ancient festivities or the presence of sombre aspects among them.[8] The *heortê*, then, was an important way of celebrating the gods, which provided a pleasant interruption to the routines of everyday life.

The fragmentation of the vocabulary of what nowadays is called 'ritual' is not a purely Greek phenomenon, but can be observed in many cultures.[9] In fact, it was only about 1900 that anthropologists and historians of religion started to use 'ritual' as the standard term for repetitive, representational behaviour that often has to be decoded.[10] In other words, by introducing a new classification based on only one aspect of a mass of heterogeneous phenomena, viz. its prescribed and repetitive character, they could reduce both single rites, such as prayer (see §2), and extended rituals, such as initiation (see §3), to a common denominator. I follow the modern categorization but keep in mind that 'ritual' is not a native category.

It is not easy to analyse ancient ritual, since the evidence usually stems from different periods, places, and genres. Moreover, the nature of the evidence rarely enables us to integrate the opinions of the participants or to describe a ritual in all its details, since ancient authors focused on the unusual and habitually considered the usual too well known to be mentioned.[11] Necessarily but regrettably, our descriptions, then, often have to focus on the structure of a ritual and to be brief on its psychological impact or historical development.

2. Prayer, procession, and sacrifice

The more elaborate Greek festivals were made up of a limited number of basic ritual acts: dances,[12] which were especially important for girls in

[6] Vernant 1990: 169–79 and 1991: 244–57; Jameson 2014: 112–26.

[7] Laxander 2000; Burkert 2001–11: vi.241–58; Parker 2011: 171–223.

[8] Mikalson 1982.

[9] See Stausberg *et al.* 2006.

[10] For the historiography of the term, see Boudewijnse 1995; Bremmer 1998: 14–24; Bremmer 2019c (earliest history of the term).

[11] See the interesting reflections of Henrichs 2019: 93–102 on insider interpretations.

[12] Delavaud-Roux 1994; Henrichs 1996a, 1996b; Ceccarelli 1998. For a good introduction and historiography, see Naerebout 1997.

the archaic period,[13] musical and athletic contests,[14] prayers and hymns, processions, and, most important of all, animal sacrifices. Prayers usually followed a structure of invocation, claim for attention, and request, as when Achilles prays to Zeus (*Il.* 16.233–48). Striking differences from Christian prayer were the lack of a feeling of gratitude (instead, the Greeks offered expressions of praise and honour), the posture (Greeks usually did not kneel but prayed with hands raised – see Appendix), the loudness (silent prayer became more usual only in late antiquity), and the regular singing of prayers in the form of hymns;[15] the latter sometimes developed into a special genre for a particular god: paeans for Apollo and dithyrambs for Dionysos.[16]

Processions were part and parcel of Greek life.[17] The sacrificial procession paraded the value of the sacrificial victim and the piety of the sacrificers (Figure 8). The wedding procession advertised the official nature of a wedding. For more than half a millennium, a yearly procession kept the memory alive of those who had fallen at the Battle of Plataea in 479 BC, even though the ritual will hardly have remained unchanged in all those years. Processions with a divine statue were often part of festivals in which the normal social order was inverted, as when slaves were free to do what they wanted or women were on top for a day (see §3). Yet they could also stress the existing order, as when, once a year, the leading Milesian aristocrats, the Molpoi, travelled in procession to Didyma singing paeans at all the sanctuaries along the road. Processions could even symbolize the restoration of the old order, as when Thrasybulus solemnized the reinstatement of Athenian democracy in 403 BC with a march from the Piraeus to the Acropolis. In short, the functions of processions were manifold.[18]

Processions were particularly suited to making symbolic statements about power relations, since they often drew large audiences. For example, during the sacrificial procession of the Panathenaea,

---

[13] Calame 1997 (≈ Calame 2019); Albertocchi 2015.

[14] Kotsidu 1991; Shapiro 1992; Rotstein 2012.

[15] On prayer, see Versnel 1981b; Mikalson 1989; Aubriot-Sévin 1992; van der Horst 1994: 252–77 (silent prayer); Pulleyn 1997; Chapot and Laurot 2001. On hymns, see Lehmann 1997; Furley and Bremer 2001; Furley 2007.

[16] For paeans, see S. Schröder 1999 (to be read with d'Alessio 2000); Rutherford 2001. For dithyrambs, see Zimmermann 1992.

[17] Graf 1996b; Kavoulaki 1999; Kubatzki 2018.

[18] For Plataea, see Yates 2019: 76–80. On Molpoi, see Herda 2006. For Thrasybulus, see Strauss 1985.

Figure 8. Sacrificial procession. Attic black-figure Siana cup by the C Painter, *c.* 570–565 BC.

Athenian colonies and allies had to parade a cow and panoply, the daughters of Athenian metics carried parasols for female citizens, and adult metics carried sacrificial equipment; colonies also had to contribute a phallus to the procession of the Great Dionysia.[19] Whereas these processions showed Athenian dominance, others could demonstrate modesty. During the Spartan Hyacinthia festival, adolescent girls rode down in a procession to Amyclae, showing themselves off to the community after, probably, an initiatory seclusion at the border area. Some aristocratic girls rode in race-carts, others in carriages with the shape of griffins or goat-stags. The daughter of the Spartan king Agesilaus went in one of the latter vehicles, a public one, which was 'no more elaborate than that of any other maiden'. Evidently, the Hyacinthia procession normally demonstrated that some Spartans were more equal than others, although Spartan ideology claimed otherwise.[20]

All these elements were important, but the pivot of Greek ritual was undoubtedly animal sacrifice.[21] In the 1970s and 1980s, both Burkert

---

[19] *IG* I³ 34.42, 46.15–16, 71.57 (cow, phallus, and panoply); *Adespota* fr. 240 Kassel/Austin; Ael. *VH* 6.1 (equipment); Miller 1992: 103–5; Neils 1992 (beautifully produced); Cole 1993.

[20] Xen. *Ag.* 8.7 (quotation); Calame 1997: 175.

[21] Most recently, see Parker 2011: 124–70; Pirenne-Delforge and Prescendi 2011; Faraone and Naiden 2012; Ekroth and Wallensten 2013; Naiden 2013; Ekroth 2014; Bielawski 2017; Hitch

and Vernant (and his school) devoted much of their scholarly efforts to
the meaning of sacrifice and its place in Greek society – although drawing very different conclusions.[22] We still lack investigations of local
practices (though a start has been made[23]), but two developments in
particular now enable us to evaluate these studies in a more satisfactory
manner than even a few decades ago. First, we now know that Attic
vases and votive reliefs are important sources for sacrificial representations,[24] even though we should realize that iconographical representations have their own problems and are not, so to say, realistic
depictions of the ritual.[25] Second, biologists have increasingly paid
attention to the faunal remains of excavated altars – a practice often
nowadays called zooarchaeology – which allows glimpses of the realities
of Greek sacrificial practice rather than the often idealizing representations of literature and vase-paintings.[26] Here, instead of a step-by-step
analysis of normative Greek animal sacrifice,[27] sacrifices at the beginning of battle, at the crossing of rivers, or at the conclusion of oaths,[28]
the difference between chthonian and Olympian sacrifice (a debate that
has much advanced in recent years),[29] the banqueting and group worshipping, or even human sacrifice,[30] space limits us to two questions.

Bearing in mind our attention to the hierarchy within the Greek pantheon (Chapter II, §3 and Chapter III, §2), I will first briefly look at the
choice of sacrificial victims. Did all divinities receive the same animals
or did some fare better than others? Although cattle constituted the
most valued victims, the preferred victims for all major gods were
sheep and goats.[31] The main exceptions to this rule were Hestia (the
goddess of the [city] hearth), who customarily received a preliminary,
usually cheap, sacrifice, and Demeter, who traditionally received a
pig(let); on Attic vases, Dionysos was also regularly associated with a

and Rutherford 2017; Lippolis, Vannicelli, and Parisi 2018; Bremmer 2019e: 303–35; Ekroth
2019; Graf 2020.
    [22] For a summary of their views, see Naiden 2015. For the reception of the Paris school in the
Anglophone world, see Ekroth 2020.
    [23] Tsoukala 2009; Bundrick 2014; Carbon 2017; Parker 2018a.
    [24] Van Straten 1995; Gebauer 2002; Hermary et al. 2004; T. Smith 2016; Klöckner 2017.
    [25] Klöckner 2006.
    [26] See Ekroth 2009, 2017.
    [27] See now, with extensive bibliography, Bremmer 2019e: 303–35, upon which I draw in this
section.
    [28] On sacrifices at the beginning of battles, see Jouan 1990–91 (also when crossing rivers);
Parker 2000b; Jameson 2014: 98–126. On sacrifices at the conclusion of oaths, see Faraone 1993.
    [29] Hägg and Alroth 2005; Parker 2011: 80–4, 283–6.
    [30] Bremmer 2019e: 349–415; Henrichs 2019: 37–68.
    [31] Jameson 2014: 215–20; Bremmer 2019e: 307–8.

pig sacrifice.[32] Polluted Eileithyia (Chapter III, §2), cruel Ares (below, §3), and spooky Hekate received dogs, of which the consumption was much more widespread than is usually thought, as recent faunal analyses show;[33] Aphrodite was honoured with birds, Asclepius with cockerels, and randy Priapus with fish.[34] Most gods, then, received cattle, sheep, and goats, whereas inedible or cheap animals were offered to those divinities that were connected with impurity and/or situated at the margin of the social order. The 'eccentric' position of Demeter and Dionysos, which was already noted during discussion of the gods (Chapter II, §3) and the locations of their sanctuaries (Chapter III, §3), is confirmed by the 'eccentricity' of their victims, the pigs, whose rooting, digging habits made them less suitable for densely populated areas.[35] Evidently, the choice of sacrificial victims reflected and helped to reinforce the divine pecking order.

The question of sacrificial hierarchy has received very little attention in recent times, but the second question goes to the heart of a long debate on Greek sacrifice: what was the significance of the ritual surrounding the killing of the sacrificial victim? Modern debate started with a highly learned study by the Swiss classicist and folklorist Karl Meuli (1891–1968), who argued that Greek sacrifice ultimately derived from hunting practices and that hunters, feeling guilty for having killed their game, regularly tried to disclaim their responsibility.[36] There can be no doubt that Meuli was partially right and partially wrong: a number of features of Greek sacrifice, such as the disclaiming of responsibility, the hanging up of the sacrificial victim's skull, the burning of small pieces of meat, the burning of bones, the tasting of the innards, and the preservation of the skin of the victim, all have their closest parallels in hunting practices. Yet the Greeks were no archaic hunters and, unlike them, broke the bones of the sacrificial victims to extract the marrow; they did not give back the bones to a Lord/Lady of the Animals; and they used grains in their sacrificial ritual – to mention only some of the differences from hunting societies.[37]

---

[32] For Hestia, see Eupolis F 301; Graf 1985: 363; Detienne 1989: 89–98. For Demeter, see, most recently, Forstenpointner 2001; Jameson 2014: 213–14; Amory 2016. For Dionysos, see Peirce 1993: 255f. In general, see Hermary *et al.* 2004: 68–95 (well documented).

[33] Most recently, see Georgoudi 2018.

[34] On birds, see Villing 2017 (with previous bibliography, also on cockerels). On fish, see *Anth. Graeca* 10.9, 14, 16; Robert and Robert 1950: 82; Mylona 2008.

[35] Jameson 2014: 213–15.

[36] Meuli 1975: ii.907–1021 (an article first published in 1946).

[37] For the continuity between hunt and sacrifice, see Bremmer 2018b: 236–43.

Walter Burkert made the feeling of guilt, as analysed by Meuli, the focus of his sacrificial theory. His crowning witness is the Dipolieia, an Athenian festival in the month Bouphonion, during which an ox was sacrificed because it had tasted sacrificial cakes. Subsequently the sacrificial knife was condemned and expelled from the city, but the ox ritually re-erected, yoked to a plough. In the aetiological myth, the killer of the ox eased his conscience by suggesting that everybody should partake in the killing of the sacrificial victim.[38] Burkert took this 'comedy of innocence' to be paradigmatic for every sacrifice: humans experience angst when actually killing the animals and have feelings of guilt over the blood which they have shed.[39]

However, Burkert's observations cannot be accepted in their totality, since there are virtually no testimonies of actual fear and guilt among the Greeks: Attic vases constantly connect sacrifice with ideas of festivity, celebrations, and blessings.[40] The question of disclaiming is also more complicated than Burkert thought.[41] The ritual of the Dipolieia cannot wholly make up for this absence: it presupposed the developed Attic rules of justice and had only limited circulation, being found only in Athens and a few neighbouring communities,[42] even though the month name Boukation, which is related to Bouphonion, in central Greece suggests that comparable festivals were more widespread once.[43] Its protagonist was a plough-ox, which, reportedly, it had once been a crime to kill at Athens.[44] Meuli considered the plough a latecomer in the ritual, but it was its vital position in Athenian society and its closeness to the farmer that made the killing of the plough-ox the subject of an elaborate ritual: Theophrastus (fr. 584A Fortenbaugh) explicitly notes that the ritual was inaugurated to enable people to eat the ox.

The expansion of the Athenian state, however, which required the sacrifice of numerous oxen in order to feed the people at the banquets

---

[38] Parker 2005: 187–91.

[39] For Burkert's views, see Burkert 1983, 1996, and the articles collected in vol. 5 of Burkert 2001–11. The expression 'comedy of innocence' (*Unschuldskomödie*) was coined by Meuli (1975: ii.1005).

[40] Peirce 1993.

[41] Georgoudi 2008; Parker 2011: 129–30.

[42] Karystos (*IG* XII 9.207), Chalkidike (*SEG* 38.671), Delos (*IG* XI 2.203 A; *SEG* 35.882), and Tenos (*IG* XII 5.842).

[43] For the month name, see Egetmeyer 2010: i.312–15.

[44] Aristoxenus fr. 29 Wehrli; Ael. *VH* 5.14; Varro, *Rust.* 2.5.3; Columella 6 *praef.* 7; Schol. *Od.* 12.353. See also Aratus 131–2; Ov. *Met.* 15.120–42, 470.

accompanying state festivals – Isocrates mentions sacrificial processions of 300 oxen (*Ar.* 29) – removed the original tie which the farmers of an earlier, smaller Athens would have felt with their plough-oxen. It is no wonder, then, that Aristophanes in his *Clouds* (984–5) considers the Dipolieia/Bouphonia an archaic affair. Yet there seem to be no really convincing arguments against the fact that we have here an ancient ritual that with its 'comedy of innocence' preserved a mode of behaviour that clearly went back to hunting practices. In other words, it is not an unusual development, as Robert Parker has stated, but an unusual survival.[45]

Finally, in explicit opposition to Meuli and Burkert, Jean-Pierre Vernant argued both that Greek sacrificial rites should not be compared with hunting rituals but resituated within their proper Greek system and that the killing of the victim does not constitute the centre of gravity of sacrifice, although he explicitly noted that rituals, myths, and representations are all painfully careful in avoiding any reference to the actual killing of the sacrificial victim. In this way, according to Vernant, the Greeks wanted to exclude the elements of violence and savagery from their sacrifice in order to differentiate it from murder.[46] Vernant was certainly right in questioning Meuli's and Burkert's all-too-strong accentuation of the influence of hunting traditions: Meuli overlooked the influence of Syro-Palestine,[47] which shows that there is not a straight line between Greek sacrificial and archaic hunting practices, and other differences with societies of hunters (see above). On the other hand, the differentiation between sacrifice and murder does indicate an underlying feeling of unease with the ritual, as is confirmed by other indications. In the myth of the Dipolieia, the killer of the ox is a foreigner and the sacrificial knife is hidden as long as possible;[48] the Greeks employed the euphemism 'to do' for sacrificing; and, without the existence of some mixed feelings about sacrificial killing, it remains hard to explain why Orphics, Pythagoreans, and Empedocles rejected animal sacrifice altogether.[49] Killing for sacrifice,

[45] For his somewhat inconclusive analysis, see Parker 2011: 129–30. See also McInerney 2014; Lebreton 2015; Humphreys 2018: ii.641–3.

[46] Detienne and Vernant 1979; Vernant 1991: 290–302 (291–2 for Vernant's opposition to Meuli and Burkert). The theses of Detienne and Vernant have received new, sometimes critical, attention in Georgoudi, Koch Piettre, and Schmidt 2005; Mehl and Brulé 2008; and Ekroth 2018c.

[47] Ekroth 2018b.

[48] Bonnechere 1999; Georgoudi 2005.

[49] For Pythagoras and the Pythagoreans, see the exhaustive bibliography of Macris 2018.

then, did not generate fear and angst, but it certainly generated feelings of unease in some circles of Greek society.

There is one last point to make. Whereas the Greeks themselves did represent gods in the act of sacrifice (Figure 9), the protagonists in the modern debates feel apparently ill at ease with the religious functions of sacrifice and approach the subject in a strikingly secular manner. For Meuli, it was nothing but ritual slaughter; for Burkert, the shared aggression of the sacrificial killing primarily leads to the founding of a community; and for Vernant sacrifice was, fundamentally, killing for eating.[50] Clearly, however, this act, which stands at the centre of Greek ritual, is much richer than these reductive formulas suggest. In order to do justice to the rich and varied evidence, studies of sacrifice will be satisfactory only if they are based on the combination of literary, epigraphical, iconographical, and osteological evidence and not if they concentrate on just one of these aspects.

3. Initiation and festivals

Regarding more elaborate rituals, modern anthropology often distinguishes between one-off rites of transition and cyclical rites that are repeated at regular intervals, such as New Year. I will conclude this chapter with a discussion of both types, paying special attention to their performance, function, symbols, and logic. I start with initiation, which has been a productive concept in the last half-century, although not uncontested.[51] Instead of the more often discussed rites of Athens and Sparta,[52] I will concentrate on Crete, as the fourth-century historian Ephoros has left us a detailed, contemporary report about its male initiation.[53] As was the case with 'ritual' (§1), the Greeks had no term for 'initiation', but Minoans and early Indo-Europeans practised it,[54] the Spartans called their initiatory process *agôgê* ('the leading of a

---

[50] Meuli 1975: ii.948: 'dass das Olympische Opfer nichts anderes sei als ein rituelles Schlachten'; Burkert 1983: 35–48; Vernant 1981: 26: 'Sacrifier, c'est fondamentalement tuer pour manger.'

[51] Versnel 1993: 48–60 (extensive bibliographies); Graf 1993c; Padilla 1999. Contested by Dodd and Faraone 2003, but see Ma 2008 (with some modifications of the model, stressing its civic nature in historical Greece) and Dowden 2011.

[52] For Sparta, see Ducat 2006. For Athens, see Vidal-Naquet 1983: 151–75 and 1992.

[53] Ephoros *FGrH* 70 F 149 (= Strabo 10.4.16–20: all quotes); Koehl 1997; Seelentag 2015.

[54] Marinatos 1993: 201–20; Bremmer and Horsfall 1987: 38–43, 53–6 (Bremmer on Indo-Europeans).

Figure 9. Sacrificing Nike. Tondo of Attic red-figure cup, Sabouroff Painter, *c.* 460 BC.

horse by the hand': see below on *agela*), and the names of various initiatory festivals have survived. We, the outsiders, construct a whole,
whereas the insiders focused more on the different parts.[55] Naturally,
there will have been local differences between the various Cretan cities.
My reconstruction should therefore be taken as an 'ideal' ritual rather
than assuming that every detail will have been practised in every Cretan
city, but the cities resembled one another sufficiently structurally to
warrant the analysis.[56]

Cretan political power was in the hands of an aristocratic elite which
dominated both the serfs (the native Cretans) and the less privileged
free. The aristocrats were organized in clubs and dined in 'men's
houses' (*andreia*), where young Cretan boys, summer and winter

[55] Anthropologists such as Geertz (1983: 56–8) have stressed that these views are two, necessary, sides of the same coin; see also Ginzburg 2013.
[56] See Chaniotis 2005; Seelentag 2015: 93–128.

dressed in the same dirty garment, waited on the adults. They received little food and drink, and their main activity was fighting.[57] At seventeen, the boys who were 'most conspicuous and also most influential' – surely the sons of the elite – collected as many boys as possible around them into an *agela* ('herd of horses'): apparently, the youths were seen as unruly foals who had to be domesticated.[58]

The 'herds' were supervised by the fathers of these boys, who also directed their most important activities: running, hunting, dancing in choruses, marching over steep roads, and fighting in gymnasia 'with the fist and with clubs, as was prescribed by law' (Heraclides Lembus fr. 15). On certain appointed days, the *agelai* fought against each other, 'marching rhythmically into battle, to the tune of pipe and lyre, as is their custom in actual war'. In addition to these physical activities, the boys had to learn their letters and songs, 'prescribed by the laws', which consisted of laws, hymns to the gods, and praises of brave men, although Plato, who still knew them, rated their quality rather low (*Laws* 2.666D).[59]

The final stage of Cretan education began with a ceremonial casting off of the dirty garment: in fact, in various Cretan cities the technical term for leaving the *agela* was 'to undress'. The change is firmly located in an initiatory setting by the aetiological myth of the Ekdysia ('Undressing') festival at Phaistos for Leto, an initiatory goddess (Chapter II, §3): a girl who had been brought up as a boy actually changed into a real boy the moment she became an adolescent. Transvestism seems indeed to have been a common feature in archaic initiation, which survived in classical times only at a few places, such as in the Athenian Oschophoria festival, where two youths dressed as girls performed, which, hardly fortuitously, was connected with the initiatory myth of Theseus (Chapter V, §3).[60] Further Cretan details are absent, but both the names 'nude ones' and 'very nude ones' for adolescents near maturation, and the existence of a 'Festival of the Garment' (Periblemaia) at Lyttos, strongly suggest that the order of the final stage of initiation was: undressing, being nude, and donning the new adult garment. The focus on the garment during the 'graduation' is

[57] For this early stage, see also Seelentag 2015: 446–53.
[58] For this important metaphor in Greek initiation, see Calame 1997: 215–16; this volume, Chapter VI, §1.
[59] Seelentag 2015: 453–8.
[60] For the Oschophoria, see Pilz 2011b; Humphreys 2018: ii.671–3. In general, see Bremmer 1999c.

hardly surprising, since Ephoros tells us that the elite were characterized by a distinctive dress. Clearly, the transition from dirty garment to adult dress was too great to be made in one step. It had to be eased and dramatized by a series of festivals.[61] In Sparta, where the difference between youths and adults was even more strongly marked, initiation was also concluded with a series of festivals, but in Athens, where the difference was much less strong, a concluding festival no longer existed.

In addition to nudity, the contrast with the future status was expressed in a different manner. Ephoros tells us that shortly before official adulthood the aristocratic boys were 'kidnapped' for a brief pederastic relationship; in fact, in more or less formalized ways pederasty was widespread in the Greek world. As, ideologically, the boys could only play a passive role in the relationship, this part of the ritual stressed their non-manhood before they became real males, just as was done by the myth about the transformation from a girl into a man.[62]

The physical side of Cretan initiation, then, prepared the boys for a life in which fighting was of the utmost importance, while songs helped to instil the corresponding ideology. At the same time, the initiatory process had been adapted to the political situation of Crete. The prominent position of the elite's sons and the focus on the garment impressed the domination of the elite on their inferiors but, by incorporating the latter into the *agela*, feudal ties were promoted which helped to support the political system. As ritual often pretends to be of great antiquity, it is equally important to note its innovative powers and flexibility. This is shown by the introduction of literacy in the training (though this did not pre-date the fifth century), and the stress on running, which was absent from Athenian and Spartan initiation. Crete is very mountainous and Cretans could hardly have survived as soldiers without the ability to run. In fact, running was so important that the Cretan term for adult was *dromeus* ('runner'): even ecology can be a factor in the shaping of a particular ritual.[63]

---

[61] For the Ekdysia, see Waldner 2009; Bremmer 2019e: 436–9. 'To undress': *IC* I.ix (Dreros).1.A.99–100; I.xix (Malla).1.17–18, etc. 'Nude ones': *IC* I.ix (Dreros).1.D.140–1 (*azôstoi*). 'Very nude ones': *IC* I.ix (Dreros).1 A.I 11–12 (*panazôstoi*). Periblemaia: *IC* I.xix (Malla).19.1.

[62] Bremmer 1991; Davidson 2007: 304–15; Link 2009. On 'kidnap', see Bremmer and Horsfall 1987: 105–11 (Bremmer). The analysis in Seelentag 2015: 464–85 insufficiently takes into account all the available Cretan evidence and the comparable customs in other Greek cities.

[63] Brelich 1969: 204f.

Contrasts not only played a role in the logic of rites of transition; we also find them in cyclical rituals, as a Theban festival may illustrate. According to Xenophon (*Hell.* 5.4.4–6), Theban *polemarchs* (generals) customarily celebrated a festival of Aphrodite at the end of their period in office. In the winter of 379, the pro-Spartan *polemarchs* were promised a night with women and wine, but the veiled women turned out to be conspirators in disguise, who efficiently disposed of their opponents and liberated the town from the Spartans. How do we explain this connection of the military with the goddess of love?

The connection is less surprising than might be expected at first sight. Aphrodite was associated with the god of war, Ares, in literature (witness Homer's delightful story of their liaison), in art (witness the representation of Ares assisting with Aphrodite's birth), and in cult (witness their communal temples and altars). Moreover, Aphrodite was widely associated with magistrates, both civilian and military, whose harmonious cooperation she was believed to promote. Yet the goddess was also sometimes contrasted with Ares because in the *Homeric Hymn to Aphrodite* (9–10, with Faulkner *ad loc.*) Athena states that she took no pleasure 'in the works of golden Aphrodite but liked wars and the work of Ares'.[64] So how do we approach the Theban case?

The answer is found on Aegina, the island from which Plutarch explains the otherwise unknown ritual of the 'solitary eaters' in his *Greek Questions* (301e–f). The male Aeginetans celebrated a festival of Poseidon by isolating themselves in their homes and by feasting in silence without the presence of non-kinsmen and slaves for sixteen days. The festival shows all the signs of a disturbance of the social order: normally the Greeks feasted uproariously in the company of family and friends. Interestingly, the festival was terminated with the Aphrodisia before the return of normal life. Since Poseidon was also a macho god (Chapter III, §3), he was in various ways comparable to Ares. So in both cases the transition from the sphere of war and virility to peace was eased by passing through the opposite of war: love.[65] At the same time, we may assume that the juxtaposition of the two festivals put their contrasting contents in sharper relief: the significance of

---

[64] For Ares and Aphrodite, see Delivorrias 1984: 123–5; Bruneau 1984: 482–3; Graf 1985: 264 (magistrates); this volume, Chapter II, §3. For Ares, see Wathelet 1992. For Aphrodite, see Pirenne-Delforge 1994; Pironti 2007.

[65] See also Polinskaya 2013: 201–2, 313f.

individual parts of a more elaborate ritual cannot be separated from their position within the ritual.

We now turn to more elaborate festivals, the analysis of which has made much progress in recent decades. Festivals are shorter or longer periods of intense worship, usually local by nature and celebrated at a certain date in the year. Modern anthropologists and scholars of religion stress their community-affirming nature, but this function was long ago seen by Plato: 'so that...people may fraternize with one another at the sacrifices, and gain knowledge and familiarity, since nothing is of more benefit to the *polis* than this mutual acquaintance' (*Laws* 5.738d–e, trans. Bury 1926, adapted).[66] The mention of sacrifices shows that the shared consumption of meat was considered a prominent part of the festivals. Burkert's *Homo necans* (1983) and Graf's *Nordionische Kulte* (1985) still provide some of the best discussions of festivals, although at the time the former's combination of structuralism, functionalism, and ethology was deemed so revolutionary that the leading German review journal *Gnomon* was unable to find a reviewer for the original German edition of *Homo necans* (1972).[67] I will try to build upon these insights in an analysis of what is perhaps the most complex Greek festival we know of, the Athenian Anthesteria. As is often the case with Greek festivals, we partially depend on later sources for our reconstruction, not all events are securely attested, and we cannot be certain that all elements were integral to the festival from the very beginning, which goes back to the second millennium BC.[68]

The festival took place on three successive days in the month Anthesterion, roughly the end of February, which were called Pithoigia, Choes, and Chytroi. The first day, 'The opening of the wine jars', dramatized the opening of the festival, as did the first day of the Thesmophoria (Chapter VI, §3). On that day, the farmers of Attica brought their jars with new wine to the sanctuary of the god of the wine, Dionysos 'in the marshes' (Chapter III, §2), to have the wine ceremonially opened, mixed with water, and tasted for the first time. This was also the moment of celebrating the god. As a fourth-century eyewitness noted, 'delighted then with the mixture, the people

---

[66] For an enlightening comparison of Greek and Hittite festivals, see Rutherford 2020: 226–45.
[67] See Parker 1999; see also my reviews in Bremmer 1985 (Burkert) and 1990 (Graf).
[68] Burkert 1983: 213–43; Hamilton 1992: 149–71; Noel 1999; Humphreys 2004: 223–75; Parker 2005: 290–316; Valdés Guía 2015; Heinemann 2016: 467–87.

celebrated Dionysos in song, dancing, and calling upon him as Flowery, Dithyrambos [see §2], the Frenzied One and the Roarer' (Phanodemus *FGrH* 325 F 12). Wine mixed with water was the main drink in Greece and an indispensable part of libations.[69] It is therefore not surprising that the advent of new wine was a matter of general concern and controlled by the community.

But, as with the Cretan 'graduation', the advent of such an important drink as new wine had to be extended in time. The next day, the Choes ('Jugs'), which often gave its name to the whole festival (see §1), started with the chewing of leaves of buckthorn (a rather unappetising plant). Doors were smeared with pitch, temples were closed (with the exception of that of Dionysos), and men on wagons reviled passers-by. This dissolution of the social order preceded a strange drinking contest in the late afternoon, which was held both centrally, supervised by the highest magistrate, and at home in the various Attic demes (districts and villages).[70] Contrary to custom, the Athenians brought unmixed wine and their own large jug (*chous*), and were seated at separate tables, whereas normally guests were regaled, drank mixed wine from cups, and reclined together on couches: the separateness of the drinkers must have even been so striking that it is reflected on the vase-paintings of the Choes jugs.[71] Crowned with ivy, the plant dear to Dionysos, the banqueters awaited the sign of a trumpet, seen as an uncanny instrument by the Greeks, before trying to drain their 3.28 litres (!) as quickly as possible in complete silence.[72]

The ritual shows a clear resemblance to that of the Aeginetan 'solitary eaters' and illustrates how the Greeks shaped a 'negative' (part of a) ritual by a reversal of normal practices. Other means are the absence of wreaths; libations of unmixed wine, water, or oil instead of mixed wine;[73] or the dark colour and/or holocaust of the sacrificial victim instead of a sacrifice ending in a banquet.[74] It was the presence and intensity of these ritual markers that determined the nature, positive or negative, of a ritual.

The resemblance with Aegina extended to the level of myth. The Aeginetans explained their festival as recalling the return of the

---

[69] Gaifman 2018.
[70] On contests at home, see Parker 2005: 293–4; Heinemann 2016: 468.
[71] See Heinemann 2016: 468–70 (size of the jugs, unmixed wine, separateness).
[72] For the trumpet, see Graf 1985: 245; Krentz 1991; Neils 2014.
[73] Graf 1985: 28 (wreaths, libations); Henrichs 2019: 69–83 (wine).
[74] For holocausts, see Parker 2011: 144–50; Ekroth 2018b.

survivors of the Trojan War. Since they had no wish to hurt the feelings of those whose relatives had not returned, they feasted separately and secretly. In a comparable way, the Athenian custom of silent drinking was explained by the arrival of the matricide Orestes, whom Athenians did not want to entertain except in silence and at a separate table.[75] A different, perhaps later, aetiology connected the strange features with the Athenian murder of Aetolians who had brought them the wine. These myths can be used as a substitute for the unknown reactions of participants, since they tell us how the atmosphere was perceived. We have another indication of the sombre mood: we are told that at the time of the Choes Sophocles had choked on an unripe grape. Since at that time of year grapevines could hardly have finished blossoming, the anecdote is most likely not historical – the more so since Anacreon reportedly also choked on a grape. Yet it is important to note that the sad event was said to have occurred during the Choes, thus fitting the sombre atmosphere of the ritual.[76] The myth of Orestes focused on the strange nature of the contest, which can only have lasted a few minutes. Afterwards everybody indulged in a copious dinner and even a misanthrope would have at least one table companion. The picture of the banquet in Aristophanes' *Acharnians* is a happy one, and that is obviously how the Athenians abroad remembered the festival (see below).[77]

So far one might have thought that the festival was only for Athenian male citizens, but nothing would be further from the truth. Miniature jugs, confusingly also called *choes*, show that children of all ages received such jugs as toys and were probably the centre of special attention on this day. The festival is attested as a milestone in a small boy's life in Roman times, but this should not be retrojected to classical Athens.[78] Slaves, too, had a good time and their licence was explained by the great number of Carians among them or the one-time Carian ownership of a part of Attica: the stress on Carians seems to suggest mumming by the enslaved. Another, late explanation spoke of the Keres, spirits of the dead. It is hard to choose from these explanations

[75] For the literary evidence, see Harder on Call. fr. 178.2. For the iconographical representation of this solitary drinking, see Heinemann 2016: 470–4.

[76] Sad or glad events were often remembered on ominous or felicitous days: see Grafton and Swerdlow 1988; Chaniotis 1991.

[77] Buxton 1984: 4; Val. Max. 9.8 (Anacreon). For *Acharnians*, see N. Fisher 1993. For misanthropes, see Plut. *Vit. Ant.* 70.

[78] *Contra* Parker 2005: 297–301. Cf. Schmidt 2005: 2016–6; Heinemann 2006, 2016: 439.

and perhaps unnecessary, since (ancestral) Carians and spirits of the dead are structurally equivalent: both are entities normally absent from ordered Athenian life.[79]

The licence permitted to the enslaved was one more sign of the dissolution of the social order. Their inclusion in the general atmosphere of merriment may well have contributed to better relations with their owners, since such festivals of reversal could work as a safety valve, as the testimony of former American enslaved people confirms. But did they also have a legitimizing function as has been suggested? Perhaps in the eyes of the ruling classes, but hardly from the point of view of the enslaved. Such a view could only be sustained if Athens had been a relatively static society. The enslaved in Athens, however, had often been imported during their own lifetimes, and their massive flight during the Peloponnesian War shows their refusal to accept the existing order. In fact, several of these festivals of reversal became the scene of revolution, as they have been in more modern times, which is hard to explain if they really helped to legitimize the existing order.[80]

The discovery of a sacrificial calendar in Thorikos, dating from the 430s or 420s, shows that during the Choes this deme sacrificed to Dionysos a tawny (or perhaps black) billy goat that had lost its milk teeth. The dark colour fits the character of the day and the small size of the victim seems to suggest the absence of a public banquet: such a goat can hardly have fed many stomachs. Apparently, the Attic demes contributed a modest public supplement to the many festivities at home.[81]

Yet society cannot live in permanent disorder and at the end of the Choes a herald announced the third day of the festival, the Chytroi ('Pots'). Although the event has sometimes been called into doubt,[82] it is certain that the return to order was celebrated by a symbolic wedding between the wife of the highest magistrate and the god, which is reflected on vase-paintings at a mythological level by Dionysos' wedding with Ariadne.[83] At home, the 'Pots' was celebrated

[79] Regarding Carians/Keres the matter is contested: compare Bremmer 1983: 113–18 and Parker 2005: 297.

[80] *Contra* Versnel 1993: 116–17 (cf. Bremmer and Horsfall 1987: 86–7), although his observations on festivals of reversal (115–21) are of interest. On scenes of revolution, see Graf 1985: 245–6; on early modern times, see Le Roy Ladurie 1979.

[81] For Thorikos, see *CGRN* 32; Henrichs 1990: 262–3.

[82] Hamilton 1992: 55–6, but see Kapparis 1999: 324f.

[83] Burkert 1983: 235 mistakenly suggests that Aristotle speaks of a sexual act: cf. Parker 2005: 303–5. On Dionysos, see Heinemann 2016: 449–52.

by remembering the flood.[84] People ate a stew of all kinds of vegetables cooked in earthenware pots and sacrificed to Hermes Chthonios, the god associated with the victims of the flood.[85] Aristophanes' *Frogs* mentions a procession with drunken people on the Chytroi (211–19) and thus the festival seems to have been officially concluded with choruses at the place where it had all begun: the sanctuary of Dionysos.[86]

For the Athenians themselves, one of the most striking features of the festival must have been the licence accorded to the enslaved. It is therefore not surprising that their return to normality had to be dramatized. So at the end of the festival the owners, presumably, said: 'Begone ye Carians/ Keres. [It's] no longer Anthesteria.' Similarly, the enormous phallus which had been carried round Athens during the Dionysia was ceremoniously burned at the end of that festival.[87]

On the third day, another feast also took place. Girls commemorated the maiden Erigone by swinging: she had hanged herself after shepherds had murdered her father, Ikarios, who had introduced wine to them. This feast, the Aiora, is not found in non-Athenian Anthesteria festivals and is not attested in literature before the Hellenistic era, but iconographical evidence for the swinging attests to its celebration in the fifth century. Although the myth fits the Dionysiac themes of the festival, and the special place of the girls fits that of young children and enslaved people, this part seems to be a later addition from a particular local festival: one more testimony to the flexibility of ritual.[88]

Of all their festivals, the Anthesteria perhaps lay closest to the Athenians' hearts. As a political refugee, Themistocles introduced it to Magnesia, which he had received as a fiefdom from the Persian king. It was also celebrated at the court of the Sicilian tyrant Dionysius, where it may well have been organized for, or perhaps by, Plato during his stay in Sicily. This feeling lasted into the third century, since the followers of Epicurus countered accusations of atheism against their master with the argument that he had celebrated the Choes and had advised his pupils to do likewise. And Callimachus mentions an Athenian who celebrated the Anthesteria in Alexandria

---

[84] For Greek traditions of the flood, which eventually derive from the Near East, see Bremmer 2008: 101–16.

[85] Parker 2005: 295f.

[86] For choruses, see Hamilton 1992: 38–42.

[87] On the phallus, see *PCG* Adesp. 154. In general on Dionysos and the phallus, see Csapo 1997.

[88] Harder on Call. fr. 178.3 (literary evidence); Heinemann 2016: 435–42 (iconography).

in Ptolemaic times. Clearly, the festival had become part and parcel of Athenian identity, like Christmas once for European colonists, or, today, Ramadan for many Muslims in the West.[89]

The Anthesteria displays the typical signs of *la grande festa*, as ethnologists have called the type of festival which all over the world dramatized the advent of the new harvest/fruit/wine by a sharp break with the existing order. The festival therefore resembled a New Year celebration, and this may explain why teachers were paid during it (Eubulides, fr. 1). Yet its New Year character was naturally stressed less than that of the official Athenian New Year, which was celebrated in Hekatombaion, a month marked by two official New Year festivals, Synoikia and Panathenaea (see §2), and preceded by two festivals characterized by a dissolution of the social order, the Kronia (Chapter V, §3), with the role reversal of the enslaved, and the Skira, with the women on top (Chapter VI, §3).[90]

As was customary in Greece, the Anthesteria had given its name to the month in which it was celebrated: Anthesterion. This old Ionian month went back to the period before the Ionian colonization (around 1000 BC), as Thucydides realized; we may thus safely assume that the Anthesteria was one of the oldest Greek festivals. Its Ionian occurrence perhaps explains that several elements look like imports from the Near East (see the Appendix), such as the Sacred Marriage, a household festival that celebrated the institution of marriage,[91] and, perhaps, the expulsion of the Carians.[92] Greek calendars are under-researched, but they can be important for determining the connotations, positive or negative, attached to a festival and for the varying positions of divinities in Greek cities. Yet here, too, we have to be careful. The month Anthesterion, like other months, did not occupy the same place in the year in the calendar of every Ionian city: evidently, names of months were moved around and could even change in the course of the centuries, thus altering their original characters.[93]

We have seen that the study of smaller and larger rituals has to take into account different aspects: the calendrical order, the spatial

---

[89] Call. fr. 178; Possis *FGrH* 480 F 1; Philodemus, *De pietate*, 806–8, 865–9 (Epicurus: to be added to the sources in Hamilton 1992); Plut. *Vit. Ant.* 70.3; Diog. Laert. 4.8.

[90] On *la grande festa*, see Versnel 1993: 127–8. On Synoikia, see Graf 1985: 167; Hornblower 1991–2009: i.265; Parker 2005: 480–1. On the Skira, see Parker 2005: 173–7.

[91] Parker 2005: 76.

[92] See Avagianou 1991; Garthwaite 2010.

[93] Thuc. 2.14.4, but see Hornblower 1991–2009: i.266–7. On month names, see Trümpy 1997; Burkert 2001–11: vi.208–30.

organization, gender, social groups and relations, systems of classification, psychological and emotional features, power aspects, the place of
divinities, local peculiarities, the internal logic, and commentaries of
participants. The fragmentary state of our tradition often makes it
impossible to pay attention to all these aspects or to apply all modern
insights, such as those of performance theory and cognitive science
(but see Chapter VI, §3),[94] but we should at least try. In many ways,
the study of Greek ritual has only just begun.

---

[94] On performance, see Hall and Harrop 2010; Oschema 2015. For cognitive science, see
Meineck, Short, and Devereaux 2019.

V. MYTHOLOGY

Myth played an important role in Greek religion: it illustrated and defined the roles of gods and heroes (Chapter II, §1); it also explained aspects of rituals (Chapter IV, §3), showed correct or deviant patterns of behaviour, and reflected on human conduct and the cosmos.[1] Since, of all aspects of Greek religion, myth has perhaps drawn the greatest attention and the largest number of different approaches,[2] I start with a short historical survey of these approaches and a brief discussion of recent definitions (§1). I then analyse origins and uses of myth (§2), study the relations between myth and ritual (§3), and conclude by looking at some changes in the popularity of myths, as reflected by the visual arts, and the nature of myth itself (§4).

1. A mini-history and a definition

After the Renaissance, which preferred an allegorical interpretation of Greek myth, as exemplified by the successful handbook of Natale Conti (*c.* 1520–1600),[3] and the ahistorical use of Greek mythology as material for literature in the seventeenth century,[4] modern research started at the beginning of the eighteenth century.[5] Pioneers were the Frenchmen Bernard de Fontenelle (1657–1757) and Nicolas Fréret (1688–1749). The former postulated a kind of 'primitive' mentality, initiated comparative mythology, reflected about the transmission of myths, and, last but not least, recognized the fatal influence of writing on mythology – all this in a small treatise.[6] The latter saw mythology as

---

[1] Despite its importance, there is no chapter on mythology in Nilsson 1967; Burkert 1985; Jost 1992; Rudhardt 1992; Parker 2011; or Larson 2016, although the last has good observations throughout (see the index s.v. 'myth').

[2] Good introductions, each with a different approach: Dowden 1992; Graf 1993b; Buxton 1994, 2004; Saïd 2008. There are stimulating collections in Bremmer 1988a; Calame 1988, 2015; Woodard 2007; Dowden and Livingstone 2011.

[3] Natale Conti 1567 (translated as Mulryan and Brown 2006); Costa 2004; Hartmann 2018: 17–52.

[4] Starobinski 1989: 233–62 ('Fable et mythologie aux XVIIᵉ et XVIIIᵉ siècles').

[5] For historical surveys, see Graf 1993b: 9–56; Jamme 1995; Bremmer 2019e: 511–31, which I use and update in this section.

[6] De Fontenelle 1989: 197–202 ('De l'origine des fables') (translated in Feldman and Richardson 1972: 7–18); Krauss 1989 (a good German translation and an important study).

the expression of the culture, customs, and social order of a specific community.[7]

Despite this promising start there was insufficient philological expertise in France to develop these ideas. The situation was different in Germany, where the Göttingen professor of Greek, Christian G. Heyne (1729–1812), introduced the term *mythus* to stress that he was not dealing with a *fabula*, the invention or fiction of a poet. According to Heyne, myth was the expression of a specific *Volksgeist*, it explained the admirable or frightening aspects of nature, and (although this is less marked in his work) it was a means to preserve the memories of great exploits.[8] In the nineteenth century, two Müllers (no relation) further developed Heyne's insights. The first, Karl Otfried Müller (1797–1840), stressed that myth was the reflection of a national (= tribal) identity and various historical periods. The second, Friedrich Max Müller (1823–1900), saw an important clue in the use of etymologies and directed his attention to the connection between myth and nature.[9] The dominance of these approaches came to an end when the unification of Germany (1870) lessened interest in the political background of Greek myth, and new insights in comparative linguistics destroyed the basis of most etymologies produced by Max Müller and his followers.[10] Instead of nature, attention was now focused on fertility and agriculture.

The stress on fertility was very successful and became canonized in the writings of James G. Frazer (1854–1941), the famous author of *The Golden Bough* (1890), and Martin P. Nilsson (1874–1967), who dominated the study of Greek religion in the middle of the twentieth century.[11] A link of myth with ritual was tentatively explored only late in his life by the learned German Hermann Usener (1834–1905), but especially elaborated in England by the so-called Cambridge ritualists, whose most famous representative, Jane Harrison (1850–1928), eventually discredited this approach by some all-too-fanciful analyses.[12]

---

[7] Fréret 1756; see also Grell and Volpilhac-Auger 1994.

[8] Most recently, Scheer 2014.

[9] For this development and its prehistory, see, from different angles, Humphreys 2004: 197–222; Gordon 2019.

[10] On Karl Müller, see Momigliano 1984: 271–86; Calder and Schlesier 1998. On Max Müller, see Lloyd-Jones 1982: 155–64; Stocking 1987: 56–62; van den Bosch 2002; Segal 2016.

[11] On Frazer, see most recently Rosa 1997; Stocking 2001: 147–61. For Nilsson, see Bremmer 2019e: 13–16.

[12] Calder 1991; Bremmer 2011a. For Harrison in particular, see Bremmer 2019e: 533–7.

After the First World War, the excesses of the ritualists and the rejection of comparative studies by Classicists strongly diminished interest in Greek mythology, but in the middle of the 1960s structuralism promoted new interests, which came to the fore in the works of Walter Burkert (1931–2015), Jean-Pierre Vernant (1914–2007), and Marcel Detienne (1935–2019). Whereas Burkert's main interest has been in links between myth and ritual (see §3), Vernant and Detienne focused on those aspects of myth that elucidate aspects of Greek culture and society, such as the position of women (Chapter VI, §2), values of plants and animals (see §2), or the role and place of sacrifice (Chapter IV, §2).

Although the insights of Burkert and of Vernant and Detienne remain productive, the last two decades have seen two new developments in particular. The first one is an increasing attention to the mythographers: that is, those early Greeks, such as Hekataios and Akousilaos, who around 500 BC started to collect myths and write them down in readable and accessible prose. They emerged at more or less the same time as the tragedians; thus, both provide evidence of the distinctive cultural importance of these stories, and their recognition as a category of tale we call 'myth'. The books of the mythographers mainly concentrated on what they considered 'history' and therefore, somewhat surprisingly to modern students of myth, hardly focused on the gods: a theogony is mostly absent from their writings.[13] A second striking feature is their often rationalizing approach. It is quite amazing to see how early Greek intellectuals started to systematize and rationalize features of Greek myth before the more radical rationalizers of the fourth century and later, such as Palaephatus.[14]

A second development is the focus on myths as stories, an important mode of transmission and reflection within Greek religion that has not yet received the attention it deserves.[15] Indeed, the concentration on myth's connection to ritual and its importance for reconstructing ancient Greek culture and society made students neglect the simple fact that for a very long time Greek myths were told to an audience,[16] whose composition and circumstances were continually changing. In fact, each time a myth was related it had to be adapted to the

---

[13] For the texts, with monumental commentary, see Fowler 2000–13.
[14] Hawes 2014.
[15] See Kindt 2016.
[16] See Fowler 2017; W. Hansen 2017; S. Johnston 2018. Scobie 1979 is still interesting.

conventions of the genre, which could be epic, choral lyric, hymns, drama, or just private telling, such as by women at the loom.[17] From the few surviving fragments of the early mythographers, we can still see that competing versions of Greek myths often circulated without seemingly bothering the Greeks themselves: the Athenians told at least three different myths to explain the origin of the Panathenaea.[18] Consequently, there was no one authoritative version of a myth. Professional and private storytellers knew standard plots, which they constantly had to adapt. Variation, therefore, is an important characteristic of Greek myth.

From the 1980s onwards, scholars started to call into question the validity of the notion of myth.[19] And, indeed, Greek *mythos* does not mean 'myth' but 'is, in Homer, a speech-act indicating authority, performed at length, usually in public, with a focus on full attention to every detail'. However, in the course of the early classical period, we can gradually observe a shift in meaning of *mythos* from 'authoritative speech' to 'imaginative tale', as more and more intellectuals contested the authority of fellow historians and poets when speaking about gods and heroes.[20]

All these developments once again force us to ask what we mean by 'myth' in early Greece. Burkert once proposed the definition 'myth is a traditional tale with secondary, partial reference to something of collective importance', but later suggested 'traditional tales of special "significance"', which comes very near to my own 'traditional tales relevant to society'. In other words, the definition alerts us to those tales which are traditional (even new myths tend to follow patterns of old myths), are of collective importance (they are meant for public performance and not a vehicle for private views), and are transferable from one society to another (Greek mythology is not a closed corpus).[21]

[17] For women as myth-tellers, see S. West 2003; Tuck 2009; Heath 2011; Bremmer 2019e: 248–50.
[18] Parker 2005: 254–6.
[19] See especially Detienne 1981 (translated as Detienne 1986).
[20] R. Martin 1989: 12 (quotation); Beck 2004. For developments, see Buxton 1999; Fowler 2009, 2011.
[21] Burkert 1979: 23 and 2001–11: iv.105 (definitions); Bremmer 2019e: 419–26 (also on differences between myth and other types of traditional tales, such as legends, *Sagen*, and fairy-tales). My definition is similar to that of Fowler 2017: 7: 'a myth is a story offering an explanation about something of collective importance'.

2. Origins and uses

Greek mythology of the archaic and classical periods was a conglomerate
of old and new, indigenous and imported.[22] The myths of Achilles, Arion
(the first horse: see Chapter II, §3), Helen (Chapter VI, §1), and the
cattle-raiding Heracles (Chapter II, §2) all seem to go back to
Indo-European times (and Heracles perhaps even further).[23] It is their
concentration on prime interests of early societies – initiation, horses,
marriage, food – which explains their continuity. Unfortunately, other
old myths, such as the strange birth of Erichthonius/Erechtheus
(Chapter VI, §1) from the seed of Hephaistos, and the mythical complex
of Demeter and Persephone (Chapter II, §3), which was closely connected with the Thesmophoria (Chapter VI, §3), remain hard to date.[24]
New imports were Oriental theogonic and cosmogonic myths
(Chapter I, §3), but poets also borrowed individual motifs, as in the
case of Bellerophontes. Out of spite for rejection by the hero with
whom she was in love, King Proitos' wife had denounced him before
her husband. To appease her, the king sent Bellerophontes to his
father-in-law, the King of Lycia, with a letter containing 'many
life-destroying things' (Il. 6.152–210). Homer's version of the myth
contains two motifs which are most likely derived from the Near
East, since both occur in the Old Testament: the Potiphar episode
from the story of Joseph (Genesis 39) and the fateful letter that
David sent to his chief-of-staff to get rid of the man whose wife,
Bathsheba, he wanted to marry (2 Samuel 11–12). But when, why,
how, and where did these Oriental borrowings take place?[25]
Originally, the Greeks were less concerned with the creation of the
world than with the origin of their own cities, which presupposed the
existence of the gods,[26] but interest in the creation of gods and the cosmos fitted the new interest in the world which became visible in Ionia in
the archaic period. The date fits the fact that borrowings of Oriental
myths most likely postdate the Mycenaean period: there is no influence
from Canaanite myths, although the powerful city of Ugarit flourished
until the invasions of the Sea Peoples, and the version of the

[22] Burkert 2001–11: i.1–12; Bremmer 2019e: 419–22.
[23] Graf 1993b: 74 (Achilles); Jackson 2006 (Helen); Burkert 1979: 78–98 (Heracles).
[24] For Erichthonius/Erechtheus, see Kearns 1989: 16; Meyer 2017: 313–17, 362–77.
[25] Frei 1993; note also Burkert 2001–11: ii.48–72; Simon 2009; Fowler 2000–13: ii.183–4; Calame 2015: 117–53.
[26] See López-Ruiz 2010.

Mesopotamian epic *Enuma Elish* which is quoted by the *Iliad* (Chapter I, §3) is unlikely to have been composed before 1100 BC. The varying geographical origins of the myths (Anatolia, Mesopotamia, and the Syro-Phoenician coastal area) all point to transmission routes via both Anatolia and the Levant, where Greek traders and mercenaries will have heard Oriental bards or storytellers and, in turn, told their myths to poets at home. The various transmissions must have been an important factor in the origin of the many differences between Greek and Oriental versions, the precise origins of which remain impossible to trace at the moment.[27]

What were the uses of myth? One answer would surely have to be: pure entertainment. Choral lyric with its combination of music, dance, and song provided quite a spectacle, and for thousands of Athenians the dramatic performances must have been welcome breaks in the winter months. However, myths were also a serious matter. As mentioned in the Introduction, in addition to defining the gods (Chapter II, §1) and illuminating rituals (below, §3), they supplied arguments in debates, served as models of ethical and religious behaviour, helped to establish political identities or advance political claims, and contributed towards the Greek *mentalité*. Let us look at a few examples.

When Achilles had withdrawn into his tent in anger and the Trojans were threatening the Greek camp, an embassy came to Achilles in a last attempt at persuading him to renounce his anger. His old tutor, Phoenix, then told him the myth of Meleager, who had not only killed the Calydonian boar (Figure 10) but also his mother's brother in a battle over the spoils. When his mother cursed him, Meleager became very angry and withdrew from the battle in which the Kouretes threatened to take his town, Calydon in Aetolia. Only at the very last moment did Meleager rejoin the battle, but by his prolonged withdrawal he had forfeited the presents which had been promised to him (*Il.* 9.529–99).

The passage is illustrative in more than one aspect. First, it strongly suggests that myths could be told to persuade people to change their actions. Second, the anger of Meleager is hardly mentioned in other versions and is likely, therefore, to be Homer's invention to make the myth more suitable to its context. Third, myths could be continually adapted, since only from about 500 BC do we find versions in which

---

[27] See Rutherford 2009, 2018.

Figure 10. Terracotta representing the Calydonian Hunt. The so-called Melian relief, *c.* 460 BC.

the fate of Meleager was connected with a log of wood which his mother threw into the fire after she had heard about her brother's death.[28] Apparently, this spectacular motif appealed to the changing tastes of the Greek public, which had become interested in a 'more emotional, even larmoyant appeal'.[29]

The Calydonian boar had been sent by Artemis, whom the father of Meleager, King Oeneus, had forgotten during a sacrifice. The omission was not unique. Tyndareus once forgot to include Aphrodite, which angered the goddess to such an extent that she made his daughters Helen and Clytaemnestra desert or even deceive their husbands: in other words, Tyndareus' omission eventually led to the Trojan War; and Hera's anger at Pelias for not having been honoured set off the expedition of the Argonauts. These myths, then, also showed the terrible consequences of not giving the gods their proper due.[30]

[28] The late date makes it unlikely that Homer left out the motif on purpose: see March 1987: 27–46; Bremmer 1988b; Woodford *et al.* 1992. For a different view, see Grossardt 2001. In general, see also Arrigoni 2019: 11–63.

[29] Burkert 2001–11: i.211.

[30] For Aphrodite, see Stesichorus, fr. 223 Davies = 85 Finglass. For Hera, see Ap. Rhod. *Argon.* 1.14; Apollod. 1.9.16; Bremmer 2019e: 325.

Instead of focusing on Panhellenic expeditions, such as the Trojan War or the Seven against Thebes, myths could also advance social and political claims of families and cities, sometimes via genealogies.[31] Hippocrates' family was traced back to the healing hero Asclepius, and that of the Athenian priests of Poseidon Erechtheus to Erechtheus, son of Ge (Earth) and Hephaistos. The Athenians promoted Ion's ancestorship of the Ionians to win their support against the Spartans during the Peloponnesian War. In his tragedy *Ion*, Euripides even went as far as having Creusa conceive Ion by Apollo but his brother Dorus, the ancestor of the Dorian Spartans, by a mortal, whereas traditionally Dorus was the maternal uncle of Ion. One could also adduce foul play in the past. The Spartans underpinned their possession of Messene by claiming that, after the return of the Heraclids, who had divided the Peloponnese among themselves, Kresphontes received Messene via tricks: Sparta's conquest of this area was thus fully justified.[32]

The political side of Greek myth has often been discussed, but until very recently much less attention had been given to ways in which myth was shaped by and articulated the Greek mental landscape.[33] Its pictures of cities and crossroads,[34] warriors and women (Chapter VI, §2), meadows and mountains,[35] plants,[36] and animals[37] can help us to see how the Greeks perceived their world. For instance, when Inachus, the main river of the Argolid, was worshipped as the first king of Argos and ancestor of the Argives, or when Acheloos, the largest river of northern Greece, was closely connected with the education of boys, it is clear that the Greeks perceived their rivers rather differently from, say, those living close to the Thames, Seine, or Mississippi.[38] More investigations in this direction will eventually enable the

---

[31] Fowler 1998; for Hellenistic times, see Scheer 1993.

[32] On families, see Thomas 1989: 155–95. For Athens, see Meyer 2017: 244–56. For Ion and Kresphontes, see Zingg 2016: 25–65 (Kresphontes); Bremmer 2019e: 463–74.

[33] Hawes 2017.

[34] On cities, see Zeitlin 1990; Saïd 1993; Rosenbloom 2013. On crossroads, see S. Johnston 1991.

[35] Motte 1973. Buxton 2013: 9–31 ('Imaginary Greek Mountains') is exemplary; Viscardi 2020 (mountains and caves).

[36] Gartziou-Tatti and Zografou 2019.

[37] Detienne 1972; Buxton 2013: 33–51 ('Wolves and Werewolves in Greek Thought'); Gordon 2015; Kindt 2020; Ogden 2021.

[38] On Inachus, see Dowden 1989: 123–4; Katalis 1990. For Acheloos, see Graf 1985: 104–6.

reconstruction of a 'mythical Greece': that is, the way in which Greece was represented in myth.[39]

Rather optimistically, earlier generations thought that Greek myth could also be used to reconstruct past events, but Greek oral tradition was probably 'of the most fluid kind, its transmission casual, and its lifespan usually short', as can indeed be demonstrated for Athens.[40] On the other hand, myth does reflect customs, relations, institutions, and perceptions of early Greece; in some cases, it even preserved extinct institutions. Myth reveals that heroes such as Hippolytus and Theseus were educated by their maternal kin, and this type of education (fosterage) lasted in western Europe into the Middle Ages, although it did not survive into classical Greece.[41]

Yet when using myth for the reconstruction of social life in early Greece, we must be very attentive to genre and ideology, as myths about the family may illustrate. The *Iliad* tended to avoid focusing on family conflict, but Attic tragedy pictured struggles within the family in the most sombre colours. And whereas father–son hostility usually ended badly,[42] the brother–sister relationship was invariably good. The brother was the protector of his sister's honour: Achilles could ambush Troilus when he accompanied his sister Polyxena to a fountain (Figure 11). Even when, in Euripides' *Helen*, the priestess Theonoe opposes her brother, she is reconciled with him at the end of the play. In both cases, myth does not reflect the realities but the imperatives of life in a society with weak legal institutions. In such a society, families need one another in order to survive and prosper, and that is an important message of these myths.[43]

3. Myth and ritual

In recent decades, scholars have paid much attention to the relation between myth and ritual. Although myths existed without rituals and rituals without myths, the two symbolic systems were often interrelated.

[39] There are good observations towards such a project in Dowden 1992: 121–49; Buxton, 1994: 80–113.

[40] On oral tradition, see Thomas 1989: 283 (quotation).

[41] For fosterage, see Bremmer and Horsfall 1987: 53–6 (Bremmer); Bremmer 1999a.

[42] On this genre, see Seaford 2018: 300–22.

[43] For father–son hostility, see Sourvinou-Inwood 1991: 244–84. For brother–sister relationships, see Bremmer 2008: 325–33. On Troilus, see Kossatz-Deissman 1981: nos. 206–388 and Kossatz-Deissman 1997; Wathelet 1988: s.v. Troilos.

Figure 11. Polyxena and Achilles, who is waiting in ambush for her brother Troilus. Black-figure lekythos, Athena Painter, *c.* 490 BC.

This relationship is only gradually becoming clearer and is still the subject of lively debates. In the course of time, three possibilities have been suggested: ritual follows the pattern of myth; ritual generates myth; and ritual and myth arise at the same time, *pari passu*. We will look at all three possibilities and start with the influence of myth.[44]

Cities not infrequently appropriated figures from Panhellenic mythology for a local cult. So Athens instituted a cult for Theban Oedipus and, in the mid-sixth century BC, Argos founded a *heroön* for the Seven against Thebes and in this way 'claimed' these warriors. In Tarentum we can see a more specific influence of myth, since women were excluded from the cult of Agamemnon – surely in memory of his murder by Clytaemnestra. However, this was the proverbial exception proving the rule: in general, such cults did not display details characteristic of their myth.[45]

More complicated are myths produced by rituals. An interesting example is the myth of Perseus. When this hero of Mykenai beheaded the Gorgon Medusa with a sickle, 'out jumped big Chrysaor and the horse Pegasus' (Hesiod, *Theog.* 281). The winged horse enabled Perseus to rescue the maiden Andromeda from a sea monster in Joppa-Jaffa, where in Roman times the 'huge bones' (prehistoric

---

[44] For a history of the debates, see Versnel 1993: 15–88; Bremmer 2019e: 435–44.
[45] For Athens, see Lardinois 1992. For Argos, see *SEG* 42.274; also Pariente 1992. For Tarentum, see Graf 1985: 391. In general, see Richardson 1983.

fossils?) of the monster were shown to tourists – an often neglected use of mythology. Burkert rightly noted that 'the steed and the warrior are indicative of a trial of initiation', but he overlooked important testimony in support of his interpretation, as in 1892 the following, early fifth-century Mycenaean inscription had been published: 'If there is no *damiorgia* [a Doric office], the *iaromnamones* [recorders of sacred matters] for Perseus are to serve as judges for the parents, according to what has been decided' (trans. Jameson 2014).[46] Apparently, Perseus was closely connected with contests of boys, whose role model he will have been.

In the sanctuary of the initiatory Spartan goddess Ortheia masks have been found of old women and of a handsome young man; moreover, Spartan boys engaged in contests and, when victorious, dedicated iron sickles to the goddess. As Michael Jameson perceptively observed, these Spartan initiatory customs must form the ritual counterpart of Perseus' myth: Mycenaean boys took leave of the world of the females with a sham fight in which masks of terrifying females played an important role. We may even wonder whether this use of masks in ritual is not also the background for Theseus' victory over the Minotaur with the help of Ariadne: another initiatory fight (Chapter IV, §3). The Minotaur is often pictured as a man with a bull's head and we know that in Cypriot Amathus priests officiated with bull's masks in a sanctuary of Aphrodite Ariadne. But, whereas Perseus' fight seems to reflect the break with the world of women, Theseus' victory signifies the entry into the world of adults: some Greek warriors wore bull helmets, and on his return Theseus became king of Athens.[47]

Versnel has strongly argued that in some cases myths and rituals were formed *pari passu*. His main witness is the myth and ritual complex of Kronos and the Kronia. Versnel approached this complex as follows. First, he gathered all mythical traditions about Kronos, which show that myth depicts this god sometimes negatively (from parricide to general lawlessness) and sometimes positively (king of a golden age). Subsequently, he collected the ritual testimonia, which

---

[46] Burkert 1992: 83–5; also Pomponius Mela 1.64 (tourists); Kaizer 2011. In general, see Hartmann 2010; Osborne 2010b.

[47] On Perseus see Ogden 2008; Fowler 2000–13: ii.253–8; Jameson 2014: 22–40 (Mycenaean inscription). For bulls' masks, see Ovid, *Met.* 10.222–37; Graf 1985: 415–16 (also bull warriors); Hermary 1986: 164–6; Hermary and Masson 1990. For helmets, see Brijder 1991: 430–2. On Theseus and the Minotaur, see Fowler 2000–13: ii.468–74; Giudice and Giudice 2018: 166–7 (iconographical evidence).

at Rhodes speak of human sacrifice but in Athens of a very happy atmosphere, since, during the festival, masters and slaves happily dined together. Surveying the myth and the ritual, he concluded that 'Kronian ritual is just as ambiguous as Kronian myth'.

Regarding the historical development, Versnel suggests that the rite started with an agricultural festival (for obscure reasons devoted to Kronos), which in historical times 'was firmly anchored in a festive complex which marked the transition from the old to the new year and that, accordingly, it was celebrated with rites of role reversal'. In cult, Kronos developed into the 'mythical' god of the precosmic era with its utopian and catastrophic aspects. Consequently, according to Versnel, we find in this complex a correspondence between myth and ritual in structure and atmosphere in such a way that both deal with the same type of experience in the same affective mode and this *pari passu*.

However, Versnel neglected to study the origin of the Kronia festival and overlooked the fact that we do not have sufficient information to conclude that the myth and the ritual of the Kronia originated along-side each other. Moreover, he did not take into account that, in the cases of human sacrifice, Kronos is usually the *interpretatio Graeca* of a Carthaginian or Semitic god, whereas, in the case of abundance, Kronos is sometimes the Greek interpretation of the Egyptian god Geb. In fact, the traditions of Kronos seem to have entered Greek mythology from Anatolia, plausibly Lycia, not before the eighth century, with the ritual of the Kronia only being celebrated in a very limited area. Despite his impressive erudition, in the end Versnel's attempt at proving a *pari passu* origin of Greek myth and ritual fails to convince.[48]

Finally, Claude Calame has suggested replacing the terms 'myth' and 'ritual' by a single new expression: 'symbolic process'.[49] Yet the myth and ritual of Perseus illustrate at least four important differences between these two symbolic systems.[50] First, whereas the ritual was acted out by boys and men with masks, myth speaks of a real fight between a young man and an old hag, Medusa: what is symbolic and reversible in ritual becomes realistic and irreversible in myth. Second,

---

[48] Versnel 1993: 88–135. For a reinterpretation of the complex of Kronos and the Kronia, see Bremmer 2008: 82–7; and 2019c: 289–91.

[49] Calame 1991 (reprinted in Calame 2008: 43–62).

[50] For the complicated relations between myth and ritual, see Bremmer 2010 and 2019c: 427–45; Larson 2016: 84–8.

myth is selective: it mentions only Perseus' fight, whereas the ritual must have been quite a spectacle, with judges, spectators, and contestants. This selectivity can be quite remarkable. On the island of Lemnos, there was a temporary separation of the sexes during the period leading up to the yearly arrival of new fire. The corresponding myth speaks of a murder of the husbands by their wives but has no mention whatsoever of fire: clearly, a ritual should not be reconstructed on the basis of a myth only. Third, myth bestows significance on ritual. The contest in the ritual for Perseus was not just any game, since the winner became, so to speak, a Perseus-to-be. The significance could also be of an explanatory manner, since many a myth explained striking details of the ritual. Fourth, the name Pegasus and the idea of a winged horse most likely derive from the Near East, as does the location of Andromeda in Joppa/Jaffa. Evidently, myth can incorporate motifs from other myths and be removed from its ritual basis; in fact, whole myths migrated from one cult to another.[51]

4. Visual arts and changes

Our concentration on the performative and literary aspects of myth should not conceal the great importance of the visual arts for the study of myth.[52] The splendid iconographical encyclopaedia of classical mythology, the *Lexicon Iconographicum Mythologiae Classicae* (1981–2009), now enables a more intensive 'cross-fertilization' between literature and the visual arts, which in antiquity hardly constituted two independent streams of tradition.[53] In fact, we can sometimes notice a virtually immediate response of artists to poets. After Pindar had described the throttling of serpents by young Heracles in his *First Nemean Ode*, Attic painters represented the feat within a few years of the poem being premiered in Sikyon shortly after 470 BC.[54] Painters may even have invented versions of myths which are absent from the literary tradition. On a Douris cup, datable

---

[51] On Lemnos, see Burkert 2000 (= Burkert 2001–11: v.186–205); Fowler 2000–13: ii.217. On Pegasus, see Schürr 2014. For migrating myths, see Graf 1979b and 1993: 116–17; Audley-Miller and Dignas 2018.

[52] From the many studies on art and myth, note especially Knell 1990; Carpenter 1991; Shapiro 1994b; Junker 2012.

[53] See also the excellent handbook Gantz 1993.

[54] Moret 1992.

to 480–470 BC, a dragon disgorges Jason in the presence of Athena, and a similar scene already occurs on a late seventh-century Corinthian alabastron, although extant literature never mentions this detail. On the other hand, the early archaic poet Eumelos wrote an epic, *Corinthiaca*, in which Medea played a considerable role, and vase-painters may have taken the scene from this epic or from similar archaic Argonautic poetry.[55] However this may be, the interaction between poetry and the figurative arts remains a vexing problem and deserves further attention.

In the course of time some myths declined in popularity, whereas others suddenly caught the Greek imagination. In contrast to the fragmentary state of the literary tradition, the enormous output of vase-painters allows us to trace such changes in Athens, the main producer of vases, in chronological detail. By simply counting surviving vases, even though these are only a fraction of the archaic production, we can see the emergence around 560 BC of a new preference in Athens for myths with specifically Attic associations, such as Theseus and the Minotaur (Chapter IV, §3), or those Panhellenic myths which the Athenians in some sense adopted as their own, such as the ones about Heracles (Chapter II, §1). This popularity can be correlated with the reconstruction of the Panathenaea (Chapter IV, §2) in the 560s and thus testifies to a new spirit in contemporary Athens. Other cases are less easy to explain. Why did maenads suddenly become popular in Athenian imagery towards the end of the sixth century? The question is more easily posed than answered.[56]

Attic vase-painters' interest in mythological scenes strongly diminished after 480 BC, but myth remained popular in literature, although in changing ways. In the course of the classical period, the position of the poet as the main producer and innovator of religious traditions started to lose importance, and by the Hellenistic age his function had been largely taken over by philosophers and historians. This development also influenced the status of myth, which no longer had the same relevance to society; typically, in the fourth century myths started

---

[55] Neils 1992; Moreau 1994; Clauss and Johnston 1997; Fowler 2000–13: ii.195–234. *POxy.* 53.3698 adds a small fragment of archaic Argonautic poetry, mentioning Orpheus, Mopsus, and Aeëtes. For Eumelos, see Fowler 2000–13: ii.656–7; M. West 2011: 367–79; Debiasi 2015: 15–150 and 2020.

[56] Shapiro 1990. Note also the table with changes regarding Attic panel amphoras in Scheibler 1987: 89. For maenads, see Osborne 2010a: 382–7.

to be called 'old wives' tales'.[57] It can hardly have been chance that in the same century Asclepiades of Tragilus published *Subjects of Tragedy*, the first book in which tragedies were retold and compared with earlier versions.[58] In the Hellenistic and Roman periods, myths were collected as background material for the explanation of great poets or organized around a uniform theme, such as the *Library* ascribed to Apollodorus which is arranged genealogically by mythical families.[59] The myths now often served the need to possess cultural capital, as people liked to quiz one another regarding obscure mythological details, but in Roman times painters also decorated the walls of houses with mythological scenes, as the influential wall paintings of Pompeii show, and mosaicists created floors with mythological scenes, examples of which keep turning up in excavations.[60] The mythographical collections, in which myths have been reduced to fixed, sometimes rather dry texts, are now our main source for the knowledge of Greek mythology.[61] Yet we should always remember that these texts are only pale reflections of the performances which once brought these myths to life.

This analysis has shown a variety of approaches to myth in the course of time. Gradually, methodological pitfalls and possibilities are becoming clearer, but we are still far from a scholarly consensus regarding the best methods. The plasticity, multifunctionality, and many meanings of myth always make its analysis a hazardous undertaking.

---

[57] Heath 2017; Bremmer 2019e: 240–2.

[58] For Asclepiades, see *FGrH/BNJ* 12; Villagra 2012.

[59] Pàmias 2017; Acerbo 2019.

[60] Muth 1998; Bowersock 2006: 31–63; Hodske 2007; Lorenz 2008.

[61] For the Hellenistic and Roman mythographers, see, most recently, van Rossum-Steenbeek 1997; Cameron 2004; Trzaskoma and Smith 2013 (with a useful bibliography); Zucker *et al.* 2016; Romano and Marincola 2019; Smith and Trzaskoma forthcoming; many studies in the journal *Polymnia*, https://polymnia-revue.univ-lille3.fr/index.php/en/this-journal-home/ (accessed 20 January 2021).

VI. GENDER

In the West, recent years have witnessed a big increase in accepting sexual fluidity, as manifested in the growing visibility of the LGBT community. It was different in antiquity, where a binary culture of masculinity and femininity prevailed, although reality will have been more diverse. Ancient historians and literary scholars have worked on concepts of masculinity in antiquity,[1] but more recent studies of Greek religion have mainly analysed positions and representations of women, in so far as they have focused on gender differences at all.[2] I will therefore first look at some elements of the female life cycle and daily life (§1), then consider representations of women in art and myth, and goddesses as possible role models (§2), and conclude with a discussion of the most important women's festivals (§3).[3] At all times, we should keep in mind, however, that the real life of women probably differed significantly from male ideologies of their worth and proper place. This means that, although I focus on female gendered roles, male gendered roles will play a role too, even if more indirectly than directly in this chapter.[4]

1. The life cycle and daily life

In Athens, gender differentiation was immediately apparent at birth,[5] since parents hung a woollen fillet on the doorpost for girls and an olive wreath for boys.[6] The symbolism seems clear: weaving and spinning were among the main activities of Greek women, whereas an olive wreath was the prize given to meritorious citizens in Athens and the male winners of the Olympic and Panathenaic Games. Regarding

---

[1] Rosen and Sluiter 2003; Van Nortwick 2008; Rubarth 2014.

[2] For surveys, see Scheer 2011; Foxhall 2013. Bjork-James 2019 provides a useful online bibliography.

[3] As with the chapter on myth, no modern study of Greek religion has a chapter on gender. This absence is also noted by Georgoudi 2005: 70 n. 6, but see Goff and Taylor 2004; Bodiou and Mehl 2009; Dillon, Eidinow, and Maurizio 2017.

[4] For a good introduction to many aspects of gender and history, see Downs and Rubin 2019.

[5] For birth, see Bremmer 2020a.

[6] Ephippus fr. 3; Nonnus, *Dion.* 25.220; Hesychius σ 1981. It is unknown whether this custom was widespread.

young girls, little is known about religious activities in general, but we are reasonably well informed about their coming-of-age rituals, which have been well researched.[7]

But before we come to these, we have to note a typically Greek manner of looking at girls. As was the case with boys (Chapter IV, §3), adolescent girls were seen as 'untamed' fillies or deer and their initiation as a kind of 'domestication', which on vases was often represented as a 'capture' of a fleeing girl by a youth.[8] The metaphor is very clearly expressed in Euripides' *Hippolytus* when the chorus evokes how Aphrodite gave the girl Iole to Heracles, 'a filly, unyoked to the marriage bed, husbandless before' (546–7). Moreover, girls were compared to unruly heifers, and myth pictured both Io and the daughters of Proitos wandering around as cows.[9] Yet the metaphor of the marriage yoke suggests an important difference from boys' initiation. Despite the similarities, boys became free men on adulthood, whereas women were always imagined as being 'yoked'.

The 'domesticating' function of marriage was represented on the level of cult and ritual as well. Spartan girls worshipped certain prenuptial heroines, the Leukippides, whose name, 'White Mares', reflected their transitional position between youth and married adulthood, as did their sometime appearance as adolescents and as newlyweds. Myth also related their capture by the Dioskouroi, the mythical models of the young Spartan males, whom Alcman significantly calls 'tamers of fast horses' (fr. 2 Calame = 2 Page/Davies). The capture ended in marriage, which was a direct reflection of the Spartan wedding custom of 'kidnapping' the bride. The Thessalians even acted out the equestrian metaphor in their wedding ritual. Here, as Aelian (*c.* AD 170–240) relates

a man about to marry, when offering the wedding sacrifice, brings in a war-horse bitted and even fully equipped with all its gear; then when he has completed the sacrifice and poured the libation, he leads the horse by the rein and hands it to his bride. The significance of this the Thessalians must explain. (*NA* 12.34)

---

[7] Calame 1997 (≈ Calame 2019) is still seminal. See also Sourvinou-Inwood 1988; Dowden 1989; Dillon 2003; Neils and Oakley 2003.

[8] For vases, see Sourvinou-Inwood 1991: 58–98; Stansbury-O'Donnell 2009; Klinger 2009: 104; Bernhardt 2014; Tsiafakis 2019: no. 5 (with further bibliography). On 'taming', see Calame 1997: 238–44; Topper 2010 (with latest bibliography).

[9] For Io, see Yalouris 1990. For Proitos, see, most recently, Cairns 2005; Fowler 2000–13: ii.169–78, 239–40; Bremmer 2019e: 40f.

We need not share Aelian's despair, since the meaning of the gesture seems clear: among the horse-loving Thessalians a man expected his wife to act like a completely domesticated and tamed horse.[10]

Typical motifs of Greek female initiations were the prominence of aristocratic girls, seclusion, humiliation, choral dancing, physical exercise, and attention to beauty, as the following examples may illustrate. In Athens, four girls of noble families, the *arrhêphoroi*, lived on the Acropolis for a number of months (see below). In Attic Brauron, noble girls stayed for a while as *arktoi* ('she-bears'), in the sanctuary of Artemis, where they passed their time with dancing, running, and weaving. In Corinth, seven boys and seven girls of the most prominent families spent a year in the temple of Hera Akraia on the Acropolis dressed in black clothes and with close-cropped hair. In Ilion, two maidens of the best families of Locri had to spend one year in the temple of Athena Ilias, which they had to keep clean, while being barefoot, their hair cut short, and with only one dress to wear. Finally, on Keos marriageable girls had to spend the day in sanctuaries with sport and dancing, but at night they had to perform menial duties in other people's homes. All these rituals are most easily understood as transformations of initiations, since these are their closest parallels.[11]

In Sparta, female initiation lasted longer than anywhere else in Greece. Here the girls received a thorough physical training in palaestras and racing courses to become fit for producing firm and vigorous children. During the later part of their initiation some girls received a female lover. The seventh-century poet Alcman describes the principal girls of a chorus, Hagesichora and Agido, as being in love with each other (fr. 3 Calame = 1 Page/Davies).[12] Comparable 'lesbian' relationships existed on the island of Lesbos, where girls received prematrimonial training by means of dance and song in various circles: the poems of Sappho, the 'mistress' of one of these circles, testify to her passionate love for some of her pupils.[13]

---

[10] For the Leukippides, see Prange 1992; Calame 1997: 185–91; Baldassi 2018. On 'kidnapping', see Bremmer and Horsfall 1987: 110 (Bremmer). For Thessaly, see Aelian as translated by Scholfield 1959.

[11] For Athens/Attica, see Burkert 2004b: 119–21; Parker 2005: 228–49. For Corinth, see Calame 1997: 120–1. For Ilion, see Graf 2000a. For Keos, see Plut. *Mor.* 249. For Magna Graecia, see Kleibrink 2017.

[12] For Sparta, see Ducat 2006: 241–5, 261–77; Nobili 2014; Calame 1997. For 'lesbian' love in myth and Sparta, see Calame 1997: 252–5.

[13] See Lardinois 1989, 2010; duBois 1995; Caciagli 2011: 97–133.

In the final part of their initiation, Spartan girls participated in the cult of Helen, who in Sparta was worshipped as a goddess. An important element in her service was running, which was not unique to Sparta: girls in Brauron ran races (see above); in Chios girls ran against boys, and during Hera's festival in Elis girls ran in a very short dress, hair loosened, and right shoulder and breast bare.[14] In Helen's service, the girls also performed choral dances during which these 'little Helens' sang patriotic songs and displayed their beauty. This connection between beauty and female adolescence was widespread. In Athens, it is well illustrated by the maidens on the Parthenon frieze, and an aristocratic, marriageable girl could simply qualify her function as carrier of the sacrificial basket in processions (*kanêphoros*) with 'when I was a beautiful girl'. In Arcadian myth, the exemplary female novice was significantly called Kallisto, or 'the most beautiful'. In fact, in several places female initiation ended with a beauty contest. The parallels suggest that originally the situation in Sparta had not been all that different, but Spartan males, being a minority, had intensified the traditional physical exercise and concern for beauty to ensure that their domination over the Messenian helots was supported in all possible ways.[15]

Although the ritual elements were largely comparable, local myths varied widely and tied the rites more closely to their communities. For example, in the myth of the *arrhêphoria*, which is widely but not universally believed to reflect an initiation scenario, the three daughters of Athens' first king Kekrops (Aglauros,[16] Pandrosos, and Herse), also called the Aglaurides,[17] grew up in the palace on the Acropolis. The goddess Athena gave them a basket to guard and sternly forbade them to look inside it, but one night the sisters opened the basket and saw the child Erichthonius/Erechtheus and two snakes. Panic-stricken by this view they cast themselves from the Acropolis. In addition to explaining the presence of precincts of Aglauros and Pandrosos on the heights and slopes of the Acropolis, this myth

[14] For Chios, see Ath. 13.566E. For, Elis, see Paus. 5.16; also Calame 1990; Serwint 1993; Mirón 2004–5 [2007].

[15] For Helen, see *SEG* 26.457f, 35.320 (?); Kahil 1988; Calame 1997: 191–202. On *kanêphoros*, see Roccos 1995. For Kallisto, see Henrichs 1988: 254–67; Dowden 1989: 182–91; McPhee 1992; Fowler 2000–13: ii.107–8. On beauty contests, see Graf 1985: 275; Gherchanoc 2016.

[16] For her name, which is sometimes spelled as Agraulos, see Fowler 2000–13: ii.454.

[17] *Pace* Parker 2005: 222 n. 17; cf. Eur. *Ion* 23; Hesychius α 611: Ἀγλαυρίδες· νύμφαι παρὰ Ἀθηναίοις.

associated the *arrhêphoroi* with the heart of the Athenian tradition and motherhood: Erichthonius/Erechtheus was the first human king; a snake who was believed to guard the city was the most famous inhabitant of the Acropolis; and Athenian women put gold amulets in the form of snakes around their own babies, 'observing the custom of their forefathers and of earth-born Erichthonius' (Euripides, *Ion*, 20–1).[18]

Why did only a few aristocratic girls usually participate in these 'initiatory' rites and why was the coming of age of 'lower-class' girls not ritualized? An answer to this difficult question may perhaps be found in Crete, where only the aristocratic boy had a pederastic relationship, even though the other boys 'graduated' with him (Chapter IV, §3). Similarly, the relationship of Hagesichora and Agido seems to have been paradigmatic for the other Spartan girls. Evidently, aristocratic youths played a more prominent role in the ancient puberty rites than other adolescents. When in the course of the archaic period the puberty rites lost their original significance, perhaps because of urbanization, they were not totally abolished but reduced to a symbolic participation of a few boys and/or girls. It is only understandable that these few 'exemplary' youths were recruited from the nobility, considering its dominant position. In democratic Athens, such an exclusively aristocratic privilege became no longer tolerable, as is shown by a vote that all Athenian girls had to be a 'bear' at Brauron, reported by the fourth-century historian Krateros (*FGrH* 342 F 9). This discontent in Athens with the prominent place of aristocratic girls had already come to the fore in the archaic period, when non-aristocrats frequently dedicated statues of their daughters (*korai*) on the Acropolis to advertise their own status.[19] In many places in Greece, however, after the disintegration of the puberty rites the wedding seems to have become the main rite dramatizing the transition from youth to adulthood for girls of all classes.[20]

Married Greek women would soon experience how religion helped to sustain a social system in which they occupied an inferior position, but which, paradoxically, also enabled them temporarily to escape

[18] For this much discussed ritual and myth, see, most recently, Parker 2005: 219–23; Sourvinou-Inwood 2011: 36–50; Räuchle 2015; Meyer 2017: 267–88 (with detailed discussion of the literary, iconographical, and topographical evidence); Mackin Roberts 2019. There are also interesting observations in Sonnino 2010.
[19] Holloway 1992; Meyer 2007. Rühfel 1992, notes that girls' marble statues were often smaller than those of boys; see also Osborne 1994.
[20] Many studies, but see, especially, Oakley and Sinos 1993; Vérilhac and Vial 1998.

from that system. Women were considered to be more susceptible to impurity and pollution, and giving birth was sometimes linked with defecating and urinating as the three important taboos on sacred ground, which illustrates a regular association of women with 'dirt' and pollution. This association also spilled over into secular life. In the Hippocratic tradition, for example, only female patients were 'purified' with excrements. These negative associations appeared in other ways too. Statues of goddesses were more often washed than those of gods, sexual abstention seems to have been more strictly enforced for priestesses than for priests, and women were more often excluded from sanctuaries, especially from those of macho gods and heroes, like Poseidon (Chapter II, §3) and Heracles (Chapter II, §2).[21]

Still, it was not all gloom for women in religion. Priestesses must have been respected everywhere, and decrees praising their services were widespread in all regions of Greece.[22] Some of them clearly fulfilled highly important positions. The priestesses of Hera in Argos were the basis for Hellanicus of Lesbos in creating 'a chronological scaffolding upon which to hang the events of Greek history from the very beginning'; Aristophanes' Lysistrata is widely, and probably rightly, believed to have been modelled on Athena Polias' long-serving priestess Lysimache; and in Delphi the Pythia must have been a prestigious position for local women, just as another ecstatic seer, the Sibyl, seems to have been active in (especially western) Anatolia. More recently, several inscriptions have shown that female seers were more active than the literary evidence would suggest. It may well be that our male-dominated evidence has given us a skewed idea of the importance of women in religious functions.[23]

As regards female sociability, fetching water from fountains must have long provided an opportunity for women to meet and exchange views and gossip. The importance of the fountain is well illustrated on vase-paintings and in mythology, where fountains are places for gods and heroes to meet mortal women, such as Poseidon and Amymone, Achilles and Polyxena, or Heracles and Auge.[24] Female

---

[21] On women and dirt, see Parker 1983: 84–5; Cole 1992; von Staden 1992b; Carson 1999.

[22] See Kron 1996: 140–55; Lindner 2003; Pirenne-Delforge 2005; J. Connelly 2007; Bruit Zaidman 2013; Leventis 2019.

[23] For Hera's priestesses, see Fowler 2000–13: ii.683–5 (quotation). For Lysimache, see Thonemann 2020. For the Pythia, see, most recently, Graf 2011; Chalupa 2014. For female seers, see Bremmer 2019e: 153–5.

[24] Richardson 1974: 179–80; Manfrini 1992; Pfisterer-Haas 2002; Kosso and Lawton 2009.

festivals likewise enabled women to move among other women, albeit
for a limited period only (below, §3). Greek males must have realized
the importance that women attached to these events. We hear that
Democritus did his utmost not to die during the most important
women's festival, the Thesmophoria (§3), in order that his sister
would not be prevented from attending (Diog. Laert. 9.43).

Women could also show their activities and trades by way of votives,
as the many loom weights in sanctuaries show.[25] More importantly,
they could even found private shrines and play an important role in
the new cults and 'sects' that gradually infiltrated the Greek world –
a phenomenon well attested for late antiquity, when women were
instrumental in the spread of Manichaeism, a post-Christian world religion which survived until about 1500 in China and Japan, and, in particular, for early Christianity itself. Older Athenian women, who
actively used their possibilities of wandering more freely in the streets
than was allowed to pre-menopause women, propagated cults of
Kybele and Sabazios (Chapter VII, §2).[26] If these women often give
the impression of belonging to the lower social strata, this cannot be
said of those who were interested in Bacchic teachings. It is rather striking that several of the Orphic Gold Leaves, which derived from Bacchic
groups (Chapter VII, §2), have been found in graves of wealthy women
in various parts of the Greek world.[27]

From a religious point of view, clearly more went on behind the
closed doors of Greek women's quarters than was dreamt of in most
scholars' philosophies. Yet male Greeks were not prepared to allow
women too much freedom in religion, and festivals such as the
Thesmophoria were closely supervised by males. In the fourth century
the Athenians executed at least two women for introducing new cults
and would have put to death the courtesan Phryne for the same reason,
if her lawyer had not spectacularly bared her breasts in front of the male
jury.[28]

---

[25] Ferrandini Troisi 1986; Sofroniew 2012.

[26] On private shrines, see Purvis 2003; Blok 2018. For late antiquity, see Bremmer 2017: 33–41.
For old women, see Bremmer 2019e: 234.

[27] On Orphism and women, see Bremmer, 2019c: 80.

[28] On supervision of women, see Cole 1992: 113–14. For Phryne, see Gherchanoc 2012;
Eidinow 2016: 23–30; Bremmer 2020c.

2. Representations and role models

What images, attitudes, and associations of Greek women were mediated through religion? An answer cannot be exhaustive, but two areas especially deserve our attention.[29] Numerous Attic vases display women, especially young ones,[30] practising or participating in various rites, especially wedding rites (above, §1). They often mark the bride's beauty and thus reflect the Greek view of upper-class female adolescents (§1). These vases were given as a wedding present to the bride, and women may well have internalized this view and appreciated these gifts. Equally popular were vase-paintings of women performing libations for departing warriors or participating in funerals as mourners and, especially after the first half of the fifth century, as visitors at a grave. These vases present us with positive roles of women but nearly always being subject to or serving men.[31] This subordinated position also appears on Athenian marble votive reliefs of women, where they are portrayed more often than men in a suppliant position, although their clothing shows a greater variety than that of the males, thus granting them a certain degree of self-expression.[32]

Although positive images of women, then, were not absent, they did not dominate. Mythology, in particular, played an important role in spreading and sustaining negative images of women in all stages of their lives, starting with the myths surrounding the first woman, Pandora, who was credited with bringing evils such as disease and old age to humanity through her curiosity.[33] The recurrent motif of young girls falling in love and betraying their own family presents a more negative portrayal. It is already alluded to in the *Odyssey* (11.321–5), where Odysseus sees Ariadne, whose assistance had been decisive in Theseus' conquest of the Minotaur (Chapter V, §3). Another early example is Medea, who had helped Jason to procure the Golden Fleece. Neither girl fared well after her betrayal, as was to be expected: Greek myth could hardly have condoned such

[29] For Athens, see the nicely produced Kaltsas and Shapiro 2008.
[30] Meyer 2014.
[31] Bérard 1984; Shapiro 1991; Lissarrague 1992 (funeral, libation, marriage, and more); Merthen 2014; E. Giudice 2015: 127–54 (richly illustrated); Gaifman 2018: 74–9 (departure of warriors).
[32] Klöckner 2002.
[33] For the role of mythology, see Gould 2001: 112–57. For Pandora, see Bremmer 2008: 19–34; Steiner 2013.

behaviour. In these and similar cases, the ambiguous action of the girls (helping and betraying) reflected the ambiguous position between their own and (future) husbands' families in an early society where the support of the family was all-important (Chapter V, §2).[34] In writing his *Antigone*, Sophocles shifted this type of family conflict to a level that fitted the occasion of a public festival attended by many Athenians, perhaps even by many Athenian women, as Antigone has to choose between her brother and the *polis*, a conflict that still elicits many differing reactions among modern students of the play.[35]

Sophocles had probably been inspired by Herodotus' account of Intaphernes' wife, who preferred her brother over her husband (3.119).[36] Other adult women were pictured as betraying their husbands, witness Eriphyle's betrayal of the seer Amphiaraos (Chapter III, §3) for a golden necklace, whereas other women, such as the Lemnian ones and the Danaids, murdered their husbands.[37] Similarly terribly, in the myths of the Phineids the sons are blinded by their mother or, sometimes, their stepmother, and in the myth of Ino Themisto killed her own children by accident while trying to murder her stepchildren. The collective imagination probably considered a murdering mother too harsh and therefore constructed the killing as an accident or replaced the mother by a stepmother, since in some versions of these myths the mother alternates with the stepmother. But they are not the only mothers who killed their children. Greek tragedy even put killing mothers, such as Medea and Procne, on the stage as, presumably, frightening examples. The message seems clear: Greek males and their offspring were highly vulnerable in the family sphere and the loyalty of their wives was never to be taken for granted, despite such positive examples as Penelope.[38]

We find similar ideas about women well beyond child-bearing age, as can be seen from the number of terrifying females who were represented as old women: Empousa, Erinyes, Graiai, Lamia, and Moirai.[39] From adolescence to old age, then, myth regularly depicted

[34] Bernhard and Daszewski 1986 (Ariadne); Neils 1990 (Medea). For betrayal, see Bremmer 2019e: 245.
[35] For opposing views, compare Sourvinou-Inwood 1990 with Foley 1996.
[36] For this example, with ethnographical parallels, see Bremmer 2008: 329–33.
[37] See Fowler 2000–13: ii.217 (Lemnian women); Villagra 2018.
[38] On Eriphyle, see Buxton 1982: 37. For the Phineids and Themisto, see Watson 1995: 236–7 and 224–5, respectively. For Medea and Procne, see Klöckner 2005; E. Giudice 2008; Räuchle 2008.
[39] For old women, see Bremmer 2019e: 244.

women in more or less negative ways, even though some women could be monstrous and beautiful at the same time. It is important to note that these mythical representations were not seen as something from a distant past but explicitly connected with the present. When Odysseus meets Agamemnon in the underworld, the latter complains about his murder by his wife, Clytaemnestra, and comments: 'she has brought shame on herself and future generations of women, even if one of these were to be honest' (*Od.* 11.433–4, trans. Heubeck and Hoekstra 1989).

Myth not only depicted women as threatening the male order (of the city), but even located them outside the borders of the Greek world. The *Iliad* (3.189, 6.186) only alludes to a tribe of warrior women, the Amazons, 'women equal to men', but the formula looks old and Homer may not have told everything he knew. Other epics were more informative, and the *Aethiopis* related the fight between Achilles and Penthesileia, the queen of the Amazons.[40] In the archaic period, Heracles' battle against the Amazons became one of the most popular feats in the visual arts (Figure 12), only to be succeeded by Theseus. The few data from the tradition made the Amazons into a myth without much content which could be filled by successive periods with their most favourite heroes. This 'emptiness' is also reflected in the widely diverging interpretations of modern scholars: from nineteenth-century matriarchy via initiation to the contemporary 'Other'. Every age gets the Amazons it deserves.[41]

If mythology supplied few females as attractive role models for Greek women,[42] what about goddesses?[43] The armed Athena did not conform to a stereotypical femininity, and Hera's marriage to Zeus was not a real model of harmony, whereas Aphrodite was probably too much associated with physical love to be a proper example. Eileithyia, the goddess presiding over birth (Chapter III, §2), seems to have played only a functional role in the lives of Greek women, but Demeter, the goddess by whom women swore oaths, must have been more attractive to them, in particular because of her Thesmophoria festivals (below, §3). However, Greek parents never gave their daughters the name Demeter, since the distance between gods and mortals was normally

---

[40] See Pilz 2011a; M. West 2013: 129–62.
[41] Blok 1995 (with bibliography); Dowden 1997; Wünsche 2008; Martini 2013.
[42] See also Meyer 2010.
[43] Loraux 1992 is still fundamental.

Figure 12. Battle of the Amazons against Heracles (whose head is missing) with his
heroic friends. One side of an Attic black-figure band-cup, Phrynos Painter, c. 555 BC.

too great to give a child the name of a god (Chapter II, §1). In the classical era, the only exception to this rule was Artemis. From the fourth
century onwards, girls could be called after the goddess, although perhaps not daughters of Athenian citizens, and the reason seems apparent. In the *Odyssey*, Nausicaa's pre-eminence among her friends is
compared to Artemis' position among her nymphs (6.102–9). By nam-
ing a daughter Artemis, parents probably hoped for a similar pre-
eminence among her contemporaries.[44]

The reason why goddesses were hardly satisfactory role models lies
in one of the peculiarities of the Greek pantheon which we have not
yet mentioned: representations of gods and goddesses in no way directly reflected the common role patterns of the sexes in human life.
On the contrary, the Greek pantheon contained a striking asymmetry.
Whereas the gods did not play important roles in typically female activities, goddesses were often connected with typically male ones.
Admittedly, Athena supervised spinning and weaving, but she was
also the goddess of artisans, closely connected with war, and always
represented in armour (Chapter II, §3). Hera and Aphrodite
(Chapter IV, §3) were also, in varying ways, connected with war,[45]
and Artemis was the goddess of the hunt (Chapter II, §2). Burkert
once argued that archaeological findings prove that this prominent position of goddesses in the male world goes back to pre-agricultural

[44] Masson 1990: 543–7.
[45] Argive initiates received a shield during the Heraia: see Burkert 1983: 163–4; Moretti 1991.

hunting cultures, but the darkness of prehistory prevents any further understanding.[46] Greek mythology, then, did not offer many positive female role models, and this makes the role of female festivals even more important.

3. Women's festivals

The most widespread women's festivals were the Thesmophoria festivals.[47] I purposely use the plural because modern research regularly discusses the festival in the singular as if it was the same all over Greece, which clearly was not the case. I will sketch the festivals in outline and apply a certain 'ritual logic' in my reconstruction of the order of events during the festivals, but we have to remain aware that they were old, Panhellenic, and displayed local differences.

The festivals generally lasted three days, for which the Athenian names have been preserved, but they were celebrated in Sicily for ten days, since here Demeter and Kore occupied important positions in the local pantheon. In Athens participation was restricted to married women from noble families, but such social differentiation need not have taken place always and everywhere; in some places, girls also seem to have attended.[48] In Athens, the first day was known as Anodos because it started with the 'Ascent' of the women with their equipment, food, and shrieking piglets to the sanctuaries of Demeter, which were often situated on the tops or slopes of hills (Chapter III, §2). They built huts in which they stayed during the festivals, and made beds with twigs of withy, fleabane, and certain types of laurel – all antaphrodisiac plants.[49] On the level of myth, this absence of sexuality was symbolized in Demeter's gift of the Thesmophoria to an old woman (Corinth) or to the maiden daughters of the first king (Paros) – both belonging to categories on either side of licit sexuality. In a Peloponnesian version, the

---

[46] Burkert 2001–11: vi.104–21.

[47] See, most recently, Parker 2005: 270–83; Chlup 2007 (a sophisticated article to which I refer for the various levels of meaning of the Thesmophoria); Bremmer 2014: 170–7 (thick description). Also Ruscillo 2013; Osek 2018; Patera 2020. I refer to these studies for the sources.

[48] Demetrios of Kallatis *FGrH* 86 F 6 (death of twenty-five girls during the festival); Cic. *Verr.* 4.99 (women and maidens perform sacrifices for Demeter in Sicilian Catane); Lucian, *Dial. meret.* 2.1 (courtesan and virgin attendance); Schol. Theocr. 4.25c (participation by maidens and women), if in garbled and clearly late text, which still suggests the possibility of local varieties and/or later developments.

[49] On huts and beds, see Kron 1988 and 1992: 620–3; von Staden 1992a.

Danaids who had murdered their husbands during their wedding night had brought the festival from Egypt: an interesting indication of the festival's perceived 'otherness'.[50] Since the women had temporarily deserted marriage, the absence of sexuality was heavily marked during the seclusion – which may well have reassured the husbands.

The second day was called Nesteia, or 'Fasting', which the women spent without food, sitting on the ground, and without the usual flowery garlands. This is the day on which Aristophanes has situated a meeting of all Athenian women in his *Thesmophoriazusae*, although in reality Athenian women never celebrated the festival together but met only in their own demes.[51] As Versnel suggests, it fits the 'abnormal' character of the day that on this day Athens released its prisoners and suspended court sessions and council meetings: the 'reversals' strongly contrasted the 'Fasting' with the return to 'normality' on the last day, when fertility of land and humans became the main focus of activities.[52] And just as the death of Sophocles occurred on the most sombre day of the Anthesteria (Chapter IV, §3), so Plutarch located the death of Demosthenes on 'the most gloomy day of the Thesmophoria' in his *Life of Demosthenes* (30), even if probably wrongly.

Demeter's fasting during her search for Persephone came to an end when, in one version of the myth, an old lady, Baubo, made her laugh by lifting her skirt. As the Demeter myth was closely connected with the Thesmophoria in various places in Greece, it is attractive to connect the lifting of the ritual fasting with the reports about mocking, sham fights, and indecent speech during the festivals: the return to 'normality' had to be marked by a period of highly 'abnormal' female behaviour. Herodotus (2.171.2) mentions that not everything about the Thesmophoria could be freely told, and these 'secrets' may well relate to this part of the festivals. In any case, secrecy was an important part of the festival as the sanctuaries often had high walls, and various anecdotes told of the bad end of males who had tried to break that secrecy.[53]

On the third day, the Kalligeneia, decayed remains of piglets were fetched up from subterranean pits (*megara* or *magara*),[54] where they

---

[50] Serv. *Aen.* 1.430 (Corinth); Apollodorus *FGrH* 244 F 89 (Paros); Hdt. 2.171 (Danaids).

[51] On play and festival, see Bowie 1993: 205–27; Zeitlin 1996: 375–416. On meeting in their own demes, see Clinton 1996.

[52] Versnel 1993: 242–4.

[53] For Baubo, see Bremmer 2019e: 65 (recent bibliography). On walls and secrecy, see Bremmer 2019c.

[54] Robert 1969: 1005–7 and 1989: 289–90; McLardy 2015; Henrichs 2019: 3–9.

had been left to rot for some time, and placed on altars as future manure. In addition to this concern for the fertility of the land, there was concern for human procreation: Kalligeneia was invoked as goddess of birth in Athens on this day. It is probably these positive aspects of the day which were celebrated with the sacrifice of pigs, the sacrificial victim appropriate to Demeter (Chapter IV, §2).[55] In a famous study, Marcel Detienne once argued that women themselves were not allowed to sacrifice but that sacrifice was strictly a male business. Yet literary, epigraphical, and archaeological (see Figure 13) evidence all attest to the contrary, and in Bronze Age graves women were buried with sacrificial knives,[56] even though in Sicily quite a few terracotta figurines have been found of women offering small bread, cakes, and fruit, suggesting that women perhaps practised non-animal sacrifice more often.[57] With the sacrifices, normality returned. The women had to return to their homes and their wool baskets: the temporary reversal of the ordinary had only reformulated the status quo.

If the women at the Thesmophoria might have behaved in an unseemly way at times, it was a very different matter with the maenads, the female followers of Dionysos in myth and ritual, whose ecstatic rituals took place every other year on mountains in the winter.[58] Greek myth abounds with startling pictures of their mad behaviour, culminating in the description of their murderous ecstasy in Euripides' *Bacchae*: running over mountains, moving like birds, handling fire and snakes, attacking men, and tearing apart animals, children, and even the Theban king[59] – although more in literature than on vase-paintings.[60] Literature and art have provided us with much information about these rituals, which are also reflected in some of the names of maenads on vases, such as the references to the nightly character of the ritual in the names 'Torch' (Lampas) and 'All night long' (Pannychis): apparently, the rituals could be relatively freely observed or talked about.[61] In recent times much attention has been directed to the disentanglement of myth and ritual in these reports; to

---

[55] Clinton 1988. For the connection with fertility of the land, note the dedications of ploughs and hoes in the Thesmophoreion of Gela: Kron 1992: 636–9.

[56] Detienne 1979. *Contra*: Kron 1992: 640–3, 650; Osborne 2000. Note also Flemming 2007 (priestesses of Ceres/Demeter).

[57] See Pautasso, 2020.

[58] For Dionysiac ecstasy, see Henrichs 1994; Gödde 2016.

[59] For the *Bacchae*, see March 1989; Versnel 1990: 31–205, *passim*.

[60] As noted by Heinemann 2016: 502.

[61] Kossatz-Deissmann 1991: 175–92.

Figure 13. Girl sacrificing at an altar. Attic red-figure alabastron, Painter of Copenhagen 3830, c. 470 BC.

distinguishing those images of maenads which matched the visual experience of a contemporary viewer from those which were 'invented' by the painter or copied from other images; to the representation of the maenads in literature and art; and to the origin and function of the ritual. Let us look at a few elements of these discussions.

By taking into account distinctions between myth and ritual
(Chapter V, §3) and comparative evidence, we can often reasonably
decide in what ways the mythical imagination 'processed' elements of
ritual.[62] When in the *Bacchae* maenads are said to eat raw meat, a judicious comparison with the tasting of small portions of meat from
domesticated animals in epigraphically attested maenadic ritual shows
that the carnivorous women operated only on the level of myth. In
the case of the ritual, though, comparisons with ecstatic rituals from
all over the world strongly suggest that elements such as walking barefoot, headshaking, moving to shrill music and clappers, and singing in
high-pitched voices were not invented by the ancient sources.[63]
Regarding the representations on the vases, we can investigate which
elements are consistently attested or note the lack of functionality of
certain details. For example, long ago it was argued, not unpersuasively, that the consistency in the ways in which the women's poses
in maenadic dances were pictured and their absence in other female
Dionysiac representations implied that they reflected 'real life' dances.
And when for no obvious reasons round cakes (?) appear at the
shoulders of the 'idol' of Dionysos on the so-called Lenaean vases,
they will hardly have been invented by the painter.[64]

It is clear that poets and painters have been much intrigued by the
maenads. Homer compares Andromache to a 'maenad' when she
rushes through the house in fear for Hector's life (*Il.* 6.389), and tragedy abounds with allusions to maenadism, especially in Euripides.
Sometimes maenadism enables Euripides to let a female character
move freely outside her house, as in his *Antigone*. In other cases, mythical maenads are used as a point of comparison for the frenzied behaviour of his male protagonists, as in the *Heracles*.[65] Vase-painters also
showed great curiosity about the maenads but certainly not at all
times.[66] The high points of interest seem to have been the end of the
sixth century and the fourth century. Moreover, interest was clearly
limited to certain contexts. Maenads are absent from white-ground
lekythoi and, considering the interest of Bacchic mysteries in afterlife

[62] *Pace* Heinemann 2016: 593 n. 2.

[63] Bremmer 2019e: 251–77; McGlashan 2021 (forthcoming).

[64] I owe these examples to Osborne 2010a: 368–404 (interesting methodological reflections) at
377. For additional bibliography on the Lenaean vases and the cakes, see Tsiafakis 2019: 10,
no. 10; also Heinemann 2016: 429–33. On dance, see Delavaud-Roux 1995, 2006; Toillon 2017.

[65] Kannicht 1992; Schlesier 1993; Seaford 1993.

[66] Moraw 1998; Fahlbusch 2004; Villanueva Puig 2009; Heinemann 2016; G. Giudice 2018.

(Chapter VII, §2), it is at least noteworthy that maenads never appear on funerary pots.[67]

There is little known about the origin of maenadism, although a background in initiation is not unlikely,[68] but maenadic ritual, albeit with many local variants, was widespread in the Greek world.[69] It must have fulfilled various functions in Greek women's lives – that is, in the lives of 'upper-class' women, as the ritual was probably limited to that class. First, it gave the women the possibility of a genuine religious experience through their identification with Dionysos during the ritual. Second, the rituals provided occasions for leaving the home and staying with other women without the immediate supervision of males. Third, by going into a trance the women could perhaps reach a more authentic self-expression than in their normal fixed roles. Yet the limited occurrence of the rituals (only every other year), the restricted participation (see above), and the male supervision from a distance should warn us against overrating the importance of these rituals for Greek women, however fascinating they were for Greek males (and modern scholars!).

Our last festival is the Adonia, which took place yearly in high summer.[70] During the festival, women of all classes mourned the death of the divine youth Adonis with ecstatic, nightly dances and planted quickly germinating green salad stuff on sherds, which at the end of the festival were thrown into the sea. The cult, which served more or less the same functions as maenadic ritual, is attested first in the eastern part of the Greek Mediterranean.[71] It clearly derives from Syro-Palestine: witness the connection of Adonis' name with the Semitic title 'adôn ('Lord'), and testimonies about the offering of incense to Baal on flat rooftops (Jeremiah 32:29). The growing of the gardens seems to have originated in the widespread agricultural custom to grow a few plants in order to test the quality of seeds, but it is obscure how or why this custom was incorporated into the Adonis ritual.[72] In myth, Adonis is painted in very negative colours. He is the product of incest, the toyboy of Aphrodite, a coward who hides himself

---

[67] As observed by Osborne 2010a: 387.
[68] Bremmer 2019e: 266–9.
[69] See the survey in Versnel 1990: 134–50.
[70] Parker 2005: 283–9; Reitzammer 2016; Cook 2018: 87–110.
[71] Hes. fr. 139; Sappho fr. 140a, 168; Panyassis fr. 22b Davies = 27 Bernabé; Antimachus of Kolophon fr. 92; Epimenides fr. 13.
[72] For all texts, see Bühler 1998: 463–73. See also Hiltebeitel 1988; Holes 2004; Vajda 2008.

among lettuce plants, is passive in love affairs, and perishes in a hunt:
from a male point of view not a very threatening figure. Did the women
accept the male negative view or were there female voices whose independent opinions have been lost?

According to a female anthropologist, twentieth-century rural Greek
women seemed to have internalized the male negative views about
them.[73] There are really no indications that ancient Greek women
had developed an alternative ideology.[74] One thing seems sure. As
this discussion of the rituals, myths, and festivals has shown, cult provided only limited possibilities to Greek women for status, support, and
self-expression. Lower-class women may have fared worse than aristocratic females in this respect, although they perhaps had more possibilities for self-expression by being able to work outside the house.[75]
Mythology produced and maintained a stream of negative images
about women. In the end, Greek religion was not so very different
from the women-unfriendly spirit of Greek culture at large.

---

[73] Du Boulay 1986.
[74] *Contra* Winkler 1990: 188–209, who drew his modern parallels not from rural areas but from
circles that had already come into contact with Western ideas.
[75] E. Harris 2014.

VII. TRANSFORMATIONS

Although we have already noticed various changes in the period under survey, we have still been insufficiently able to escape a certain static view (Chapter I, §1). In this last chapter, therefore, I will concentrate on changes in Greek religion. I first discuss the Eleusinian Mysteries (§1), which became increasingly important in the fifth century, then Orphic ideas and Bacchic Mysteries (§2), which both emerged around 500 BC, and conclude with a sketch of the structural transformations during the transition to the Hellenistic period (§3).

1. The Eleusinian Mysteries

Mysteria was originally the Athenian term for the Eleusinian festival of Demeter and Kore but was later used for a whole range of cults, from Isis to Mithras, whose principal resemblances were initiation, secrecy, and a certain interest in the afterlife (the Samothracian and Mithraic Mysteries excepted).[1] The Eleusinian Mysteries were celebrated annually in the sanctuary of Demeter and her daughter, Kore/Persephone, on a hill outside Eleusis (Chapter III, §2), one of the many demes of Attica; the autumn festival lasted more than a week and knew two degrees of initiation, of which the first one seems to have focused on the finding of Persephone and the second one on the revelation of an ear of corn.[2]

After a procession from Athens to Eleusis along the (still-existing) Sacred Way and more individual rites of fasting and purification, the actual initiation took place over two consecutive nights in the main building, the *telestêrion*.[3] On the first night, the Eleusinian 'clergy' and the prospective initiates acted out the myth of the *Homeric Hymn to Demeter* (late seventh century BC), the foundation myth of the Mysteries, which relates how Hades kidnapped Persephone, and how

---

[1] See, most recently, Cosmopoulos 2003; Bowden 2010; Auffarth 2013; Bremmer 2014. Scarpi 2002 is an excellent collection of sources.

[2] See Parker 2005: 327–68; Bremmer 2014: 1–20. On degrees of initiation, see Dowden 1980. For iconography, see Clinton 1992. For the early study of the Mysteries, see Ben-Tov 2019.

[3] For the procession and the entry into the Eleusinian sanctuary, see Miles 2012; Lambert 2021: 103–5.

her mother, Demeter, wandered the earth in search of her. When Persephone had been returned to her, Demeter promised fields yellow with corn and a better afterlife. After Persephone was found, in ways that we cannot reconstruct, the ritual came to an end with 'rejoicing and brandishing of torches', as the Christian author Lactantius tells us.

The second night was reserved for the initiation into the highest degree of the Mysteries, the so-called *epopteia* ('contemplation'). As its climax, the hierophant showed 'a single harvested ear of grain' and called out at the top of his voice: 'The reverend goddess has given birth to a sacred boy, Brimo to Brimos, that is, the strong one has borne a strong child.'[4] The mention of the ear of corn seems to confirm Isocrates' words that Demeter was well disposed towards Attica 'because of benefits which only the initiated may hear' (*Paneg.* 28). It also suggests that the Mysteries did not conceal an esoteric wisdom. In fact, the *Homeric Hymn to Demeter*, the oldest source to relate the institution of the Mysteries by Demeter during her search for her kidnapped daughter (Figure 14),[5] explains the secrecy from the 'awesomeness' of the rites and states that 'a great reverence of the gods restrains utterance' (478–9).

The *Homeric Hymn of Demeter* singles out two gains for initiates: prosperity in this life and a blessed state in the life hereafter (480–9). The prosperity was reinterpreted by the Athenians as the gift of corn and connected with Triptolemos, an Eleusinian king, who is relatively unimportant in the *Hymn*. During the heyday of the Athenian empire he was promoted to great prominence as the Attic cultural hero who taught the art of agriculture to humans.[6] After the decline of the Athenian empire, the emphasis gradually seems to have shifted from agriculture to eschatological theories, but the Mysteries increased in popularity, as Plato extensively used Eleusinian realia and terminology in his *Symposium* and *Phaedrus*, and followers of Epicurus argued the 'religious correctness' of the master by his participation in the Mysteries.[7]

---

[4] The enigmatic detail is only supplied by the Gnostic 'Naassenian', who is quoted by the third-century church father Hippolytus in his *Refutation of All Heresies* (5.8.39–40), for whose sources see Mansfeld 1992: 318–23.

[5] The precise connection of the *Hymn* with the Mysteries is much debated: see Parker 1991; Clinton 1992, *passim*.

[6] Smarczyk 1990: 167–298; Raubitschek 1991: 229–38 ('The Mission of Triptolemos'); Schwarz 1997; Nesselrath 2013.

[7] For Plato, see Riedweg 1987: 1–69. For Epicurus, see Philodemus, *De pietate*, 550–9, 808–10.

Figure 14. Capture of Persephone by Hades. Fragment of south Italian (Taranto) red-figure krater, akin to Painter of the Birth of Dionysos, *c.* 380 BC.

The earliest archaeological evidence for the sanctuary dates from the late eighth century BC.[8] Yet the widespread occurrence of a Demeter Eleusinia in Ionia and the Peloponnese (the Laconian sanctuary dates from *c.* 700 BC) demonstrates an early popularity of the cult. The Peloponnese with its beauty contest (Chapter VI, §1) points to an initiatory background, whereas the Ionian connection with (royal) families (Chapter II, §2) and the administration of the Eleusinian cult by two *genê* (clans), the Eumolpids and Kerykes, suggest the cult of a *genos*.[9] If we combine these data with the presence in the Eleusinian festival of a boy 'who was initiated from the [state] hearth [at the marketplace]', it seems to follow that initiation into the Mysteries probably originated in the archaic puberty rites of a *genos*.[10]

A similar development from initiatory to Mystery cult probably took place elsewhere in Attica. In Phlya, Themistocles rebuilt a shrine of Mystery rites (*telestêrion*) for his clan, the age-old Lykomids, after it

[8] See Cosmopoulos 2015.

[9] For the early history of the Eumolpids and Kerykes, see Humphreys 2018: ii.637–40.

[10] For Demeter Eleusinia, see Graf 1985: 274–7, 490; Parker 1988; Stibbe 1993. For the boy's presence in the festival, see Burkert 1983: 280–1.

had been burnt down by the Persians. Many centuries later the traveller Pausanias reported that the Lykomids chanted songs of Orpheus and a hymn to Demeter at the ceremonies in their 'clubhouse' (*kleision*). The resemblance of this 'clubhouse' to other Greek 'men's houses', and the 'wolf' (*lykos*) in the name of the *genos*, suggest a background in tribal initiation. Apparently, some Attic initiatory cults were reconstructed and reinterpreted as Mysteries after the disintegration of male puberty rites in the course of the archaic period.[11]

Unfortunately, much less is known about three other public Mysteries in the classical period – those of Samothrace, Lemnos, and Thebes – even though we know that the first two had been influenced by the Eleusinian Mysteries. As regards Samothrace, it is unlikely that the local gods had a Greek origin, since a form of Thracian was locally used well into the Hellenistic period. Unlike Eleusis, the Samothracian Mysteries were geared towards protection at sea and not eschatological expectations. Of the Mysteries of the Kabeiroi on Lemnos and in Thebes, little is known with certainty, except that wine played an important role in these cults and that puberty rites can still be seen in the background. The consistent connection of the Kabeiroi with the Great Goddess points to an origin in a pre-Greek cult, but the lack of sufficient data makes it impossible to disentangle the mixture of non-Greek roots and Greek (re)interpretations.[12]

2. Orphic ideas and Bacchic Mysteries

If the interpretation of the Eleusinian Mysteries is only progressing at snail's pace, in the last five decades the discovery of new texts and vase-paintings has spectacularly increased our knowledge and understanding of the books, doctrines, rites, initiators, and groups connected with Orphic ideas and Bacchic Mysteries.[13] Around 500 BC, if not somewhat earlier, a new religious movement arose in southern Italy, which distributed its ideas in the form of poems ascribed to Orpheus, the archaic

---

[11] On the Lykomids, see Simonides fr. 627; Plut. *Vit. Them.* 1; Paus. 1.22.7, 31; 4.1.5–9; Humphreys 2018: ii.549, 674–5. On wolves and initiation, see Bremmer 2019e: 361–6. For the *kleision* as the 'men's house', see Gernet and Boulanger 1970: 72.

[12] For these Mysteries, see Bremmer 2014: 21–54.

[13] See the editions in Bernabé 2004–5: ii.9–79; Bernabé and Jiménez San Cristóbal 2008; Graf and Johnston 2013.

mythical singer par excellence, to legitimize the innovation.[14] The earliest sources betray influences from Anatolia and Phoenicia, but also indicate closeness to Pythagorean ideas and practices, as well as to Dionysiac cult.[15] Herodotus (2.81) identified Orphic and Bacchic rites, and in Euripides' *Hippolytus* (428 BC) Theseus uses the verb *bakcheuein* for Orphic rites (953–4); moreover, in Black-Sea Olbia, fifth-century bone plaques have been found with the mention of Orphikoi in a Dionysiac context.[16] Evidently, Orphic ideas and Bacchic mysteries belonged to the same complex. The two most popular early Mysteries, then, were cults of precisely those two divinities who were 'eccentric' in the Greek pantheon (Chapter II, §3; Chapter III, §2; Chapter IV, §2).

It was always known that the most important, original Orphic poem was a theogony. Direct knowledge, though, was lacking, and scholars had to extrapolate from reconstructions of the ever-expanding Hellenistic and late antique Orphic theogonies.[17] Thanks to the publication of a papyrus (*c.* 325 BC) from Derveni (Macedonia) that contains a commentary on the oldest Orphic theogony, we now have direct access to a number of its verses.[18] The papyrus shows that Orphic theogony contained a succession myth *à la* Hesiod but with more scandalous details, such as Zeus's incest with his mother. The actual theogony probably started with Night, since the papyrus mentions 'Night-born heaven, who was the first king' (XIV.6 Kouremenos = §43 Kotwick). Such a beginning is supported by the birth of Aristophanes' Orphic egg of Night in the *Birds* (693–7) and by the fourth-century philosopher Eudemus' knowledge of a theogony beginning with Night; after two introductory hymns, the imperial collection of Orphic Hymns also starts with a hymn to Night.[19] However, a Protogonos is mentioned as first

[14] See vol. 3 of Burkert 2001–11 (many fundamental articles); Bernabé and Casadesús 2009; Herrero de Jáuregui *et al.* 2011; Edmonds 2013 (too minimalistic); Bremmer 2014: 55–80.
[15] On Anatolia and Phoenicia, see López-Ruiz 2010; Rutherford 2018. For Pythagoreanism, see Bremmer 1999b.
[16] For *bakcheuein*, see Henrichs 1994: 47–51; Jiménez San Cristóbal 2009. For bone plaques, see *Orph. frag.* 463–5 (500–450 BC) = Dubois 1996: 154–5, no. 94a–c.
[17] For these later poems, see the many studies of Luc Brisson, now conveniently collected in Brisson 1995. For their transmission, see Trzcionkowski 2018.
[18] The official first edition is Kouremenos, Parássoglou, and Tsantsanoglou 2006, but the best edition with commentary is Kotwick 2017; see also Piano 2016; Santamaría 2019 (with a good bibliography, 151–7). The commentary was probably written in Athens: see Bremmer 2019b.
[19] On Night, see Bremmer 2008: 5; also Euripides fr. 758a.1106 Kannicht = *Orph. frag.* 65. Night was also first with Silence in Antiphanes' comedy *Theogonia* (?): see Kassel and Austin 1991: 366–7. For the Orphic Hymns, see Robert 1990: 569–73, with a discussion of, surely Orphic, dedications to Night.

king in the so-called rhapsodic Orphic theogony, which is possibly as early as the Attic historian Clidemus (c. 350 BC: *FGrH* 323 F 25).[20] We may therefore conclude that competing versions already existed at an early stage of the 'movement'.

The papyrus breaks off at the moment of Zeus's incest with his mother. In later versions Zeus mated with the product of this union, Persephone, and begot Dionysos, whom the Titans slew but who was restored to life with the help of Athena or Demeter-Rhea, a sequence of motifs that seems to have been influenced by the Egyptian myth of the dismemberment of Osiris. This 'ancient grief of Persephone' is mentioned by Pindar (fr. 133): it was therefore, presumably, already part of the Derveni theogony.[21] The meaning of the episode is clarified by the climax of the rhapsodic theogony, which dealt with the origin of humankind, as perhaps in the oldest theogony: as descendants of the Titans, humans were of tainted but divine origin.[22] Unfortunately, the fragmentary state of the papyrus does not allow us to see whether the theogony also referred to reincarnation, a doctrine attributed to Orphism by later sources.[23]

In addition to the papyrus, recent years have witnessed the discovery of a number of so-called Orphic gold tablets. These minute tablets were, so to speak, passports to the underworld and have been found in graves in Italy, Crete, Thessaly, and Lesbos, but not in Attica. Here the prestige of the Eleusinian Mysteries must have blocked any competition in the area of afterlife expectations. Around 1970, the then available texts (which presuppose oral circulation[24]) had been classified into two groups: in one (A) the soul addresses the powers of the underworld; the other group (B) contains instructions to the dead person.[25] But the Pelinna gold tablets published in 1987 (Figure 15) bridged the differences between the two groups and also provided additional evidence for the connection between Orphic anthropogony and Bacchic mysteries, since the dead person has been instructed: 'Tell Persephone that Bakchios [in Orphism Persephone's son: see above] himself has set you free' (line 2) – a line understandable in the light

---

[20] Compare Obbink 1994 with M. West 1983: 251.

[21] Lloyd-Jones 1990: 80–105 (Pindar); Burkert 2004a: 71–98 ('Orpheus and Egypt').

[22] For the chronology of this myth, see Henrichs 2011, which appeared too late for Gagné 2013: 455–60.

[23] Bremmer 2002: 11–26.

[24] Janko 1984.

[25] Zuntz 1971: 277–393.

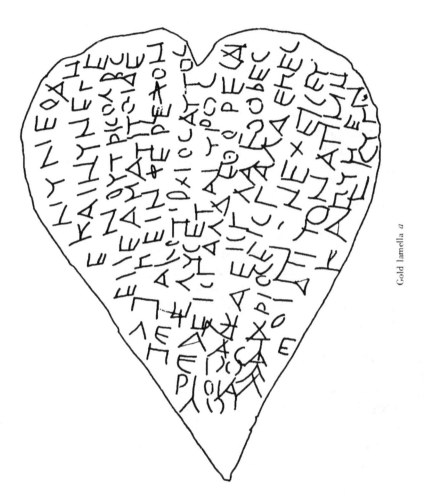

Gold lamella *a*

Figure 15. Pelinna gold tablet (no. a) in the shape of an ivy-leaf, the plant sacred to Dionysos. After Tsantsanoglou and Parâssoglou 1987: 7.

of Persephone's 'ancient grief'.[26] New discoveries complicate the matter even further, since the most recently published tablets not only mention Brimo and thus seem to indicate Eleusinian influence

---

[26] *Orph. frag.* 485–6; see also Bremmer 2002: 18–19.

(see above), but also Chthonic Demeter and the Mountain Mother, thus pointing to ecstatic rites (below, §3).[27]

The literary evidence for Bacchic mysteries is rather poor and the gold tablets provide few pointers to Bacchic ritual, although a reference to purity suggests purifications. In fact, it is not even clear in what ritual context the tablets were used: initiation into the Mysteries or funerals?[28] The Derveni papyrus suggests a ritual setting for the Orphic theogony, since its first line states: 'I will speak for those that understand. Close the doors, ye profane' (*Orph. frag.* 1). Moreover, if we may compare the end of the so-called Jewish-Hellenistic *Testament of Orpheus*, the theogony would have closed with a call for secrecy.[29] Since the commentator mentions that the initiates had to pay for their ceremony but failed to achieve understanding (XX.3–12 Kouremenos = §§67–8 Kotwick), Bacchic initiates probably had to listen to the theogony during initiation but did not interpret it correctly in the eyes of the commentator.

The mention of pay suggests that, in the time of the commentator, Orphic/Bacchic initiators demanded money for their services. This fits with Plato's denigratory remarks about Orphic 'begging priests and soothsayers' at 'rich men's doors', who used Orphic books in their ritual and performed sacrifices for purifications and special rites for the dead (*Resp.* 2.364D–E).[30] Plato's observations also indicate that the clientele was rich, which is confirmed by the discovery of tablets in graves of wealthy women (Chapter VI, §1) and by Herodotus' mention of the Bacchic initiation of the Scythian king Skyles in Olbia (4.78–80). Two tantalizing testimonia even suggest the existence of 'congregations': the Olbian mention of Orphikoi and the statement in a fifth-century inscription from Italian Cumae that 'it is not lawful for anyone to be deposited here [presumably a burial plot] unless he has been initiated to Bakchos (*bebakcheumenon*)'.[31] Yet

---

[27] For Brimo, see *Orph. frag.* 493. For Chthonic Demeter and the Mountain Mother, see *Orph. frag.* 493a; also Henrichs 2019: 201–3.

[28] Versnel 1990: 150–5; Burkert 2001–11: iii.120–36.

[29] Riedweg 1993: 47–48 (beginning), 52 (end); Bremmer 2011b.

[30] This may confirm the suggestion, with some hesitations, of Graf 1993a: 250 that the leaves presuppose the funeral. But would these 'priests' always have been available in the case of sudden deaths outside big cities? Or were the leaves sometimes handed out during an initiation for later use at the funeral?

[31] For Orphikoi, see Henrichs 2019: 205–6. For Cumae, see *Orph. frag.* 652; also Casadio 2009.

it seems hardly permissible to extrapolate from these two examples to a more general model.

As often with new cults, Orphism was a mixture of old and new. While using the traditional idea of genealogy, it presented a somewhat more streamlined succession. The Derveni papyrus also reminds us of Xenophanes' philosophy (fr. 23) with its stress on the position of Zeus: 'Zeus is the head, Zeus the middle, through Zeus all things come to pass' (XVII.12 Kouremenos = §55 Kotwick).[32] At the same time, it presented an explanation of the origin of humanity and some eschatological comfort. By preaching an ancient guilt and practising vegetarianism, Orphism directly opposed the this-worldly spirit of Greek religion (Chapter I, §2) and its community-supporting practice of sacrifice (Chapter IV, §2). Moreover, Euripides' mention of a variety of Orphic books in his *Hippolytus* (954) points to another striking difference from mainstream religion. The books were clearly considered offensive in the predominantly oral society of ancient Greece, just as sceptical Sophists were negatively associated with books.[33] Despite these 'deviations', the 'movement' was successful and by the fifth century Orphic ideas had penetrated the Eleusinian and Theban Mysteries (see above).[34]

The new discoveries, then, have greatly illuminated the early history of Orphism, even though the reasons for its origin, popularity, transmission of ideas, connection with Bacchic Mysteries, and social location still pose many questions.[35]

3. Structural changes

The rise of Orphic ideas and connected practices was only one of the developments which gradually changed the face of traditional religion. I will therefore close this chapter by sketching some of those transformations, while focusing on the gods, the area in which arguably most changes occurred. Xenophanes' critique of divine anthropomorphism (Chapter II, §1) and Orphic changes in divine genealogy show that around 500 BC the Homeric picture of the gods no longer satisfied

---

[32] For the Orphic gods, see Herrero de Jáuregui 2010; Bremmer 2019e: 61–83.

[33] For Orphic books, see Henrichs 2003; in general, see Parker 2011: 18–20.

[34] On Eleusis, see Graf 1974. On Thebes, see Moret 1991.

[35] For a good overview, see Parker 1995, to which I am indebted, updated in Parker 2011: 255–8.

intellectuals. In the following century this dissatisfaction only intensified, if in various different ways. To start with, we can notice a blurring
of identity of some divinities. In Aeschylus' Lycurgus trilogy,[36] Orpheus
probably calls Apollo Helios,[37] and the connection with Orpheus may
not be Aeschylus' innovation, since the Derveni commentator quotes
an Orphic hymn that equates Demeter with Rhea, Ge (= Gaia),
Meter, Hestia, and Deio. Similar equations also occurred in Pindar,
Sophocles, and Euripides, but in all these cases they remained limited
to Demeter and less important divinities such as Rhea, Ge, and the
Mother of the Gods.[38] There was more to come.

It had always been known that the Sophist Prodicus first denied the
essential qualities of the gods but subsequently invested them with a
new identity by claiming that they had been deified by their admiring
contemporaries because of their discoveries of 'foods, shelter and the
other practical skills'. A papyrus from Herculaneum shows, that
according to Prodicus, in an earlier stage of cultural evolution 'primitive man, [out of admiration, deified] the fruits of the earth and virtually everything that contributed to his subsistence'.[39] These views were
an instant success in Athens and are parodied in Aristophanes' Birds
(414 BC; 685ff) and Euripides' Bacchae (c. 406 BC; 274–85).[40] Their
mention in comedy and tragedy shows that Greek intellectuals not
only discussed these ideas in private but brought them out in the
open to be discussed by the whole of Athens.[41] Prodicus, however,
remained an honoured citizen on his home island of Keos and nothing
suggests that he had drawn consequences from his theoretical views for
ritual practice; in fact, except for Orphics and Pythagoreans, few philosophers seem to have been critical of animal sacrifice before
Theophrastus' On Piety (fr. 584 Fortenbaugh), although in his last
work, the Laws, Plato calls non-animal sacrifice 'pure' (6.782C).[42]

On the other hand, we should not underestimate the impact of these
'atheistic' views. Admittedly, the regular atheistic statements in
Euripides' tragedies do not show that the poet actually was an atheist,

[36] Radt 1985: 138–9.
[37] For Apollo, see M. West 1990: 34–43.
[38] For the Derveni commentary, see XXII.12 Kouremenos = §77 Kotwick, with an illuminating commentary; in general, see Allan 2005.
[39] For Prodicus, see Henrichs 1975, 1976 (quotation from papyrus), and 1984b (first quotation).
[40] Notomi 2010.
[41] See the important discussion in Humphreys 2004: 51–76.
[42] Sfameni Gasparro 1987.

as has often been thought, but they do demonstrate that such views could be debated and formed part of contemporary discourse.[43] In addition, Euripides' late tragedies problematize the position of the gods. His *Ion* and *Orestes* show the protagonists Creusa and Orestes deserted by the gods, and in his *Helen* and *Iphigeneia in Tauris* gods no longer play a significant role.[44] It is even more telling that in Thucydides they are virtually absent, and the religious factor is largely neglected in his work.[45] Others went beyond intellectual scepsis: the mutilation of the statues of Hermes and the profanation of the Eleusinian mysteries in 415 BC, just like the founding of sacrilegious clubs like the Kakodaimonistai ('Worshippers of bad luck'), show to what extent sections of the upper classes had been estranged from traditional religion.[46]

If the existence of the gods becomes problematic in certain circles, interest in divine intervention in the public sphere will soon diminish. After the catastrophic Athenian expedition to Sicily in 415, Aristophanes all but neglected the seers who for so long had been one of the main targets of his mockery; Thucydides no longer paid attention to oracles in the part of his work that covered the period after 416; and they are absent from New Comedy.[47] Oracles returned to favour around the fateful time of the Battle of Chaeronea (338), when the Greek cities lost their independence to Philip and his Macedonians. As Plutarch notes in his biography, Demosthenes argued that the Athenians of Pericles had 'regarded things of this kind as pretexts for cowardice, and therefore followed the dictates of reason' (*Vit. Dem.* 19–20, trans. Perrin 1919). Such a strong contrast between reason and divination would hardly have been possible in the fifth century.

Religious developments, however, are rarely straightforward. If intellectuals could be dismissive of the gods, others welcomed them. In the second half of the fifth century, various new gods, healing and ecstatic, made their entry into Athens, the city about which we are best informed. Just before 420, the healing god Asclepius from

---

[43] For 'atheism', see Bremmer 2007 and 2020; Brulé 2009; Whitmarsh 2015, to be read with Bremmer 2018a; Winiarczyk 2016; Meert 2017: 240–438.

[44] Yunis 1988; Lefkowitz 2016.

[45] Hornblower 2010: 25–53 ('The Religious Dimension to the Peloponnesian War, or, What Thucydides Does Not Tell Us').

[46] For these much-discussed scandals, see most recently Graf 2000b; Todd 2004; Hornblower 1991–2009: iii.372–81; Osborne 2010a: 341–67 (on the Herms); Rubel 2014: 74–98; Kousser 2015.

[47] N. Smith 1989; Dover 1988: 72 (Thucydides).

Epidaurus arrived at Athens, accompanied by his sacred snake, which Sophocles supposedly welcomed into his house. The cult of the god immediately became very popular, although it was not free: in many sanctuaries of healing gods, excavations have uncovered 'treasuries' in which grateful patients had to leave donations – an interesting indication of the monetization of cult that started to spread from central Greece and the Peloponnese from the later fifth century. This particular attention to the body is typical of a growing interest in the private sphere, which becomes more noticeable in the fourth century, and can hardly be separated from an increasing individualism, just as we can observe an increasing interest in physical fitness in our own individualizing times.[48]

The growing interest in divinities with ecstatic cults reflects a similar movement away from the ordered public sphere, but also, perhaps, from too great a distance between gods and worshippers, as suggested by votive reliefs and vase-paintings.[49] From Phrygia, via Ionia and southern Italy, the goddess Kybele (Figure 16) had gradually migrated towards mainland Greece, where the aspect of ecstasy in her cult became visible in Athens around 420, when her name is first mentioned in Attic comedy.[50] Other divinities who seem to have entered Athens at about the same time or slightly later were Adonis (Chapter VI, §3), Bendis, and Sabazios.[51] All these gods have in common both an ecstatic cult and, apparently, often a female clientele. Sally Humphreys has attractively suggested that the male attention of vase-painters and play-wrights shows a deep but ambiguous attraction to these rites, in which one could become completely possessed by a god and escape from the framework of the *polis*. In the same way, we can consider Euripides' portrayal of the maenads (Chapter VI, §3) and Pentheus' initiation in his *Bacchae* as a kind of mental experiment in such an escape and loss of self. But it would still be some time before male citizens could openly practise such possession cults. One exception occurred in Attica, around 400, when a certain Archedemos of Thera decorated a cave of Pan (Figure 17) for the Nymphs and composed a number of

---

[48] Versnel 1990: 102–23 (new gods); Riethmüller 2005; Wickkiser 2008. For Sophocles, see Henrichs 1985: 298–301; A. Connelly 1998 (to be read with Parker 2011: 122 n. 45). On dona-tions, see Kaminski 1991; Zoumbaki 2019.

[49] Klöckner 2010; Baumer 2013.

[50] For the early stages of Kybele, see Bremmer 2020b.

[51] Parker 1996: 170–5 (Bendis); Planeaux 2000 (Bendis); Delneri 2006: 15–81 (Sabazios), 125–213 (Bendis).

Figure 16. Marble statue of Kybele as 'Lady of Animals', *c.* 330 BC.

inscriptions, in which he calls himself *nympholeptos*, or 'seized (possessed) by the Nymphs'.[52]

It was not only ecstasy which distinguished these new cults from
those of the traditional gods. As Euripides' *Bacchae* shows, the new

---

[52] On attraction to the rites, see Humphreys 2004: 71–2. For Pan and Nymphs, see van Straten
1976; Larson 2001; Purvis 2003: 33–64; Giacobello and Schirripa 2009.

Figure 17. The oldest-known representation of Pan playing on his pipes. Fragment of Attic black-figure krater, *c.* 490–485 BC.

gods also required to be praised.[53] The chorus names Dionysos 'the foremost divinity of the blessed ones' (377–8) and 'not less than any of the gods' (777), and calls him 'Lord, Lord' (583). Words even fail Teiresias to describe 'how great he will be throughout Hellas' (173). This aspect foreshadows a feature of the gods which becomes much more prominent in Hellenistic times.[54] The elevation of one god over all the others also entails a more exclusive affection for one god. The believer wants 'to serve' the god and becomes his 'servant' or 'slave'. This feature, too, only becomes prominent in Hellenistic times, but Euripides already presents us with Hippolytus' love for Artemis and Ion's devotion to Apollo. Both protagonists are youths, as is

---

[53] For the increase in praise, see Parker 2017: 149–53 and Belayche 2020, both with nuanced approaches. The translations of the *Bacchae* are from Kirk 1970.
[54] Belayche 2010; Chaniotis 2010; Versnel 2011: 239–307; Parker 2017: 113–53 (with a judicious review of recent scholarship).

Pentheus in the *Bacchae*: apparently, the playwright found it difficult to imagine adult males in such religiously dependent roles.[55]

A preference for one god became more common in Hellenistic times, when religion as embedded in the *polis* increasingly became religion as the choice of differentiated groups.[56] This tendency was already apparent in the middle of the fourth century when in his *Laws* Plato proposed a law that

> no man shall possess a shrine in his private house; when a man feels himself moved to offer sacrifice, he shall go to the public temples for that purpose and deliver his offerings to the priests of either sex whose business is to consecrate them.   (10.909D)[57]

It is intriguing that according to Plato's *Laws* this 'privatization' of religion went hand in hand with a growing interest in magic (11.933A). Magic is one of those contested terms, like religion, which a number of scholars want to banish from scholarly discussions,[58] although, as with religion (Chapter 1, §1), we can hardly do without the term. It does denote a series of oppositions that were negatively valued in Greek society, such as public/secret, night/day, individual/collective, anti-social/social or *voces magicae*/understandable language. Yet these practices and discourses should not be contrasted with religion, as frequently happened in the twentieth century.[59] Admittedly, the fringes of magic are often fuzzy and a precise definition is virtually impossible to give, especially since its meaning developed over the centuries and was never permanently fixed. But we have no convincing alternative. Thus, when using the term, we should always remain conscious of whether we use it in an emic or etic sense: that is, whether we follow ancient concepts and judgements or apply our own modern ideas.

Despite its age-old traditions, magic became increasingly marginalized in the public arena through the attacks of philosophers and doctors, who in some ways competed for the same clientele.[60] Plato prescribes solitary confinement for those who

---

[55] Pleket 1981; Versnel 1990: 169–70, 194–7.

[56] See the perceptive remarks in North 1992.

[57] Translation from Taylor 1934.

[58] For a convincing discussion and rejection of such proposals, see Sanzo 2020.

[59] See Fowler 2000; Bremmer 2008: 235–47 (origin of the term 'magic'), 347–52 (magic and religion).

[60] There has been a flood of books on ancient magic in the last three decades, but see especially Graf 1997; Boschung and Bremmer 2015; Edmonds 2019; Frankfurter 2019.

in their contempt of mankind bewitch so many of the living by the pretence of evoking
the dead [necromancy] and the promise of winning the gods by the supposed sorceries
of prayer, sacrifice, and incantations, and thus do their best for lucre to ruin individuals,
whole families, and communities.   (*Laws* 10.909B)[61]

Yet the increasing number of recent discoveries of curse tablets (*defix-iones*) shows magic to have been pervasive in all strata of society, and several tablets curse leading politicians of late fourth-century Athens.[62]

It is not easy to trace the causes of all these transformations. Historical developments, such as the democratic ideology and war-weariness in Athens, promoted the new goddess Demokratia and increased the popularity of the goddess Eirene ('Peace'), but these divinities always remained marginal.[63] Ideas about the traditional gods clearly changed under the influence of philosophers and playwrights, but the increasing interest in private religion is more difficult to explain. An important factor must have been the gradual change in the political situation in Greece, which developed into large blocks, such as the Athenians and Spartans with their respective allies. This development promoted a growing professionalization in war and politics of one part of the upper classes but estranged another part from public life and the *polis* itself. This development also reflected itself in growing cultic honours for the few powerful individuals. Whereas the Spartan general Brasidas was only worshipped after his death in 422, his colleague Lysander, who for a time was the most powerful individual in the eastern Aegean, received divine cult on Samos at the end of the fifth century.[64] Ruler cult would not become popular before Alexander the Great, but the way was paved for a completely new relationship between Greek *poleis* and their rulers.[65]

It is time to come to a close. At the end of the classical period, Greek religion showed all the signs of a religion in transition. Although ritual had not essentially changed, ideas about the gods certainly had, and the emphasis on public cult was partially shifting to private religious practices.[66] Yet the traditional structure was still fairly strong and would

---

[61] Translation from Taylor 1934.

[62] On curse tablets, see Eidinow 2007. For cursing of politicians, see Habicht 1994: 14–18; Nisoli 2003; Papakonstantinou 2014.

[63] For Demokratia, see Versnel 1995. For Eirene, see Meyer 2019.

[64] *IG* XII 6 1.334; Douris *FGrH* 76 F 71 (= Plut. *Vit. Lys.* 18.2–4), to be read with F 26; Athenagoras, *Leg.* 14; Paus. 6.3.14. See also Beck-Schachter 2016; Habicht 2017: 1–3, 179.

[65] Versnel 2011: 439–92; Habicht 2017; Caneva 2020.

[66] For the fourth century, see the useful study Mikalson 1983; also Auffarth 1995.

only slowly be transformed by new elements, such as ruler cult, growing social stratification, competition among cities regarding festivals, and continuing philosophical criticism.[67] The ultimate defeat by Christianity was still far away.

---

[67] A detailed study of Hellenistic religion is still lacking, but see Stewart 1977; Mikalson 1998; Deshours 2011; Chaniotis 2019: 395–442.

APPENDIX: THE GENESIS OF GREEK RELIGION

When groups of Indo-European raiders invaded Greece at the beginning of the second millennium BC, they did not arrive without religious baggage. On the contrary, it is surprising how much of later classical belief and practice goes back to this early heritage. Linguists have concluded that the early Indo-Europeans worshipped a divine family consisting of a Sky Father (*Dyeus pater*), his wife the Earth Goddess (*Pltwi mater*), a Daughter of the Sky (*Diwos dhugeter*), and twin Sons of the Sky (*Diwos sûnû*) – all figures in the Greek pantheon.[1] The Sky Father became Zeus, still the most prominent god, but the name of his one-time wife only survived in a small town, Boeotian Plataea.[2] In ancient India, the Daughter of the Sky was Dawn, Usas, whose name survived as Eos,[3] but she was no longer a 'daughter of Zeus'; that title was now used for other goddesses, such as Athena, Artemis, and, especially, Aphrodite.[4] Finally, the twin Sons survived as the Dioskouroi, whose name reflects the fact that they had become role models for the military age-set of youths beyond adolescence in pre-Homeric times, the *kouroi*.[5] In some cases, then, we note continuity in structure not name, in others continuity in name not structure, but it is important to note that in all these cases continuity does not mean lack of change: tradition always has to be appropriated.

The raiders also had a vocabulary of the sacred, as both *hagnos* and *hieros* (Chapter I, §1) go back to Indo-European times. They prayed with hands raised and practised libation: *spondê* derives from an Indo-European root *spend*, 'to make a libation', and *choê* is connected with Sanskrit *hotra*, 'sacrifice', and Iranian *zaotar*, 'sacrificial priest'.[6] Burkert has suggested that they also practised animal sacrifice, arguing from the term 'hecatomb', that is, 'an act which brings in 100 oxen'. However, the term originally meant 'a sacrifice of 100 oxen', as

---

[1] See Euler 1987: 35–56; M. West 2007: 166–92.

[2] Burkert 1979: 132–4; Janko 1992 on *Il.* 14.323–5; M. West 2007: 174–5, 178, 182.

[3] M. West 2007: 217–27; Pronk 2018.

[4] See Dunkel 1988–90.

[5] The importance of this age group was already waning in Homer (see Hoekstra 1981: 76–81), thus illustrating the early disintegration of the age-old rites of initiation.

[6] On hands raised in prayer, see Dunkel 1993: 111–14; J. Fisher 2014: 141–5. On libation, see Polomé 1987: 208. For all the terms, see Beekes 2010, s.v. Although Beekes's (1937–2017) work has been criticized, especially for its claims regarding a pre-Greek influence (see, for example, Simkin 2011; Meissner 2013), this hardly affects his Indo-European etymologies in these cases.

additional evidence has since shown, but the continuity between hunt and sacrifice (Chapter IV, §2) further supports Burkert's suggestion.[7]

Finally, the invaders brought a poetic tradition, which transmitted not only myths about great heroes and the prime interests of their society (Chapter V, §2),[8] but probably also contained traditions about the gods, since their Homeric epithet *dotêres eaôn*, 'givers of good things', suggests poets singing of the gifts of the gods.[9] The same conclusion is suggested by the presence in Linear B texts of formulae such as 'Mother of the Gods' and 'Drimios, the son of Zeus', which presuppose a divine genealogy.[10]

After their invasion on the mainland, the proto-Greeks merged with the existing population, of whose religious tradition there is not much to say given the absence of any early texts or pictorial representations. The Linear B texts which survived the fires that destroyed the Minoan and Mycenaean palaces in the fourteenth and thirteenth centuries already suggest a unified pantheon which had incorporated Indo-European and autochthonous gods: Zeus but also Athena and Hera. We see here the contours of later Greek religion appearing. But what about the influence of Minoan Crete or Santorini, where the discovery of wall frescoes has shown a high standard of culture? The patient work of archaeologists is making it increasingly clear that Minoan elements on the mainland were more a veneer than integrated parts of a religious system, but, contrary to long-received wisdom, there never was a Minoan–Mycenaean religion. The Cretan legacy to Greek religion was relatively small, though not negligible.[11]

Especially during the archaic age, but probably also earlier, Greece experienced considerable religious influence from Anatolia, of which the ancient languages have become increasingly well understood in the last three decades, and from the Orient (Chapter 1, §3). It is probable that the familiar picture of the Homeric assembly of the gods, but also the phenomenon of divine epithets, such as 'cloud-gathering' Zeus, derived from Oriental epic. On the ritual level, there seem to have been wandering Oriental healers and diviners, who imported into Greece ritual techniques that are clearly recognisable as

---

[7] Burkert 1985: 18; Oettinger 2008; Zimmer 2009.

[8] As is suggested by the formulae *kleos aphthiton* ('imperishable fame') and *klea andrôn* ('glories of men'): see Watkins 1995: 173–8; Massetti 2019: 113–38.

[9] *Od.* 8.325; see also M. West 2007: 132.

[10] For the Indo-European heritage of the Greek gods, see Bremmer 2019e: 3–7.

[11] Marinatos 1993.

Oriental,[12] such as hepatoscopy (divination from livers of sacrificed animals), foundation deposits, rites of purification, and technologies of magic. Greek religion, then, was the composite product of many traditions.

---

[12] For the influence of the Ancient Near East see, most recently, Bremmer 2019e: 279–300; Rutherford 2020.

BIBLIOGRAPHY

Journal titles are abbreviated as in *L'Année philologique*.

Accorinti, D. 2010. 'La montagna e il sacro nel mondo greco', in A. Grossato (ed.), *La montagna cosmica*. Milan, Medusa: 17–42.

Acerbo, S. 2019. *Le tradizioni mitiche nella Biblioteca dello ps. Apollodoro. Percorsi nella mitografia di età imperiale*. Amsterdam, Adolf M. Hakkert.

Albertocchi, M. 2015. 'Shall We Dance? Terracotta Dancing Groups of the Archaic Period in the Aegean World', in S. Huysecom-Haxhi and A. Muller (eds.), *Figurines grecques en contexte. Présence muette dans le sanctuaire, la tombe et la maison*. Villeneuve d'Ascq, Presses Universitaires du Septentrion: 13–24.

Aleshire, S. B. 1989. *The Athenian Asklepieion. The People, Their Dedications, and the Inventories*. Amsterdam, Gieben.

——— 1991. *Asklepios at Athens. Epigraphic and Prosopographic Essays on the Athenian Healing Cults*. Amsterdam, Gieben.

Allan, W. 2005. 'Religious Syncretism: The New Gods of Greek Tragedy', *HSCP* 102: 113–55.

Alroth, B. 1989. *Greek Gods and Figurines. Aspects of Anthropomorphic Dedications*. Uppsala, Uppsala University.

——— 1989–90. 'Visiting Gods', *Scienze dell'Antichità* 3–4: 301–10.

Amory, A. 2016. 'Les figurines comme ex-voto en Grèce ancienne: le cas des animaux chez Déméter', *RAPic, special issue* 31: 157–67.

Ampolo, C. 1989–90. 'Fra economia, religione e politica: tesori e offerte nei santuari greci', *Scienze dell'Antichità* 3–4: 271–79.

Arafat, K. W. 1990. *Classical Zeus. A Study in Art and Literature*. Oxford, Clarendon Press.

Arrigoni, G. 2019. *Atalanta e le altre. Scritti editi e inediti*. Bergamo, Sestante.

Aston, E. 2011. *Mixanthrôpoi: Animal–Human Hybrid Deities in Greek Religion*. Liège, Centre International d'Étude de la Religion Grecque Antique.

Aubriot-Sévin, D. 1992. *Prière et conceptions religieuses en Grèce ancienne jusqu'à la fin du Ve siècle av. J.-C..* Lyon, Maison de l'Orient Méditerranéen.

Audley-Miller, L. and Dignas, B. (eds.) 2018. *Wandering Myths. Transcultural Uses of Myth in the Ancient World*. Berlin and Boston, MA, De Gruyter.

Auffarth, C. 1995. 'Aufnahme und Zurückweisung "Neuer Götter" im spätklassischen Athen: Religion gegen die Krise, Religion in der

Krise?', in W. Eder (ed.), *Die athenische Demokratie im 4. Jahrhundert v. Chr.* Stuttgart, Franz Steiner: 337–65.

———— 2012. 'Religious Education in Classical Greece', in M. Döbler and I. Tanaseanu-Döbler (eds.), *Religious Education in Pre-Modern Europe.* Leiden and Boston, MA, Brill: 39–61.

———— 2013. 'Mysterien (Mysterienkulte)', in *RAC* 25: 422–71.

Avagianou, A. 1991. *Sacred Marriage in the Rituals of Greek Religion.* Bern, Peter Lang.

Bader, F. 1989. *La langue des dieux, ou l'hermétisme des poètes indo-européens.* Pisa, Giardini.

Baitinger, H. 2011. *Waffenweihungen in griechischen Heiligtümern.* Mainz, Römisch-Germanisches Zentralmuseum.

Baldassi, C. 2018. '*The Leucippides in Greek Myth: Abductions, Rituals and Weddings*'. PhD thesis, University of Edinburgh.

Baratz, A. 2015. 'The Source of Divine Immortality in Archaic Greek Literature', *SCO* 34: 151–64.

Barringer, J. 2010. 'Zeus at Olympia', in Bremmer and Erskine 2010: 155–77.

Bassi, K. 2014. 'Croesus' Offerings and the Value of the Past in Herodotus' Histories', in J. Ker and C. Pieper (eds.), *Valuing the Past in the Greco-Roman World.* Leiden, Brill: 173–219.

Baumbach, J. 2004. *The Significance of Votive Offerings in Selected Hera Sanctuaries in the Peloponnese, Ionia and Western Greece.* Oxford, Archaeopress.

Baumer, L. E. 2004. *Kult im Kleinen. Ländliche Heiligtümer spätarchaischer bis hellenistischer Zeit. Attika–Arkadien–Argolis–Kynouria.* Rahden: Verlag Marie Leidorf.

———— 2013. 'Entre dieux et mortels: le contact visuel sur les reliefs votifs grecs classiques', *Pallas* 92: 43–54.

Beck, W. A. 2004. 'Μύθος', in *Das Lexikon des frühgriechischen Epos 3.* Göttingen, Vandenhoeck: 271–8.

Beck-Schachter, A. 2016. 'The Lysandreia', in T. J. Figueira (ed.), *Myth, Text, and History at Sparta.* Piscataway, NJ, Gorgias Press: 105–67.

Beekes, R. 2010. *Etymological Dictionary of Greek.* 2 vols, Leiden, Brill.

Beerden, K. 2013. *Worlds Full of Signs. Ancient Greek Divination in Context.* Leiden and Boston, MA, Brill.

Belayche, N. 2010. '*Deus deum … summorum maximus* (Apuleius): Ritual Expressions of Distinction in the Divine World in the Imperial Period', in S. Mitchell and P. Van Nuffelen (eds.), *One God. Pagan Monotheism in the Roman Empire.* Cambridge, Cambridge University Press: 141–66.

—————— 2020. 'L'*eulogia* dans l'épigraphie religieuse de l'Anatolie impériale', in P. Hoffmann and A. Timotin (eds.), *Théories et pratiques de la prière dans l'antiquité tardive (IIe–VIe s.)*. Turnhout, Brepols: 17–38.

Ben-Tov, A. 2019. 'The Eleusinian Mysteries in the Age of Reason', in M. Mulsow and A. Ben-Tov (eds.), *Knowledge and Profanation. Transgressing the Boundaries of Religion in Premodern Scholarship*. Leiden and Boston, MA, Brill: 197–227.

Bentz, M. and Bumke, H. 2013. 'Mahlzeiten in rituellen Kontexten', in Gerlach and Raue 2013: 275–90.

Bérard, C. 1976. 'Axie taure', in P. Ducrey, et al. (eds.), *Mélanges d'histoire ancienne et d'archéologie offerts à Paul Collart*. Lausanne, Bibliothèque Historique Vaudoise: 61–73.

—————— 1983. 'Iconographie–iconologie–iconologique', *Études de Lettres* 199: 5–37.

—————— 1984. 'L'ordre des femmes', in C. Bérard et al., *La cité des images. Religion et société en Grèce*. Lausanne, Éditions de la Tour: 85–104.

—————— 1989. 'Hommes, prêtres, dieux', in J. Waardenburg (ed.), *L'Islam. Une religion*. Geneva, Labor et Fides: 95–120.

Bernabé, A. 2004–5. *Poetae epici Graeci. Testimonia et Fragmenta. Pars II.* 2 vols, Munich and Leipzig, Saur.

—————— 2013. 'Dionysos in the Mycenaean World', in Bernabé et al. 2013: 23–37.

—————— and Casadesús, F. (eds.) 2009. *Orfeo y la tradicion órfica. Un reencuentro.* 2 vols, Madrid, Akal.

—————— and Jiménez San Cristóbal, A. I. 2008. *Instructions for the Netherworld. The Orphic Gold Tablets.* Leiden and Boston, MA, Brill.

——————, Herrero de Jáuregui, M., Jiménez San Cristóbal, A. I., and Martín Hernández, R. (eds.) 2013. *Redefining Dionysos*. Berlin and Boston, MA, Brill.

Bernhard, M.-L. and Daszewski, W. 1986. 'Ariadne', in *LIMC* III.1: 1050–70.

Bernhardt, K. 2014. 'Mädchen im Bild: der Status der *parthenos* in den sogenannten Frauenraubdarstellungen', in Moraw and Kieburg 2014: 185–204.

Bettinetti, S. 2001. *La statua di culto nella pratica rituale greca*. Bari, Levante.

Bielawski, K. (ed.) 2017. *Animal Sacrifice in Ancient Greece*. Warsaw, Global Scientific Platform.

Birge, D. E. 1982. '*Sacred Groves in the Ancient Greek World*'. PhD thesis, University of California, Berkeley.

Bjork-James, S. 2019. 'Gender and Religion', *Oxford Bibliographies*, https:// doi.org/10.1093/obo/9780199766567-0202 (accessed 26 January 2021).

Blok, J. 1995. *The Early Amazons. Modern and Ancient Perspectives on a Persistent Myth.* Leiden, Brill.

———— 2018. 'An Athenian Woman's Competence: The Case of Xenokrateia', *EuGeStA* 8: 1–48.

Bodiou, L. and Mehl, V. (eds.) 2009. *La religion des femmes en Grèce ancienne. Mythes, cultes et société.* Rennes, Presses Universitaires de Rennes.

Boedeker, D. 2008. Family Matters: Domestic Religion in Classical Greece', in J. Bodel and S. M. Olyan (eds.), *Household and Family Religion in Antiquity. Contextual and Comparative Perspectives.* Malden, MA, and Oxford: Blackwell, 229–47.

Boehringer, D. 2001. *Heroenkulte in Griechenland von der geometrischen bis zur klassischen Zeit.* Berlin, Akademie Verlag.

Boessneck, J. and von den Driesch, A. 1981. 'Reste exotischer Tiere aus dem Heraion von Samos', *Athenische Mitteilungen* 96: 245–48.

———— 1993. 'Weitere Reste exotischer Tiere aus dem Heraion auf Samos', *Athenische Mitteilungen* 98: 21–24.

Bøgh, B. S. (ed.) 2014. *Conversion and Initiation in Antiquity. Shifting Identities, Creating Change.* Frankfurt, Peter Lang.

Bonnechere, P. 1999. '"La *machaira* était dissimulée dans le *kanoun*": quelques interrogations', *REG* 101: 21–35.

———— 2003. *Trophonios de Lébadée. Cultes et mythes d'une cité béotienne au miroir de la mentalité antique.* Leiden and Boston, MA, Brill.

———— 2007. 'The Place of the Sacred Grove in the Mantic Rituals of Greece: The Example of the Oracle of Trophonios at Lebadeia (Boeotia)', in M. Conan (ed.), *Sacred Gardens and Landscapes. Ritual and Agency.* Washington, DC, Dumbarton Oaks Research Library and Collection: 17–41.

Bonnet, C. 2017. Review of Eidinow et al. 2016, *BMCRev* 2017.06.13.

———— and Lebreton, S. 2019. 'Mettre les polythéismes en formules? À propos de la Base de Données *Mapping Ancient Polytheisms*', *Kernos* 32: 267–96.

Bontempi, M. 2013. *La fiducia secondo gli antichi. 'Pistis' in Gorgia tra Parmenide e Platone. Pensiero giuridico e politico.* Naples, Editoriale Scientifica.

Borg, B. 2002. *Der Logos des Mythos. Allegorien und Personifikationen in der frühen griechischen Kunst.* Munich, Fink.

Boschung, D. 2015. 'Unheimliche Statuen und ihre Bändigung', in D. Boschung and C. Vorster (eds.), *Leibhafte Kunst. Statuen und kulturelle Identität.* Paderborn, Fink: 281–305.

—— and Bremmer, J. N. (eds.) 2015. *The Materiality of Magic*. Paderborn, Wilhelm Fink.

Boudewijnse, B. 1995. 'The Conceptualization of Ritual', *Jaarboek voor Liturgie-onderzoek* 11: 31–56.

Bowden, H. 2010. *Mystery Cults in the Ancient World*. London, Thames & Hudson.

Bowersock, G. 2006. *Mosaics as History. The Near East from Late Antiquity to Early Islam*. Cambridge, MA, and London, Belknap.

Bowie, A. 1993. *Aristophanes. Myth, Ritual and Comedy*. Cambridge, Cambridge University Press.

Brelich, A. 1956. *Gli eroi greci. Un problema storico-religioso*. Rome, Edizioni dell'Ateneo.

—— 1969. *Paides e parthenoi*. Rome, Edizioni dell'Ateneo.

Bremer, J. M. 1991. 'Poets and Their Patrons', in H. Hofmann and M. A. Harder (eds.), *Fragmenta dramatica. Beiträge zur Interpretation der griechischen Tragikerfragmente und ihrer Wirkungsgeschichte*. Göttingen, Vandenhoeck & Ruprecht: 39–60.

Bremmer, J. N. 1983. *The Early Greek Concept of the Soul*. Princeton, NJ, Princeton University Press.

—— 1985. Review of Burkert 1983. *CR* 35: 312–13.

—— (ed.) 1988a. *Interpretations of Greek Mythology*. Second edition, London and New York, Routledge.

—— 1988b. 'La plasticité du mythe: Méléagre dans la poésie homérique', in Calame 1988: 37–56.

—— 1990a. 'Oedipus and the Greek Oedipus Complex', in Bremmer 1990a: 41–59.

—— 1990b. Review of Graf 1985. *Mnemosyne* 4th ser., 43: 260–3.

—— 1991. 'Greek Pederasty and Modern Homosexuality', in J. N. Bremmer (ed.), *From Sappho to De Sade. Moments in the History of Sexuality*. Second edition, London, Routledge: 1–14.

—— 1993. 'The Skins of Pherekydes and Epimenides', *Mnemosyne*, 4th ser., 46: 234–6.

—— 1998. '"Religion", "Ritual" and the Opposition "Sacred vs. Profane": Notes towards a Terminological "Genealogy"', in F. Graf (ed.), *Ansichten griechischer Rituale. Geburtstagssymposium für Walter Burkert*. Stuttgart and Leipzig, Teubner: 9–32.

—— 1999a. 'Fosterage, Kinship and the Circulation of Children in Ancient Greece', *Dialogos* 6: 1–20.

—— 1999b. 'Rationalization and Disenchantment in Ancient Greece: Max Weber among the Pythagoreans and Orphics?', in Buxton 1999: 71–83.

—— 1999c. 'Transvestite Dionysos', *Bucknell Review* 43: 183–200.

—— 2002. *The Rise and Fall of the Afterlife*. London and New York, Routledge.

—— 2007. 'Atheism in Antiquity', in M. Martin (ed.), *The Cambridge Companion to Atheism*. Cambridge, Cambridge University Press: 11–26.

—— 2008. *Greek Religion and Culture, the Bible, and the Ancient Near East*. Leiden and Boston, MA, Brill.

—— 2010. 'Walter Burkert on Ancient Myth and Ritual: Some Personal Observations', in A. Bierl and W. Braungart (eds.), *Gewalt und Opfer. Im Dialog mit Walter Burkert*. Berlin and New York, De Gruyter: 71–86.

—— 2011a. 'Hermann Usener between British Anthropology, Dutch History and French Sociology', in M. Espagne and P. Rabault-Feuerhahn (eds.), *Hermann Usener und die Metamorphosen der Philologie*. Wiesbaden, Harrassowitz: 77–87.

—— 2011b. 'The Place of Performance of Orphic Poetry (*OF* 1)', in Herrero de Jáuregui et al. 2011: 1–6.

—— 2012. 'Athenian Civic Priests from Classical Times to Late Antiquity: Some Considerations', in Horster and Klöckner 2012: 219–35.

—— 2014. *Initiation into the Mysteries of the Ancient World*. Berlin and Boston, MA, De Gruyter.

—— 2016. 'Arthur Darby Nock's *Conversion* (1933): A Balance', in J. Weitbrecht, W. Röcke, and R. von Bernuth (eds.), *Zwischen Ereignis und Erzählung. Konversion als Medium der Selbstbeschreibung in Mittelalter und Früher Neuzeit*. Berlin, De Gruyter: 9–29.

—— 2017. *Maidens, Magic and Martyrs in Early Christianity. Collected Essays I*. Tübingen, Mohr Siebeck.

—— 2018a. Review of Whitmarsh 2015. *CPh* 113: 373–9.

—— 2018b. 'Transformations and Decline of Sacrifice in Imperial Rome and Late Antiquity', in M. Blömer and B. Eckhardt (eds.), *Transformationen paganer Religion in der Kaiserzeit. Rahmenbedingungen und Konzepte*. Berlin and Boston, MA, De Gruyter: 215–56.

—— 2019a. 'Demons: An Epilogue', in E. Elm and N. Hartmann (eds.), *Demons in Late Antiquity*. Berlin and Boston, MA, : 167–73.

—— 2019b. 'The First Columns of the Derveni Papyrus and *Polis* Religion', *Eirene* 55: 127–41.

—— 2019c. 'Ritual and Its Transgressions in Ancient Greece', in C. Ginzburg (ed.), *A Historical Approach to Casuistry. Norms and Exceptions in a Comparative Perspective*. London, : 47–64.

—— 2019d. 'Rivers and River Gods in Ancient Greek Religion and Culture', in Scheer 2019: 89–112.

—— 2019e. *The World of Greek Religion and Mythology. Collected Essays II*. Tübingen, Mohr Siebeck.

—— 2020a. 'The Greek Birth: A Thick Description', in G. Pedrucci (ed.), *Pregnancies, Childbirths, and Religions*. Rome, Scienze e Lettere: 39–54.

—— 2020b. 'Kubaba, Kybele and Mater Magna: The Long March of Two Anatolian Goddesses to Rome', in M. Kerschner (ed.), *The Cult of Meter/Kybele in Western Anatolia*. Vienna, Holzhausen: 13–32.

—— 2020c. 'Religion and the Limits of Individualisation in Ancient Athens: Andocides, Socrates and the Fair-Breasted Phryne', in M. Fuchs et al.. (eds.), *Religious Individualisation. Historical and Comparative Perspectives*. Berlin and Boston, MA, De Gruyter: 1009–32.

—— 2020d. 'The Theriomorphism of the Major Greek Gods', in Kindt 2020: 102–25.

—— 2020e. 'Youth, Atheism and (Un)Belief in Late Fifth-Century Athens', in B. Edelmann-Singer et al. (eds.), *Sceptic and Believer in Ancient Mediterranean Religions*. Tübingen, Mohr Siebeck: 53–68.

—— and Erskine, A. (eds.) 2010. *The Gods of Ancient Greece. Identities and Transformations*. Edinburgh, Edinburgh University Press.

—— Horsfall, N. M. 1987. *Roman Myth and Mythography*. London, Institute of Classical Studies, University of London.

Brijder, H. A. G. 1983. *Siana Cups I and Komast Cups*. Amsterdam, Allard Pierson Series.

—— 1991. *Siana Cups II. The Heidelberg Painter*. Amsterdam, Allard Pierson Series.

Brinkman, V. and Scholl, A. (eds.) 2010. *Bunte Götter. Die Farbigkeit antiker Skulptur*. Munich, Hirmer.

Brisson, L. 1995. *Orphée et l'Orphisme dans l'antiquité gréco-romaine*. Aldershot, Variorum.

Bron, C. and Kassapoglou, E. (eds.) 1992. *L'image en jeu. De l'antiquité à Paul Klee*. Yens-sur-Morges, Cabédita.

Brøns, C. 2016. *Gods and Garments. Textiles in Greek Sanctuaries in the 7th to the 1st Centuries bc*. Oxford, Oxbow Books.

Bruit Zaidman, L. 2013. 'La prêtresse et le roi: réflexions sur les rapports entre prêtrise feminine et pouvoir', in S. Boehringer and V. Sebillotte Cuchet (eds.), *Des femmes en action. L'individu et la function en Grèce antique*. Paris and Athens, Éditions de l'École des hautes études en sciences sociales: 87–100.

—— and Schmitt Pantel, P. 1992. *Religion in the Ancient Greek City*. Translated by P. Cartledge. Cambridge, Cambridge University Press.

Brulé, P. 2009. 'Contribution des *Nuées* au problème de l'incroyance au Ve siècle', in P. Brulé (ed.), *La norme en matière religieuse en Grèce ancienne*. Liège, Presses universitaires de Liège: 49–67.

—— 2012. *Comment percevoir le sanctuaire grec? Une analyse sensorielle du paysage sacré*. Paris, Les Belles Lettres.

Bruneau, P. 1984. 'Ares', in *LIMC* II.1: 478–92.

Brunet, M. 1990. 'Contribution à l'histoire rurale de Délos aux époques classiques et hellénistiques', *BCH* 114: 669–82.

Bühler, W. 1998. *Zenobii Athoi proverbia V.* Göttingen, Vandenhoeck & Ruprecht.

Bumke, H. 2007. 'Fremde Weihungen für griechische Götter: Überlegungen zu den Bronzestatuetten ägyptischer Götter und Priester im Heraion von Samos', in C. Frevel and H. von Hesberg (eds.), *Kult und Kommunikation. Medien in Heiligtümern der Antike.* Wiesbaden, Reichert: 349–80.

Bundrick, S. 2014. 'Selling Sacrifice on Classical Athenian Vases', *Hesperia* 83: 653–708.

Burkert, W. 1979. *Structure and History in Greek Mythology and Ritual.* Berkeley, CA, University of California Press.

—— 1983. *Homo necans. Interpretations of Ancient Greek Sacrificial Ritual and Myth.* Translated by P. Bing. Berkeley, University of California Press.

—— 1985. *Greek Religion. Archaic and Classical.* Oxford, Blackwell.

—— 1992. *The Orientalizing Revolution. Near Eastern Influence on Greek Culture in the Early Archaic Age.* Translated by M. E. Pinder and W. Burkert. Cambridge, MA, Harvard University Press.

—— 1996. *Creation of the Sacred. Tracks of Biology in Early Religions.* Cambridge, MA, Harvard University Press.

—— 2000. 'Jason, Hypsipyle, and New Fire at Lemnos: A Study in Myth and Ritual', in Buxton 2000: 227–49.

—— 2001–11. *Kleine Schriften.* 8 vols, Göttingen, Vandenhoeck & Ruprecht.

—— 2004a. *Babylon, Memphis, Persepolis.* Cambridge, MA, Harvard University Press.

—— 2004b. 'Initiation', in *ThesCRA* II: 118–24.

Bury, R. G. (ed. and trans.) 1926. *Plato. Laws, Volume I. Books 1–6.* Loeb Classical Library 187. Cambridge, MA, Harvard University Press.

Buxton, R. 1982. *Persuasion in Greek Tragedy. A Study of 'Peitho'.* Cambridge, Cambridge University Press.

—— 1984. *Sophocles.* Oxford, Clarendon Press.

—— 1994. *Imaginary Greece. The Contexts of Mythology.* Cambridge, Cambridge University Press.

—— (ed.) 1999. *From Myth to Reason? Studies in the Development of Greek Thought.* Oxford, Oxford University Press.

—— (ed.) 2000. *Oxford Readings in Greek Religion.* Oxford, Oxford University Press.

—— 2004. *The Complete World of Greek Mythology.* London, Thames & Hudson.

—— 2013. *Myths and Tragedies in Their Ancient Greek Contexts.* Oxford, Oxford University Press.

Caciagli, S. 2011. *Poeti e società. Comunicazione poetica e formazioni sociali nella Lesbo del VII/VI secolo a.C.* Amsterdam, Hakkert.

Cairns, D. 2005. 'Myth and *Polis* in Bacchylides' Eleventh Ode', *JHS* 125: 35–50.

Calame, C. (ed.) 1988. *Métamorphoses du mythe en Grèce antique.* Geneva, Labor et Fides.

—— 1990. 'Pausanias le périégète en ethnographie', in J.-M. Adam et al. (eds.), *Le discours anthropologique. Description, narration, savoir.* Paris, Méridiens Klincksieck: 227–50.

—— 1991. '"Mythe" et "rite" en Grèce: des catégories indigènes?', *Kernos* 4: 179–204. Reprinted in Calame 2008: 43–62.

—— 1997. *Choruses of Young Women in Ancient Greece. Their Morphology, Religious Role and Function.* Translated by D. Collins and J. Orion. Lanham, MD, and London, Roman & Littlefeld.

—— 2008. *Sentiers transversaux. Entre poétiques grecques et politiques contemporaines.* Grenoble, Millon.

—— 2015. *Qu'est-ce que la mythologie grecque?* Paris, Gallimard.

—— 2018. *Thésée et l'imaginaire Athénien.* Third edition, Paris, La Découverte.

—— 2019. *Les choeurs de jeunes filles en Grèce ancienne. Morphologie, function religieuse et sociale.* Paris, Les Belles Lettres.

Calder, W. M., III (ed.) 1991. *The Cambridge Ritualists Reconsidered.* Atlanta, GA, Scholars Press.

—— and Schlesier, R. (eds.) 1998. *Zwischen Rationalismus und Romantik. Karl Otfried Müller und die antike Kultur.* Hildesheim, Weidmann.

Cameron, A. 2004. *Greek Mythography in the Roman World.* New York, Oxford University Press.

Caneva, S. G. (ed.) 2020. *The Materiality of Hellenistic Ruler Cults.* Liège, Presses universitaires de Liège.

Carbon, J.-M. 2017. 'Meaty Perks: Epichoric and Topological Trends', *in* Hitch and Rutherford 2017: 151–78.

———— and Peels, S. (eds.) 2018. *Purity and Purification in the Ancient Greek World. Texts, Rituals, and Norms.* Liège, Presses universitaires de Liège.

Carpenter, T. 1986. *Dionysian Imagery in Archaic Art. Its Development in Black-Figure Vase Painting.* Oxford, Clarendon Press.

———— 1991. *Art and Myth in Ancient Greece.* London, Thames and Hudson.

———— and Faraone, C. (eds.) 1993 *Masks of Dionysus.* Ithaca, NY, Cornell University Press.

Carson, A. 1999. 'Dirt and Desire', in J. I. Porter (ed.), *Constructions of the Classical Body.* Ann Arbor, MI, University of Michigan Press: 77–100.

Casadio, G. 2004. 'Hera a Samo', in E. Cavallini (ed.), *Samo. Storia, letteratura, scienza.* Pisa, Istituti editoriali e poligrafici internazionali: 135–55.

———— 2009. 'Dionysus in Campania: Cumae', in G. Casadio and P. A. Johnston (eds.), *Mystic Cults in Magna Graecia.* Austin, TX, University of Texas Press: 33–45.

Casevitz, M. 1984. 'Temples et sanctuaires: ce qu'apprend l'étude lexicologique', in G. Roux (ed.), *Temples et sanctuaires.* Lyon, GIS–Maison de L'Orient: 81–95.

Ceccarelli, P. 1998. *La pirrica nell'antichità greco romana, studi sulla danza armata.* Pisa, Istituti editoriali e poligrafici internazionali.

Chalupa, A. 2014. 'Pythiai and Inspired Divination in the Delphic Oracle: Can Cognitive Sciences Provide Us with an Access to "Dead Minds"?', *Journal of Cognitive Historiography* 1: 24–51.

Chaniotis, A. 1988. 'Habgierige Gütter, habgierige Städte: Heiligtumbesitz und Gebietsanspruch in den kretischen Staatsverträgen', *Ktema* 13: 21–39.

———— 1991. 'Gedenktage der Griechen', in J. Assmann (ed.), *Das Fest und das Heilige. Religiöse Kontrapunkte zur Alltagswelt.* Gütersloh, G. Mohn: 123–45.

———— 2005. 'The Great Inscription, Its Political and Social Institutions and the Common Institutions of the Cretans', in E. Greco and M. Lombardo (eds.), *La grande iscrizione di Gortyna.* Athens, Scuola archeologica italiana di Atene: 171–90.

———— 2010. 'Megatheism: The Search for the Almighty God and the Competition of Cults', in S. Mitchell and P. Van Nuffelen (eds.), *One God. Pagan Monotheism in the Roman Empire.* Cambridge, Cambridge University Press: 112–40.

———— 2017. 'The Historical Significance of the Dodona's Tablets', in K. Soueref (ed.), *Dodona.* Ioannina, Ephoreia Archaioteton Ioannina: 51–65.

———— 2019. *Die Öffnung der Welt. Eine Globalgeschichte des Hellenismus.* Darmstadt, wbg Theiss.

Chankowski, V. 2005. 'Techniques financières, influences, performances dans les activités bancaires des sanctuaires grecs', *Topoi* 12–13: 69–93.

———— 2011. 'Divine Financiers: Cults as Consumers and Generators of Value', in Z. Archibald, J. K. Davies, and V. Gabrielsen (eds.), *The Economies of Hellenistic Societies, Third to First Centuries bc.* Oxford, Oxford University Press: 142–65.

Chapot, F. and Laurot, B. (eds.) 2001. *Corpus de prières grecques et romaines.* Turnhout, Brepols.

Chlup, R. 2007. 'The Semantics of Fertility: Levels of Meaning in the Thesmophoria', *Kernos* 20: 69–95.

Christensen, K. A. 1984. 'The Theseion: A Slave Refuge at Athens', *AJAH* 9: 23–32.

Clauss, J. and Johnston, S. I. (eds.) 1997. *Medea. Essays on Medea in Myth, Literature, Philosophy, and Art.* Princeton, NJ, Princeton University Press.

Clauss, J. J., Cuypers, M., and Kahane, A. (eds.) 2016. *The Gods of Greek Hexameter Poetry. From the Archaic Age to Late Antiquity and Beyond.* Stuttgart, Franz Steiner.

Clinton, K. 1988. 'Sacrifice at the Eleusinian Mysteries', in Hägg et al. 1988: 69–80.

———— 1992. *Myth and Cult. The Iconography of the Eleusinian Mysteries.* Stockholm, Svenska institutet i Athen.

———— 1996. 'The Thesmophorion in Central Athens and the Celebration of the Thesmophoria in Attica', in R. Hägg (ed.), *The Role of Religion in the Early Greek Polis.* Stockholm, Paul Åström: 111–25.

Cole, S. G. 1988. 'The Uses of Water in Greek Sanctuaries', in Hägg et al. 1988: 161–5.

———— 1992. 'Gynaiki ou Themis: Gender Difference in the Greek Leges Sacrae', *Helios* 19: 104–22.

———— 1993. 'Procession and Celebration at the Dionysia', in R. Scodel (ed.), *Theater and Society in the Classical World.* Ann Arbor, MI, University of Michigan Press: 25–38.

———— 2000. 'Demeter in the Ancient Greek City and its Countryside', in Buxton 2000: 133–54.

———— 2004. *Landscapes, Gender, and Ritual Space. The Ancient Greek Experience.* Berkeley, CA, University of California Press.

Collard, H. 2016. *Montrer l'invisible. Rituel et présentification du divin dans l'imagerie attique.* Liège, Presses universitaires de Liège.

Connelly, A. 1998. 'Was Sophocles Heroised as Dexion?', *JHS* 118: 1–21.

Connelly, J. B. 2007. *Portrait of a Priestess. Women and Ritual in Ancient Greece.* Princeton, NJ, and Oxford, Princeton University Press.

Cook, J. G. 2018. *Empty Tomb, Resurrection, Apotheosis*. Tübingen, Mohr Siebeck.

Corso, A. 1984. 'L'Heraion di Paro', *ASAA* 62: 97–101.

Cosmopoulos, M. B. (ed.) 2003. *Greek Mysteries. The Archaeology of Ancient Greek Secret Cults*. London and New York, Routledge.

———— 2015. *Bronze Age Eleusis and the Origins of the Eleusinian Mysteries*. Cambridge, Cambridge University Press.

Costa, V. 2004. 'Natale Conti e la divulgazione della mitologia classica in Europa tra Cinquecento e Seicento', in E. Lanzillotta (ed.), *Ricerche di antichità e tradizione classica*. Tivoli, Tored: 257–307.

Csapo, E. 1997. 'Riding the Phallus for Dionysus: Iconology, Ritual, and Gender-Role De/construction', *Phoenix* 51: 253–95.

Currie, B. 2016. *Homer's Allusive Art*. Oxford, Oxford University Press.

d'Alessio, G. 2000. Review of Schröder 1999, *BMCRev* 2000.01.24.

Danner, P. 1993. 'Meniskoi and Obeloi: zum Schutz von Statuen und Bauwerken vor den Vögeln', *JÖAI* 62: 19–28.

Davidson, J. 2007. *The Greeks and Greek Love. A Radical Reappraisal of Homosexuality in Ancient Greece*. London, Weidenfeld & Nicolson.

de Fontenelle, B. 1989. *Oeuvres complètes*, vol. 3, ed. A. Niderst. Paris, Fayard.

de Jong, I. F. 2004. *Narrators and Focalizers. The Presentation of the Story of the Iliad*. Second edition, London, Bristol Classical Press.

de la Genière, J. (ed.) 1997. *Héra. Images, espaces, cultes*. Naples, Centre Jean Bérard.

De Meyer, I. 2016 'L'étymologie du mot grec "θεός"', *RPh* 90: 115–38.

Debiasi, A. 2015. *Eumelo. Un poeta per Corinto*. Rome, L'Erma di Bretschneider.

———— 2020. *Eumelo, la saga argonautica e dintorni. La documentazione papirologica*. Rome, L'Erma di Bretschneider.

Delavaud-Roux, M.-H. 1994. *Les danses pacifiques en Grèce antique*. Aix-en-Provence, Publications de l'Université de Provence.

———— 1995. *Les dances dionysiaques au Grèce antique*. Aix-en-Provence, Publications de l'Université de Provence.

———— 2006. 'Communiquer avec Dionysos: la dance des Ménades à travers l'iconographie des vases grecs', in L. Bodiou, D. Frère, and V. Mehl (eds.), *L'expression des corps. Gestes, attitudes, regards dans l'iconographie antique*. Rennes, Presses universitaires de Rennes: 153–63.

Delivorrias, A. 1984. 'Aphrodite', in *LIMC* II.1: 3–151.

Delneri, F. 2006. *I culti misterici stranieri nei frammenti della commedia attica antica*. Bologna, Pàtron.

Demetriou, D. 2017. 'Beyond *Polis* Religion: Religious Practices in the Cosmopolitan *Emporion* of Naukratis', *BABesch* 92: 49–66.

Deshours, N. 2011. *L'été indien de la religion civique. Étude sur les cultes civiques dans le monde égéen à l'époque hellénistique tardive.* Pessac, Ausonius.

Detienne, M. 1972. *Les jardins d'Adonis.* Paris, Gallimard.

——— 1979. 'Violentes "Eugenies": en pleines Thesmophories: des femmes couvertes de sang', in Detienne and Vernant 1979: 183–214.

——— 1981. *L'invention de la mythologie.* Paris, Gallimard.

——— 1986. *The Creation of Mythology.* Translated by M. Cook. Chicago, IL, University of Chicago Press.

——— 1989. *L'écriture d'Orphée.* Paris, Gallimard.

——— and Vernant, J.-P. 1978. *Cunning Intelligence in Greek Culture and Society.* Translated by J. Lloyd. Hassocks, Harvester.

——— and Vernant, J.-P. (eds.) 1979. *La cuisine du sacrifice en pays grec.* Paris, Gallimard.

Diels, H. and Kranz, W. (eds. and trans.) 1906–10. *Die Fragmente der Vorsokratiker.* Berlin, Weidmann.

Dignas, B. and Trampedach, K. (eds.) 2008. *Practitioners of the Divine. Greek Priests and Religious Officials from Homer to Heliodorus.* Washington, DC, Center for Hellenic Studies.

Dillon, M. 1997. 'The Ecology of the Greek Sanctuary', *ZPE* 118: 113–27.

——— 2003. *Girls and Women in Classical Greek Religion.* London and New York, Routledge.

———, Eidinow, E., and Maurizio, L. (eds.) 2017. *Women's Ritual Competence in the Greco-Roman Mediterranean.* London and New York, Routledge.

Dodd, D. and Faraone, C. (eds.) 2003. *Initiation in Ancient Greek Rituals and Narratives.* London and New York, Routledge.

Dodds, E. R. (ed.) 1960. *Euripides. Bacchae.* Second edition, Oxford, Clarendon Press.

Doniger O'Flaherty, W. 1980. *Women, Androgynes, and Other Mythical Beasts.* Chicago, IL, University of Chicago Press.

Dover, K. J. 1988. *The Greeks and Their Legacy.* Oxford, Basil Blackwell.

Dowden, K. 1980. 'Grades in the Eleusinian Mysteries', *RHR* 197: 409–27.

——— 1989. *Death and the Maiden. Girls' Initiation Rites in Greek Mythology.* London and New York, .

——— 1992. *The Uses of Greek Mythology.* London, Routledge.

——— 1997. 'The Amazons: Development and Functions', *RhM* 140: 97–128.

——— 2006. *Zeus.* London and New York, Routledge.

——— 2007. 'Olympian Gods, Olympian Pantheon', *in Ogden* 2007: 41–55.

———— 2011. 'Van Gennep et l'initiation dans la mythologie grecque: mort prématurée d'un paradigme?', *Gaia* 14: 171–79.

———— and Livingstone, N. R. (eds.) 2011. *A Companion to Greek Mythology*. Oxford and Malden, MA, Wiley-Blackwell.

Downs, L. L. and Rubin, M. 2019. 'Gender History', in M. Tamm and P. Burke (eds.), *Debating New Approaches to History*. London, Bloomsbury Academic: 101–25.

Doyen, C. 2011. *Poséidon souverain. Contribution à l'histoire religieuse de la Grèce mycénienne et archaïque*. Brussels, Académie royale de Belgique.

Draycott, J. and Graham, E. J. (eds.) 2017. *Bodies of Evidence. Ancient Anatomical Votives Past, Present and Future*. London, Routledge.

du Boulay, J. 1986. 'Women: Images of Their Nature and Destiny in Rural Greece', in J. Dubisch (ed.), *Gender and Power in Rural Greece*. Princeton, Princeton University Press: 139–68.

Dubois, L. 1996. *Inscriptions grecques dialectales d'Olbia du Pont*. Geneva, Librairie Droz.

duBois, P. 1995. *Sappho is Burning*. Chicago, IL, and London, University of Chicago Press.

Ducat, J. 2006. *Spartan Education. Youth and Society in the Classical Period*. Swansea, Classical Press of Wales.

Dunkel, G. 1988–90. 'Vater Himmels Gattin', *Die Sprache* 34: 1–26.

———— 1993. 'Periphrastica Homerohittitovedica', in B. Brogyanyi and R. Lipp (eds.), *Comparative-Historical Linguistics: Indo-European and Finno-Ugric*. Amsterdam, J. Benjamins Pub. Co.: 103–18.

Duplouy, A. 2006. *Le prestige des élites. Recherches sur les modes de reconnaissance sociale en Grèce entre les Xe et Ve siècles avant J.-C.* Paris, Les Belles Lettres.

Durand, J.-L. 1992. 'L'Hermès multiple', in Bron and Kassapoglou 1992: 25–34.

Eder, B. 2019. 'The Role of Sanctuaries and the Formation of Greek Identities in the Late Bronze Age/Early Iron Age Transition', *in* Lemos and Tsingarida 2019: 25–52.

Edlund, I. 1987. *The Gods and the Place. The Location and Function of Sanctuaries in the Countryside of Etruria and Magna Graecia (700–400 b.c.)*. Stockholm, Svenska Institutet i Rom.

Edmonds, R. G., III 2013. *Redefining Ancient Orphism. A Study in Greek Religion*. Cambridge, Cambridge University Press.

———— 2019. *Drawing Down the Moon. Magic in the Ancient Greco-Roman World*. Princeton, NJ, Princeton University Press.

Egetmeyer, M. 2010. *Le dialecte grec ancien de Chypre*. 2 vols, Berlin, De Gruyter.

Eich, P. 2011. *Gottesbild und Wahrnehmung. Studien zu Ambivalenzen früher griechischer Götterdarstellungen (ca. 800 v. Chr.–ca. 400 v. Chr.)*. Stuttgart, Steiner.

Eidinow, E. 2007. *Oracles, Curses, and Risk among the Ancient Greeks*. Oxford, Oxford University Press.

——— 2016. *Envy, Poison, and Death. Women on Trial in Classical Athens*. Oxford, Oxford University Press.

——— 2019 '"They Blow Now One Way, Now Another" (Hes. *Theog.* 875): Winds in the Ancient Greek Imaginary', in Scheer 2019: 113–32.

——— 2020. 'What Will You Give me? Narratives of Religious Exchange', in A. Collar and T. M. Kristensen (eds.), *Pilgrimage and Economy in the Ancient Mediterranean*. Leiden and Boston, MA, Brill: 187–203.

———, Kindt, J., and Osborne, R. (eds.) 2016. *Theologies of Ancient Greek Religion*. New York, Cambridge University Press.

Ekroth, G. 2001. 'Altars on Attic Vases: The Identification of Bomos and Eschara', in C. Scheffer (ed.), *Ceramics in Context*. Stockholm, Almqvist & Wiksell: 115–26.

——— 2002. *The Sacrificial Rituals of Greek Hero-Cults in the Archaic to the Early Hellenistic Period*. Liège, Presses universitaires de Liège.

——— 2007. 'Heroes and Hero-Cults', *in Ogden* 2007: 100–14.

——— 2009. 'Thighs or Tails? The Osteological Evidence as a Source for Greek Ritual Norms', in P. Brulé (ed.), *La norme en matière religieuse en Grèce ancienne*. Liège, Presses universitaires de Liège: 125–51.

——— 2009. 'Why (Not) Paint an Altar? A Study of When, Where and Why Altars Appear on Attic Red-Figure Vases', in V. Nørskov, L. Hannestad, C. Isler-Kerényi, and S. Lewis (eds.), *The World of Greek Vases*. Rome, Quasar: 89–114.

——— 2014. 'Animal Sacrifice in Antiquity', in G. L. Campbell (ed.), *The Oxford Handbook of Ancient Animals*. Oxford, Oxford University Press: 324–54.

——— 2017. 'Bare Bones: Zooarchaeology and Greek Sacrifice', in Hitch and Rutherford 2017: 15–47.

——— 2018a. 'The Crocodile on Samos or Africa in the Aegean', in A. Ekblom et al. (eds.), *The Resilience of Heritage. Cultivating a Future of the Past*. Uppsala, Department of Archaeology and Ancient History, Uppsala University: 61–8.

——— 2018b. 'Holocaustic Sacrifices in Ancient Greek Religion and the Ritual Relations to the Levant', in Ł. Niesiołowski-Spanò and M. Węcowski (eds.), *Change, Continuity, and Connectivity. North-Eastern Mediterranean at the Turn of the Bronze Age and in the Early Iron Age*. Wiesbaden, Harrassowitz: 308–26.

—— 2018c. 'Vernant et les os: théorie et pratique du sacrifice grec', in F. de Polignac and S. Georgoudi (eds.), *Relire Vernant*. Paris, : 83–115.

—— 2019. 'Why Does Zeus Care about Burnt Thighbones from Sheep? Defining the Divine and Structuring the World through Animal Sacrifice in Ancient Greece', *HR* 58: 225–50.

—— 2020. 'École de Paris: Praising or Debasing an Approach to the Study of Greek Sacrifice', *Cahiers Mondes Anciens* 13, https://doi.org/10.4000/mondesanciens.2764.

—— and Wallensten, J. (eds.) 2013. *Bones, Behaviour and Belief*. Stockholm, .

Etienne, R. 1992. 'Autels et sacrifices', in Schachter 1992b: 291–312.

Euler, W. 1987. 'Gab es eine indogermanische Götterfamilie?', in W. Meid (ed.), *Studien zum indogermanischen Wortschatz*. Innsbruck, Institut für Sprachwissenschaft: 35–56.

Fahlbusch, G. 2004. *Die Frauen im Gefolge des Dionysos auf den attischen Vasenbildern des 6. und 5. Jhs. v. Chr. als Spiegel des weiblichen Idealbildes*. Oxford, British Archaeological Reports.

Faraone, C. A. 1992. *Talismans and Trojan Horses. Magical Statues in Ancient Greek Myth and Ritual*. New York, Oxford University Press.

—— 1993. 'Molten Wax, Spilt Wine, and Mutilated Animals: Sympathetic Magic in Near Eastern and Early Greek Oath Ceremonies', *JHS* 113: 60–80.

—— 2008. 'Family and Household Religion in Ancient Greece', in J. Bodel and S. M. Olyan (eds.), *Household and Family Religion in Antiquity. Contextual and Comparative Perspectives*. Malden, MA, and Oxford: Blackwell, 210–18.

—— and Naiden, F. S. (eds.) 2012. *Greek and Roman Sacrifice. Ancient Victims, Modern Observers*. Cambridge, Cambridge University Press.

Farnell, L. 1907. *The Cults of the Greek States*, vol. 3. Oxford, Clarendon Press.

Feeney, D. C. 1991. *The Gods in Epic. Poets and Critics of the Classical Tradition*. Oxford, Clarendon Press.

Fehr, B. 1996. 'The Greek Temple in the Early Archaic Period: Meaning, Use and Social Context', *Hephaistos* 14: 165–91.

Fehrentz, V. 1993. 'Der antike Agyieus', *JDAI* 108: 123–96.

Feil, E. 1986–2012. *Religio. Die Geschichte eines neuzeitlichen Grundbegriffs vom Frühchristentum bis zur Reformation*. 4 vols, second edition, Göttingen, Vandenhoeck & Ruprecht.

Feldman, B. and Richardson, R. D. (eds.) 1972. *The Rise of Modern Mythology (1680–1860)*. Bloomington, IN, and London, Indiana University Press.

Ferrandini Troisi, F. 1986. '"Pesi da telaio": segni e interpretazioni', in *Miscellanea greca e romana 10*. Rome, Istituto italiano per la storia antica: 91–114.

Filonik, J. 2013. 'Athenian Impiety Trials: A Reappraisal', *Dike* 16: 11–96.

———— 2016. 'Impiety Avenged: Rewriting Athenian History', in E. P. Cueva and J. Martínez (eds.), *Splendide Mendax. Rethinking Fakes and Forgeries in Classical, Late Antique, and Early Christian Literature*. Groningen, Barkhuis: 125–40.

Fischer, J. 2017. 'Sklaverei und Religion im klassischen Griechenland', in J. Fischer (ed.), *Studien zur antiken Religionsgeschichte*. Krakow, Ridero IT Publishing: 67–107.

Fisher, J. 2014. *The Annals of Quintus Ennius and the Italic Tradition*. Baltimore, MD, Johns Hopkins University Press.

Fisher, N. 1993. 'Multiple Personalities and Dionysiac Festivals: Dicaeopolis in Aristophanes' *Acharnians*', *G&R* 40: 31–47.

Flemming, R. 2007. 'Festus and Women's Role in Roman Religion', in F. Glinster and C. Woods (eds.), *Verrius, Festus, and Paul. Lexicography, Scholarship, and Society*. London, University of London, School of Advanced Study, Institute of Classical Studies: 87–108.

Flower, M. 2008. *The Seer in Ancient Greece*. Berkeley, CA, University of California Press.

Flückiger-Guggenheim, D. 1984. *Göttliche Gäste. Die Einkehr von Göttern und Heroen in der griechischen Mythologie*. Bern, Lang.

Foley, H. 1996. 'Antigone as Moral Agent', in M. S. Silk (ed.), *Tragedy and the Tragic. Greek Theatre and Beyond*. Oxford, Clarendon Press: 49–73.

Forsén, B. 1996. *Griechische Gliederweihungen. Eine Untersuchung zu ihrer Typologie und ihrer religions- und sozialgeschichtlichen Bedeutung*. Helskinki, Suomen Ateenan-instituutin säätiö.

Forstenpointner, G. 2001. 'Sacrifice for Demeter at the Artemision of Ephesos', in U. Muss (ed.), *Der Kosmos der Artemis von Ephesos*. Vienna, Österreichisches Archäologisches Institut: 49–71.

Foster, M. 2018. *The Seer and the City. Religion, Politics, and Colonial Ideology in Ancient Greece*. Oakland, CA, University of California Press.

Fowler, R. L. 1998. 'Genealogical Thinking, Hesiod's *Catalogue*, and the Creation of the Hellenes', *PCPhS* 44: 1–19.

———— 2000. 'Greek Magic, Greek Religion', in Buxton 2000: 314–44.

———— 2000–13. *Early Greek Mythography*. 2 vols, Oxford, Oxford University Press.

———— 2009. 'Thoughts on Myth and Religion in Early Greek Historiography', *Minerva* 22: 21–39.

———— 2011. '*Mythos* and *Logos*', *JHS* 131: 45–66.

———— 2017. *What's in a Myth*. Watford, Classical Association. https://www.academia.edu/36190873/Fowler_Whats_in_a_Myth (accessed 11 September 2020).

Foxhall, L. 2013. *Studying Gender in Classical Antiquity*. Cambridge, Cambridge University Press.

Frankfurter, D. (ed.) 2019. *Guide to the Study of Ancient Magic*. Leiden and Boston, MA, Brill.

Frazer, G. 1890. *The Golden Bough. A Study in Comparative Religion*. London, Macmillan & Co.

Frei, P. 1993. 'Die Bellerophontessage und das Alte Testament', in B. Janowski, K. Koch, and G. Wilhelm (eds.), *Religionsgeschichtliche Beziehungen zwischen Kleinasien, Nordsyrien und dem Alten Testament*. Freiburg, Universitätsverlag, and Göttingen, Vandenhoeck & Ruprecht: 39–65.

Freitag, K. and M. Haake (eds.) 2019. *Griechische Heiligtümer als Handlungsorte*. Stuttgart, Franz Steiner.

Fréret, N. 1756. 'Réflexions générales sur la nature de la religion des Grecs, et sur l'idée qu'on doit se former de leur mythologie', in *Histoire de l'académie royale des inscriptions et belles-lettres*, vol. 23. Paris, Imprimerie royale: 17–26.

Frey, J. 2017. *et al.* (eds.), *Glaube. Das Verständnis des Glaubens im frühen Christentum und in seiner jüdischen und hellenistisch-römischen Umwelt*. Tübingen, Mohr Siebeck.

Frielinghaus, H. 2010. 'Waffenweihungen in Delphi und Olympia: ein Vergleich', in H. Frielinghaus and J. Stroszeck (eds.), *Neue Forschungen in griechischen Städten und Heiligtümern*. Möhnesee, Bibliopolis: 93–104.

———— 2011. *Die Helme von Olympia. Ein Beitrag zu Waffenweihungen in griechischen Heiligtümern*. Berlin, De Gruyter.

———— 2013. 'Beobachtungen zum Votivspektrum Olympias in archaischer und nacharchaischer Zeit', in Gerlach and Raue 2013: 363–68.

———— 2017. 'Schiffe im Votivkontext', in H. Frielinghaus, T. Schmidts, and V. Tsamakda (eds.), *Schiffe und ihr Kontext. Darstellungen, Modelle, Bestandteile – von der Bronzezeit bis zum Ende des Byzantinischen Reiches*. Mainz, Römisch-Germanisches Zentralmuseum: 23–37.

Friese, W. 2010. *Den Göttern so nah. Architektur und Topographie griechischer Orakelheiligtümer*. Stuttgart, Franz Steiner.

Furley, W. D. 2007. 'Prayers and Hymns', *in* Ogden 2007: 117–31.

———— and Bremer, J. M. 2001. *Greek Hymns. Selected Cult Songs from the Archaic to the Hellenistic Period*. 2 vols, Tübingen, Mohr Siebeck.

Gagné, R. 2013. *Ancestral Fault in Ancient Greece.* Cambridge, Cambridge University Press.

Gagné, R. and Herrero de Jáuregui, M. (eds.) 2019. *Les dieux d'Homère,* vol. 2: *Anthropomorphismes.* Liège, Presses universitaires de Liège.

Gaifman, M. 2012. *Aniconism in Greek Antiquity.* Oxford, Oxford University Press.

——— 2017. 'Aniconism: Definitions, Examples and Comparative Perspectives', *Religion* 47: 335–52.

——— 2018. *The Art of Libation in Classical Athens.* New Haven, CT, Yale University Press.

Gantz, T. 1993. *Early Greek Myth. A Guide to Literary and Artistic Sources.* 2 vols, Baltimore, MD, and London, Johns Hopkins University Press.

García Ramón, J. L. 2007. 'Der Begriff des Heiligtums aus sprachgeschichtlicher Perspektive', in C. Frevel and H. von Hesberg (eds.), *Kult und Kommunikation. Medien in Heiligtümern der Antike.* Wiesbaden, Reichert: 17–38.

——— 2013. 'Religious Onomastics in Ancient Greece and Italy', in J. V. García and A. Ruiz (eds.), *Poetic Language and Religion in Greece and Rome.* Newcastle upon Tyne, Cambridge Scholars Publishing: 60–107.

——— 2016. 'Hera and Hero: Reconstructing Lexicon and God-Names', in D. M. Goldstein, S. W. Jamison, and B. Vine (eds.), *Proceedings of the 27th Annual UCLA Indo-European Conference.* Bremen, Hempen: 41–60.

Garland, R. 1992. *Introducing New Gods. The Politics of Athenian Religion.* London, Duckworth.

Garthwaite, J. 2010. 'The Keres of the Athenian Anthesteria and Their Near Eastern Counterparts', *Scholia* 19: 2–13.

Gartziou-Tatti, A. and Zografou, A. (eds.) 2019. *Des dieux et des plantes. Monde végétal et religion en Grèce ancienne.* Liège, Presses universitaires de Liège.

Gebauer, J. 2002. *Pompe und Thysia. Attische Tieropferdarstellungen auf schwartz- und rotfigurigen Vasen.* Münster, Ugarit-Verlag.

Geertz, C. 1983. *Local Knowledge. Further Essays in Interpretive Anthropology.* New York, Basic Books.

Gemici, K. 2008. 'Karl Polanyi and the Antinomies of Embeddedness', *Socio-Economic Review* 6: 5–33.

Genovese, G. 1999. *I santuari rurali nella Calabria greca.* Rome, L'Erma di Bretschneider.

Georgoudi, S. 2001. 'The Twelve Gods of the Greeks: Variations on a Theme', in N. Loraux, G. Nagy, and L. Slatkin (eds.), *Postwar French Thought, III, Antiquities.* New York, New Press: 346–54.

——— 2005. '*Athanatous therapeuein*: réflexions sur des femmes aux services des dieux', in V. Dasen and M. Piérart (eds.), Ἰδίᾳ καὶ δημοσίᾳ. *Les cadres 'privés' et 'publics' de la religion grecque antique.* Liège, Presses universitaires de Liège: 69–82.

——— 2005. 'L'"occultation de la violence" dans le sacrifice grec: données anciennes, discours modernes', in Georgoudi, Nagy, and Slatkin 2005: 115–47.

——— 2008. 'Le consentement de la victime sacrificielle: une question ouverte', in Mehl and Brulé 2008: 139–53.

——— 2018. 'Couper pour purifier? Le chien et autres animaux, entre pratiques rituelles et récits', in Carbon and Peels-Matthey 2018: 173–205.

Georgoudi, S., Koch Piettre, R., and Schmidt, F. (eds.) 2005. *La cuisine et l'autel. Les sacrifices en questions dans les sociétés de la méditerranée ancienne.* Turnhout, Brepols.

Gerlach, I. and Raue, D. (eds.) 2013. *Sanktuar und Ritual. Heilige Plätze im archäologischen Befund.* Rahden, Verlag Marie Leidorf.

Gernet, L. and Boulanger, A. 1970. *Le génie grec dans la religion.* Paris, Éditions Albin Michel. (First edition 1932.)

Gherchanoc, F. 2012. 'La beauté dévoilée de Phryné: de l'art d'exhiber ses seins', *Metis* n.s. 10: 199–223.

——— 2016. *Concours de beauté et beautés du corps en Grèce ancienne.* Bordeaux, Ausonius.

Ghinatti, F. 1983. 'Manifestazioni votive, iscrizioni e vita economica nei santuari della Magna Grecia', *StudPat* 30: 241–322.

Giacobello, F. and P. Schirripa (eds.) 2009. *Ninfe nel mito e nella città dalla Grecia a Roma.* Milan, Viennepierre.

Ginzburg, C. 2013. 'Our Words, and Theirs: A Reflection on the Historian's Craft, Today', *Cromohs* 18: 97–114.

Giudice, E. 2008. 'Procne sulla "rocca rotonda"', *Ostraka* 17.2: 69–89.

——— 2015. *Il tymbos, la stele, la barca di Caronte. L'immaginario della morte sulle lekythoi funerarie a fondo bianco.* Rome, L'Erma di Bretschneider.

Giudice, G. 2018. 'Una "menade" nell'oikos? Un nuovo cratere del Pittore del Dinos ad Himera', in Giudice and Giudice 2018: 29–43.

——— and Giudice, E. 2018. *I frammenti Beazley dal Persephoneion di Locri Epizefiri. Una ricostruzione iconografica.* Rome, L'Erma di Bretschneider.

Gladigow, B. 2005. *Religionswissenschaft als Kulturwissenschaft.* Stuttgart, Kohlhammer.

Gödde, S. 2016. 'Dionysische Ekstase in der griechischen Antike', in M. Schetsche and R.-B. Schmidt (eds.), *Rausch, Trance, Ekstase. Zur Kultur psychischer Ausnahmezustände.* Bielefeld, Transcript: 131–56.

Goff, B. and Taylor, T. 2004. *Citizen Bacchae. Women's Ritual Practice in Ancient Greece*. Berkeley, CA, University of California Press.

Gordon, R. 2013. 'Hero-Cults, Old and New', *JRA* 26: 852–60.

———— 2015. 'Good to Think: Wolves and Werewolves in the Graeco-Roman World', in W. de Blécourt (ed.), *Werewolf Histories*. Basingstoke, Palgrave Macmillan: 25–60.

———— 2019. 'The Greeks, Religion and Nature in German Neo-Humanist Discourse from Romanticism to Early Industrialisation', in Scheer 2019: 49–70.

Gould, J. 2001. *Myth, Ritual Memory, and Exchange. Essays in Greek Literature*. Oxford, Oxford University Press.

Graells i Fabregat, R. and F. Longo (eds.) 2018. *Armi votive in Magna Grecia*. Mainz, Römisch-Germanisches Zentralmuseum.

Graf, F. 1974. *Eleusis und die orphische Dichtung Athens*. Berlin, De Gruyter.

———— 1979a. 'Apollon Delphinios', *MH* 36: 2–22.

———— 1979b. 'Das Götterbild aus dem Taurerland', *AW* 10.4: 33–41.

———— 1982. 'Culti e credenze religiose della Magna Grecia', *Atti Taranto* 21: 157–85.

———— 1985. *Nordionische Kulte. Religionsgeschichtliche und Epigraphische Untersuchungen zu den Kulten von Chios, Erythrai, Klazomenai und Phokaia*. Rome, Schweizerisches Institut in Rom.

———— 1993a. 'Dionysian and Orphic Eschatology: New Texts and Old Questions', in Carpenter and Faraone 1993: 239–58.

———— 1993b. *Greek Mythology. An Introduction*. Translated by T. Marier. Baltimore, MD, and London, Johns Hopkins University Press.

———— 1993c. 'Initiationsriten in der antiken Mittelmeerwelt', *AU* 36.2: 29–40.

———— 1996a. 'Namen von Göttern im klassischen Altertum', in E. Eichler et al. (eds.), *Namenforschung. Ein internationales Handbuch zur Onomastik*. 2 vols, Berlin and New York, De Gruyter: ii.1823–37.

———— 1996b. '*Pompai* in Greece. Some Considerations about Space and Ritual in the Greek *polis*', in R. Hägg (ed.), *The Role of Religion in the Early Greek Polis*. Stockholm, Paul Åström: 55–65.

———— 1997. *Magic in the Ancient World*. Translated by F. Philip. Cambridge, MA, and London, Harvard University Press.

———— 2000a. 'The Locrian Maidens', in Buxton 2000: 250–70.

———— 2000b. 'Der Mysterienprozess', in L. Burckhardt and J. von Ungern-Sternberg (eds.), *Große Prozesse im antiken Athen*. Munich, Beck: 114–27.

———— 2001. 'Der Eigensinn der Götterbilder in antiken religiösen Diskursen', in G. Boehm (ed.), *Homo Pictor*. Munich, K. G. Saur: 227–43.

———— 2006. 'Der Kult des Eros in Thespiai', in H. Görgemanns et al., *Plutarch, Dialog über die Liebe*. Tübingen, Mohr Siebeck: 191–207.

———— 2009. *Apollo*. London and New York, Routledge.

———— 2010. 'Gods in Greek Inscriptions: Some Methodological Questions', in Bremmer and Erskine 2010: 55–80.

———— 2011. 'Apollo, Possession, and Prophecy', in C. Rothchild and T. W. Thompson (eds.), *Christian Body, Christian Self. Concepts of Early Christian Personhood*. Tübingen, Mohr Siebeck: 299–310.

———— 2020. 'Caloric Codes. Ancient Greek Animal Sacrifice', in Kindt 2020: 171–96.

———— and Johnston, S. I. 2013. *Ritual Texts for the Afterlife. Orpheus and the Bacchic Gold Tablets*. Second edition, London and New York, Routledge.

Grafton, A. and Swerdlow, N. 1988. 'Calendar Dates and Ominous Days in Ancient Historiography', *JWI* 51: 14–42.

Graham, E.-J. 2020. 'Hand in Hand: Rethinking Anatomical Votives as Material Things', in V. Gasparini, J. Rüpke, M. Patzelt, R. Raja, A.-K. Rieger, and E. Urciuoli (eds.), *Lived Religion in the Ancient Mediterranean World*. Berlin and Boston, MA, De Gruyter: 209–36.

Grassinger, D., de Oliveira Pinto, T., and Scholl, A. (eds.) 2008. *Die Rückkehr der Götter*. Regensburg, Schnell & Steiner.

Greco, G. and B. Ferrara (eds.) 2008. *Doni agli dei. Il sistema dei doni votivi nei santuari*. Pozzuoli, Naus.

Grell, C. and Volpilhac-Auger, C. (eds.) 1994. *Nicolas Fréret, légende et verité*. Oxford, Voltaire Foundation.

Griffin, J. 1980. *Homer on Life and Death*. Oxford, Clarendon Press.

Grossardt, P. 2001. *Die Erzählung von Meleagros zur literarischen Entwicklung der kalydonischen Kultlegende*. Leiden and Boston, MA, Brill.

Haake, M. and M. Jung (eds.) 2011. *Griechische Heiligtümer als Erinnerungsorte. Von der Archaik bis in den Hellenismus*. Stuttgart, Steiner.

Habicht, C. 1994. *Athen in hellenistischer Zeit. Gesammelte Aufsätze*. Munich, C. H. Beck.

———— 2017. *Divine Honors for Mortal Men in Greek Cities. The Early Cases*. Translated by J. N. Dillon. Ann Arbor, MI, University of Michigan Press.

Hägg, R. 1992. 'Geometric Sanctuaries in the Argolid', in M. Piérart (ed.), *Polydipsion Argos. Argos de la fin des palais mycéniens à la constitution del' état classique*. Paris, de Boccard: 9–21.

———— (ed.) 1999. *Ancient Greek Hero Cult*. Stockholm, Svenska Institutet i Athen.

———— and Alroth, B. (eds.) 2005. *Greek Sacrificial Ritual. Olympian and Chthonian.* Stockholm, Svenska Institutet i Athen.

————, Marinatos, N., and Nordquist, G. C. (ed.) 1988. *Early Greek Cult Practice.* Stockholm, Svenska Institutet i Athen.

Hall, E. and Harrop, S. (eds.) 2010. *Theorising Performance. Greek Drama, Cultural History and Critical Practice.* London, Duckworth.

Hamilton, R. 1992. *Choes and Anthesteria. Athenian Iconography and Ritual.* Ann Arbor, MI, University of Michigan Press.

Hansen, M. H. and Nielsen, T. H. (eds.) 2004. *An Inventory of Archaic and Classical Poleis.* Oxford, Oxford University Press.

Hansen, W. F. 2017. *The Book of Greek and Roman Folktales, Legends, and Myths.* Princeton, NJ, Princeton University Press.

Harris, D. 1995. *The Treasures of the Parthenon and the Erechtheion.* Oxford, Clarendon Press.

Harris, E. M. 2014. 'Wife, Household, and Marketplace: The Role of Women in the Economy of Classical Athens', in U. Bultrighini and E. Dimauro (eds.), *Donne che contano nella storia greca.* Lanciano, Carabba: 184–207.

Harrison, T. 2002. *Divinity and History. The Religion of Herodotus.* Second edition, Oxford, Oxford University Press.

———— 2015. 'Review Article: Beyond the *Polis*? New Approaches to Greek Religion', *JHS* 135: 165–80.

Hartmann, A. 2010. *Zwischen Relikt und Reliquie. Objektbezogene Erinnerungspraktiken in antiken Gesellschaften.* Berlin, Verlag Antike.

Hartmann, A.-M. 2018. *English Mythography in its European Context, 1500–1650.* Oxford, Oxford University Press.

Hawes, G. 2014. *Rationalizing Myth in Antiquity.* Oxford, Oxford University Press.

———— (ed.) 2017. *Myths on the Map. The Storied Landscape of Ancient Greece.* Oxford, Oxford University Press.

Hawke, J. 2011. *Writing Authority. Elite Competition and Written Law in Early Greece.* DeKalb, IL, Northern Illinois University.

Heath, J. 2011. 'Women's Work: Female Transmission of Mythical Narrative', *TAPA* 141: 69–104.

———— 2017. 'Corinna's "Old Wives' Tales"', *HSCP* 109: 83–130.

Hedreen, G. M. 1992. *Silens in Attic Black-Figure Vase-Painting. Myth and Performance.* Ann Arbor, MI, University of Michigan Press.

Heinemann, A. 2006. 'Chous', in *ThesCRA* V: 351–4.

———— 2016. *Der* Gott des Gelages. Dionysos, Satyrn und Mänaden auf attischem Trinkgeschirr des 5. Jahrhunderts v. Chr. Berlin and Boston, MA, De Gruyter.

Hellmann, M.-C. 1993. 'Les ouvertures des toits ou retour sur le temple hypèthre', *RA* n.s. 1: 73–90.

────── 2006. *L'architecture grecque*, vol. 2. Paris, Picard.

Henrichs, A. 1975. 'Two Doxographical Notes: Democritus and Prodicus on Religion', *HSCP* 79: 93–123.

────── 1976. 'The Atheism of Prodicus', *CErc* 6: 15–21.

────── 1982. 'Changing Dionysiac Identities', in B. Meyer and E. Sanders (eds.), *Jewish and Christian Self-Definition*, vol. 3: *Self-Definition in the Greco-Roman World*. London, SCM Press: 137–60, 213–36.

────── 1984a. 'Loss of Self, Suffering, Violence: The Modern View of Dionysus from Nietzsche to Girard', *HSCP* 88: 205–40.

────── 1984b. 'The Sophists and Hellenistic Religion: Prodicus as the Spiritual Father of the Isis Aretalogies', *HSCP* 88: 139–58.

────── 1985. '"Der Glaube der Hellenen": Religionsgeschichte als Glaubensbekenntnis und Kulturkritik', in W. M. Calder III, H. Flashar, and T. Lindken (eds.), *Wilamowitz nach 50 Jahren*. Darmstadt, Wissenschaftliche Buchgesellschaft: 262–305.

────── 1988. 'Three Approaches to Greek Mythography', in Bremmer 1988a: 242–77.

────── 1990. 'Between Country and City: Cultic Dimensions of Dionysus in Athens and Attica', in M. Griffith and D. Mastronarde (eds.), *Cabinet of the Muses*. Atlanta, GA, Scholars Press: 257–77.

────── 1993. '"He has a god in him": Human and Divine in the Modern View of Dionysus', in Carpenter and Faraone 1993: 13–43.

────── 1994. 'Der rasende Gott: zur Psychologie des Dionysos und des Dionysischen in Mythos und Literatur', *A&A* 40: 31–58.

────── 1996a. 'Dancing in Athens, Dancing on Delos: Some Patterns of Choral Projection in Euripides', *Philologus* 140: 48–62.

────── 1996b. '*Warum soll ich denn tanzen?' Dionysisches im Chor der griechischen Tragödie*. Stuttgart, Teubner.

────── 2003. '*Hieroi Logoi* and *Hierai Bibloi*: The (Un)written Margins of the Sacred in Ancient Greece', *HSCP* 101: 207–66.

────── 2011. 'Dionysos Dismembered and Restored to Life: The Earliest Evidence (*OF* 59 I–II)', in Herrero de Jáuregui et al. 2011: 59–66.

────── 2013. 'Dionysos: One or Many?', in Bernabé et al. 2013: 554–82.

────── 2019. *Greek Myth and Religion. Collected Papers II*. Berlin and Boston, MA, de Gruyter.

Herda, A. 2006. *Der Apollon-Delphinios-Kult in Milet und die Neujahrsprozession nach Didyma*. Mainz, Von Zabern.

Hermary, A. 1986. 'Divinités chypriotes II', *RDAC*: 164–72.

────── and Masson, O. 1990. 'Deux vases inscrits du sanctuaire d'Aphrodite à Amathunte', *BCH* 114: 187–214.

──────, Leguilloux, M., Chankowski, V., and Petropoulou, A. 2004. 'Les sacrifices dans le monde grec', in *ThesCRA* I: 59–134.

Herrero de Jáuregui, M. 2010. 'Orphic God(s): Theogonies and Hymns as Vehicles of Monotheism', in S. Mitchell and P. Van Nuffelen (eds.), *Monotheism between Pagans and Christians in Late Antiquity*. Leuven, Peeters: 77–99.

———, Jiménez San Cristóbal, A. I., Santamaría Álvarez, M. A., Martín Hernández, R., Luján Martínez, E. R., and Torallas Tovar, S. (eds.) 2011. *Tracing Orpheus. Studies of Orphic Fragments*. Berlin and Boston, MA, De Gruyter.

Heubeck, A. and Hoekstra, A. 1989. *A Commentary on Homer's Odyssey. Volume 2. Books IX–XVI*. Oxford, Clarendon Press.

Hiltebeitel, A. 1988. 'South Indian Gardens of Adonis Revisited', in K. Schipper and A. M. Blondeau (eds.), *Essais sur le rituel*. 2 vols, Louvain and Paris, Peeters: i.65–91.

Hitch, S. and Rutherford, I. (eds.) 2017. *Animal Sacrifice in the Ancient Greek World*. Cambridge, Cambridge University Press.

Hodske, J. 2007. *Mythologische Bildthemen in den Häusern Pompejis. Die Bedeutung der zentralen Mythenbilder für die Bewohner Pompejis*. Ruhpolding, Franz Philipp Rutzen.

Hoekstra, A. 1981. *Epic Verse before Homer. Three Studies*. Amsterdam, North-Holland.

Holes, C. 2004. 'Arabian Gulf ḥiyya biyya, Jewish Babylonian farfisa, Christian Sicilian sepolcri: Popular Customs with a Common Origin', *Journal of Semitic Studies* 49: 275–87.

Hölkeskamp, K.-J. 1992. 'Written Law in Archaic Greece', *PCPhS* 38: 87–117.

Holloway, R. R. 1992. 'Why Korai?', *OJA* 11: 267–74.

Hölscher, F. 2017. *Die Macht der Gottheit im Bild. Archäologische Studien zur griechischen Götterstatue*. Heidelberg, Verlag Antike.

Hornblower, S. 1991–2009. *A Commentary on Thucydides*. 3 vols, Oxford, Clarendon Press and Oxford University Press.

——— 2010. *Thucydidean Themes*. Oxford, Oxford University Press.

——— 2014. 'Lykophron and Epigraphy: The Value and Function of Cult Epithets in the *Alexandra*', *CQ* 64: 91–120.

Horster, M. 2004. *Landbesitz griechischer Heiligtümer in archaischer und klassischer Zeit*. Berlin and New York, De Gruyter.

——— 2010. 'Religious Landscape and Sacred Ground: Relationships between Space and Cult in the Greek World', *RHR* 227: 435–58.

——— and Klöckner, A. (eds.) 2012. *Civic Priests. Cult Personnel in Athens from the Hellenistic Period to Late Antiquity*. Berlin and Boston, MA, De Gruyter.

Hughes, J. 2017. *Votive Body Parts in Greek and Roman Religion*. Cambridge, Cambridge University Press.

Humphreys, S. C. 2004. *The Strangeness of Gods. Historical Perspectives on the Interpretation of Athenian Religion*. Oxford, Oxford University Press.
———— 2018. *Kinship in Ancient Athens*. 2 vols, Oxford, .
Hunter, R. and Laemmle, R. 2020. 'Pulling Apollo Apart', *Mnemosyne* 4th ser. 73: 377–404.
Icard-Gianolio, N. 2004. 'Statues enchaînées', in *ThesCRA* II: 468–71.
Işik, C. 2000. 'Demeter at Kaunos', in *Αγαθός δαίμων. Mythes et cultes. Études d'iconographie en l'honneur de Lilly Kahil*. Athens, École française d'Athènes: 229–40.

Jackson, P. 2006. *The Transformations of Helen. Indo-European Myth and the Roots of the Trojan Cycle*. Dettelbach, J. H. Röll.
Jaillard, D. 2007. *Configurations d'Hermès. Une 'théogonie hermaïque'*. Liège, Presses universitaires de Liège.
Jameson, M. H. 2014. *Cults and Rites in Ancient Greece. Essays on Religion and Society*. Cambridge, Cambridge University Press.
Jamme, C. 1995. *Introduction à la philosophie du mythe, vol. 2. Époque moderne et contemporaine*. Paris, J. Vrin.
Janko, R. 1984. 'Forgetfulness in the Golden Tablets of Memory', *CQ* 34: 89–100.
———— 1992. *The Iliad. A Commentary. Volume 4, Books 13–16*. Cambridge, Cambridge University Press.
Jim, T. S. F. 2014. *Sharing with the Gods. Aparchai and Dekatai in Ancient Greece*. Oxford, Oxford University Press.
Jiménez San Cristóbal, A. I. 2009. 'The Meaning of βάκχος and βακχεύειν in Orphism', in G. Casadio and P. A. Johnston (eds.), *Mystic Cults in Magna Graecia*. Austin, TX, University of Texas Press: 46–60.
Johnston, A. 1993. 'Aegina: Aphaia Tempel 17: The Laconian Pottery. Appendix on the Graffito on B 11', *AA*: 597–8.
Johnston, S. 1991. 'Crossroads', *ZPE* 88: 217–24.
———— 2008. *Ancient Greek Divination*. Oxford, Wiley-Blackwell.
———— 2018. *The Story of Myth*. Cambridge, MA, Harvard University Press.
Jones, C. P. 2010. *New Heroes in Antiquity. From Achilles to Antinoos*. Cambridge, MA, Harvard University Press.
Jordan, B. and Perlin, J. 1984. 'On the Protection of Sacred Groves', in *Studies Presented to Sterling Dow on His Eightieth Birthday*. Durham, NC, Duke University Press: 153–9.
Jost, M. 1985. *Sanctuaries et cultes d'Arcadie*. Paris, J. Vrin.
———— 1992. *Aspects de la vie religieuse en Grèce*. Second edition, Paris, SEDES.
Jouan, F. 1990–1. 'Comment partir en guerre en Grèce antique en ayant les dieux pour soi', *Revue de la Société Ernest Renan* 40: 25–42.

Jubier-Galinier, C. 2012. 'Athéna et Poséidon en conflit: adaptations céramiques à l'ombre de l'Acropole', in H. Ménard, P. Sauzeau, and J.-F. Thomas (eds.), *La pomme d'Eris, le conflit et sa représentation dans l'antiquité*. Montpellier, Presses universitaires de la Mediterranée: 273–94.

Jung, H. 1982. *Thronende und sitzende Götter. Zum griechischen Götterbild und Menschenideal in geometrischer und früharchaischer Zeit*. Bonn, Habelt.

Junker, K. 1993. *Der ältere Tempel im Heraion am Sele. Verzierte Metopen im architektonischen Kontext*. Cologne, Böhlau.

———— 2012. *Interpreting the Images of Greek Myths. An Introduction*. Translated by A. Künzl-Snodgrass and A. Snodgrass. Cambridge, Cambridge University Press.

Kahil, L. 1988. 'Helene', in *LIMC* IV.1: 498–563.

Kaizer, T. 2011. 'Interpretations of the Myth of Andromeda at Iope', *Syria* 88: 323–39.

Kaltsas, N. and Shapiro, A. (eds.) 2008. *Worshiping Women. Ritual and Reality in Classical Athens*. New York, Alexander S. Onassis Public Benefit Foundation.

Kaminski, G. 1991. 'Thesauros: Untersuchungen zum antiken Opferstock', *JDAI* 106: 63–181.

Kannicht, R. 1992. 'Antigone Bacchans', in H. Froning, T. Hölscher, and H. Mielsch (eds.), *Kotinos. Festschrift für Erika Simon*. Mainz, P. von Zabern: 252–5.

Kaplan, P. 2006. 'Dedications to Greek Sanctuaries by Foreign Kings in the Eighth through Sixth Centuries bce', *Historia* 55: 129–52.

Kapparis, K. A. (ed. and trans.) 1999. *Apollodoros 'Against Neaira' [D 59]*. Berlin, De Gruyter.

Käppel, L. 1992. *Paian. Studien zur Geschichte einer Gattung*. Berlin and New York, De Gruyter.

Karatas, A. M. S. 2019. 'Key-Bearers of Greek Temples: The Temple Key as a Symbol of Priestly Authority', *Mythos* 13, https://doi.org/10.4000/mythos.1219.

Karavas, O. 2018. 'Le procès et l'exécution de Socrate chez trois auteurs de l'époque impériale', *Mouseion*, 3rd ser. 15: 369–88.

Kassel, R. and Austin, C. 1991. *Poetae comici Graeci*, vol. 2. Berlin and New York, De Gruyter.

Katalis, S. E. 1990. 'Inachos', in *LIMC* V.1: 653–4.

Kavoulaki, A. 1999. 'Processional Performance and the Democratic Polis', in S. Goldhill and R. Osborne (eds.), *Performance Culture and Athenian Democracy*. Cambridge, Cambridge University Press: 293–320.

Kearns, E. 1989. *The Heroes of Attica*. London, University of London, Institute of Classical Studies.

—— 1992. 'Between God and Man: Status and Function of Heroes and Their Sanctuaries', in Schachter 1992b: 65–99.

Kerschner, M. 2006. 'Lydische Weihungen in griechischen Heiligtümer', in A. Naso (ed.), *Stranieri e non cittadini nei santuari greci*. Florence, Monnier università: 253–9.

Kilian-Dirlmeier, I. 1985. 'Fremde Weihungen in griechischen Heiligtümern von 8. bis zum Beginn des 7. Jahrhunderts', *JRGZ* 32: 215–54.

Kindt, J. 2012. *Rethinking Greek Religion*. Cambridge, Cambridge University Press.

—— 2015. 'Personal Religion: A Productive Category for the Study of Ancient Greek Religion?', *JHS* 135: 35–50.

—— 2016. *Revisiting Delphi. Religion and Storytelling in Ancient Greece*. Cambridge, Cambridge University Press.

—— 2019. 'Animals in Ancient Greek Religion: Divine Zoomorphism and the Anthropomorphic Divine Body', in Scheer 2019: 155–70.

—— (ed.) 2020. *Animals in Ancient Greek Religion*. London and New York, Routledge.

Kirk, G. S. (ed. and trans.) 1970. *Euripides. The Bacchae*. Englewood Cliffs, NJ, Prentice-Hall.

Kleibrink, M. 2017. 'Architettura e rituale nell'Athenaion di Lagaria: Timpone della Motta (Francavilla Marittima)', *ASMG*, 5th ser. 2: 171–233.

Klinger, S. 2009. 'Women and Deer: From Athens to Corinth and Back', in J. H. Oakley and O. Palagia (eds.), *Athenian Potters and Painters II*. Oxford, Oxbow Books: 100–7.

Klöckner, A. 2002. 'Habitus und Status: Geschlechtsspezifisches Rollenverhalten auf griechischen Weihreliefs', in F. Zimmer et al. (eds.), *Die griechische Klassik. Idee oder Wirklichkeit*. Mainz, Philipp von Zabern: 321–30.

—— 2005. 'Mordende Mütter: Medea, Prokne und das Motiv der furchtbaren Rache im klassischen Athen', in G. Fischer and S. Moraw (eds.), *Die andere Seite der Klassik. Gewalt im 5. und 4. Jahrhundert v. Chr.* Stuttgart, Franz Steiner: 247–24.

—— 2006. 'Votive als Gegenstände des Rituals – Votive als Bilder von Ritualen: das Beispiel der griechischen Weihreliefs', in J. Mylonopoulos and H. Roeder (eds.), *Archäologie und Ritual. Auf der Suche nach der rituellen Handlung in den antiken Kulturen Ägyptens und Griechenlands*. Vienna, Phoibos: 139–52.

—— 2008. 'Hera und Demeter: die Mütter', in Grassinger, de Oliveira Pinto, and Scholl 2008: 128–37.

―――― 2010. 'Getting in Contact: Concepts of Human–Divine Encounter in Classical Greek Art', in Bremmer and Erskine 2010: 106–25.

―――― 2017. 'Visualising Veneration? Images of Sacrifice on Greek Votive Reliefs', in Hitch and Rutherford 2017: 200–22.

Knell, H. 1990. *Mythos und Polis. Bildprogramme griecher Bauskulptur*. Darmstadt, Wissenschaftliche Buchgesellschaft.

Koehl, R. B. 1997. 'The Villas of Ayia Triada and Nirou Chani and the Origin of the Cretan *andreion*', in R. Hägg (ed.), *The Function of the 'Minoan Villa'*. Stockholm, Svenska Institutet i Athen: 137–47.

Konaris, M. 2016. *The Greek Gods in Modern Scholarship. Interpretation and Belief in Nineteenth- and Early Twentieth-Century Germany and Britain*. Oxford, Oxford University Press.

Korn, U. 1992. 'Frauenfeste in Demeterheiligtümern: das Thesmophorion von Bitalemi', *AA*: 611–50.

Kosmetatou, E. 2003. '"Taboo" Objects in Attic Inventory Lists', *Glotta* 79: 66–82.

Kossatz-Deissman, A. 1981. 'Achilleus', in *LIMC* I.1: nos. 206–388.

―――― 1997. 'Troilos', in *LIMC* VIII.1: 92–4.

―――― 1991. 'Satyr- und Mänadennamen auf Vasenbildern', in *Greek Vases in the J. Paul Getty Museum*, vol. 5. Malibu, CA, J. Paul Getty Museum: 131–99.

Kosso, C. and Lawton, K. 2009. 'Women at the Fountain and the Well: Imagining Experience', in C. Kosso and A. Scott (eds.), *The Nature and Function of Water, Baths, Bathing, and Hygiene from Antiquity to the Renaissance*. Leiden and Boston, MA, Brill: 87–108.

Kotsidu, H. 1991. *Die musischen Agone in archaischer und klassischer Zeit. Eine historisch-archäologische Untersuchung*. Munich, Tuduv.

Kotwick, M. E. (ed. and trans.) 2017. *Der Papyrus von Derveni*. Berlin, De Gruyter.

Kouremenos, T., Parássoglou, G. M., and Tsantsanoglou, K. (eds.) 2006. *The Derveni Papyrus*. Florence, L. S. Olschki.

Kousser, R. 2015. 'The Mutilation of the Herms: Violence toward Sculptures in the Late Fifth Century BC', in M. M. Miles (ed.), *Autopsy in Athens. Recent Archaeological Research on Athens and Attica*. Oxford, Oxbow Books: 76–84.

Kowalzig, B. 2007. *Singing for the Gods. Performances of Myth and Ritual in Archaic and Classical Greece*. Oxford, Oxford University Press.

Krauss, W. 1989. 'Fontenelle und die Aufklärung', in B. de Fontenelle, *Philosophische Neuigkeiten für Leute von Welt und für Gelehrte*, ed. H. Bergmann. Leipzig, Reclam: 371–439.

Krentz, P. 1991. 'The Salpinx in Greek Warfare', in V. D. Hanson (ed.), *Hoplites. The Classical Greek Battle Experience*. London, Routledge: 110–20.

Kreutz, N. 2007. *Zeus und die griechischen Poleis. Topographische und religionsgeschichtliche Untersuchungen von archaischer bis in hellenistische Zeit*. Rahden, Verlag Marie Leidorf.

Kreuzer, B. 2010a. '…ἐν Ἀθήναις δὲ γλαῦκας…: Eulen in der Bilderwelt Athens', *JÖAI* 79: 119–78.

——— 2010b. 'Eulen aus Athen: 520–480 v. Chr.', in C. Weiss and E. Simon (eds.), *Folia in memoriam Ruth Lindner collecta*. Dettelbach, Röll: 66–83.

Kron, U. 1988. 'Kultmahle im Heraion von Samos archaischer Zeit', in Hägg *et al*. 1988: 135–47.

——— 1996. 'Priesthoods, Dedications and Euergetism: What Part Did Religion Play in the Political and Social Status of Greek Women?', in P. Hellström and B. Alroth (eds.), *Religion and Power in the Ancient Greek World*. Uppsala, Acta Universitatis Upsaliensis: 139–82.

Krumeich, R. 1991. 'Zu den goldenen Dreifüsse der Deinomeniden in Delphi', *JDAI* 106: 37–62.

——— 2008. 'Vom Haus der Gottheit zum Museum? Zu Ausstattung und Funktion des Heraion von Olympia und des Athenatempels von Lindos', *AK* 51: 73–95.

Kubatzki, J. 2018. 'Processions and Pilgrimage in Ancient Greece: Some Iconographical Considerations', in U. Luig (ed.), *Approaching the Sacred. Pilgrimage in Historical and Intercultural Perspective*. Berlin, Edition Topoi: 129–57.

Laferrière, C. M. 2019. 'Sacred Sounds: The Cult of Pan and the Nymphs in the Vari Cave', *ClAnt* 38: 185–216.

Lambert, S. 2010. 'A Polis and Its Priests: Athenian Priesthoods before and after Pericles' Citizenship Law', *Historia* 59: 143–75.

——— 2021. 'On the Conveyance of the Sacred Objects for the Eleusinian Mysteries: An Archaising Athenian Assembly Decree of the Third Century AD', in E. Mackil and N. Papazarkadas (eds.), *Greek Epigraphy and Religion. Papers in Memory of Sara B. Aleshire from the Second North American Congress of Greek and Latin Epigraphy*. Leiden and Boston, MA, Brill: 90–107.

Lang, F. 2016. 'Felsen und Steine: Mutmaßungen über an-ikonische Kultstätten in Akarnanien', in M. Giannopoulou and C. Kallini (eds.), *Ηχάδιν 1. Τιμητικός τόμος για τη Στέλλα Δρούγου*. Athens, Tameiou Archaiologikon Poron kai Apallotrioseon: 738–58.

Langdon, M. 2000. 'Mountains in Greek Religion', *CW* 93: 461–70.

Lardinois, A. 1989. 'Lesbian Sappho and Sappho of Lesbos', in J. N. Bremmer (ed.), *From Sappho to De Sade. Moments in the History of Sexuality*. London and New York, Routledge: 15–35.

——— 1992. 'Greek Myths for Athenian Rituals', *GRBS* 33: 313–27.

──── 2010. 'Lesbian Sappho Revisited', in J. Dijkstra, J. Kroesen, and Y. Kuiper (eds.), *Myths, Martyrs and Modernity. Studies in the History of Religions in Honour of Jan N. Bremmer.* Leiden and Boston, MA, Brill: 13–30.

Larson, J. 1995. *Greek Heroine Cults.* Madison, WI, University of Wisconsin Press.

──── 2001. *Greek Nymphs. Myth, Cult, Lore.* Oxford, Oxford University Press.

──── 2016. *Understanding Greek Religion. A Cognitive Approach.* London and New York, Routledge.

Lattanzi, E. 1991. 'Recenti scoperte nei santuari di Hera Lacinia a Crotone e di Apollo Aleo a Ciro Marina', in *Cahiers du Centre Jean Bérard* 16: 67–73.

Laurens, A.-F. and Lissarrague, F. 1990. 'Entre dieux', *Metis* 5: 53–73.

Laxander, H. 2000. *Individuum und Gemeinschaft im Fest. Untersuchungen zu attischen Darstellungen von Festgeschehen im 6. und frühen 5. Jahrhundert v. Chr..* Münster, Scriptorium.

Lazzarini, M. L. 1989–90. 'Iscrizioni votive greche', *Scienze dell'Antichità* 3–4: 845–59.

Le Roy Ladurie, E. 1979. *Le carnaval de Romans. De la Chandeleur au mercredi des Cendres, 1579–1580.* Paris, Gallimard.

Lebreton, S. 2015. 'Zeus Polieus à Athènes: les Bouphonies et au-delà', *Kernos* 28: 85–110.

Lefkowitz, M. R. 2016. *Euripides and the Gods.* New York, Oxford University Press.

Lehmann, Y. 1997. *L'hymne antique et son public.* Turnhout, Brepols.

Lemos, I. S. and Tsingarida, A. (eds.) 2019. *Beyond the Polis. Rituals, Rites, and Cults in Early and Archaic Greece (12th–6th Centuries BC).* Brussels, CReA-Patrimoine.

Leschhorn, W. 1984. *Gründer der Stadt. Studien zu einem politisch-religiösen Phänomen der griechischen Geschichte.* Stuttgart, Franz Steiner.

Leventis, I. 2019. 'Godlike Images: Priestesses in Greek Sculpture', in R. Morais, D. Leão Ferreira, and D. Rodriguez Pérez (eds.), *Greek Art in Motion.* Oxford, Archaeopress: 69–77.

Leypold, C. 2008. *Bankettgebäude in griechischen Heiligtümern.* Wiesbaden, Reichert.

Linant de Bellefonds, P., et al. 2004. 'Rites et activités relatifs aux images de culte', in *ThesCRA* II: 417–507.

Lindner, R. 2003. 'Priesterinnen: Bildzeugnisse zum griechischen Götterkult', in E. Klinger, S. Böhm, and T. Franz (eds.), *Geschlechterdifferenz, Ritual und Religion.* Würzburg, Echter: 53–66.

Lindström, G. and Pilz, O. 2013. 'Votivspektren in Heiligtümern', in Gerlach and Raue 2013: 267–74.

Link, S. 2009. 'Education and Pederasty in Spartan and Cretan society', in S. Hodkinson (ed.), *Sparta. Comparative Approaches*. Swansea, Classical Press of Wales: 89–111.

Lippolis, E., Vannicelli, P., and Parisi, V. (eds.) 2018. *Il sacrificio. Forme rituali, linguaggi e strutture sociali*. Rome: Edizioni Quasar.

Lissarrague, F. 1990. 'The Sexual Life of Satyrs', in D. M. Halperin, J. J. Winkler, and F. I. Zeitlin (eds.), *Before Sexuality. The Construction of Erotic Experience in the Ancient Greek World*. Princeton, NJ, Princeton University Press: 53–81.

———— 1992. 'Figures of Women', in P. Schmitt Pantel (ed.), *A History of Women in the West*, vol. 1: *From Ancient Goddesses to Christian Saints*. Cambridge, MA, and London, Belknap Press: 139–229.

Lloyd-Jones, H. 1982. *Blood for the Ghosts*. London, Duckworth.

———— 1983. *The Justice of Zeus*. Second edition, Berkeley, CA, University of California Press.

———— 1990. *Greek Epic, Lyric, and Tragedy*. Oxford, Clarendon Press.

López-Ruiz, C. 2010. *When the Gods Were Born. Greek Cosmogonies and the Near East*. Cambridge, MA, and London, Harvard University Press.

Loraux, N. 1992. 'What is a Goddess?', in P. Schmitt Pantel (ed.), *A History of Women in the West*, vol. 1: *From Ancient Goddesses to Christian Saints*. Cambridge, MA, and London, Belknap Press: 11–44.

Lorenz, K. 2008. *Bilder machen Räume. Mythenbilder in pompeianischen Häusern*. Berlin and New York, De Gruyter.

Lyons, D. 1997. *Gender and Immortality. Heroines in Ancient Greek Myth and Cult*. Princeton, NJ, Princeton University Press.

Ma, J. 2008. 'The Return of the Black Hunter', *Cambridge Classical Journal* 54: 188–208.

Mackin Roberts, E. 2019. 'Weaving for Athena: The *Arrhephoroi* and Mundane Acts of Religious Devotion', *Journal of Hellenic Religion* 12: 61–84.

———— 2020. *Underworld Gods in Ancient Greek Religion. Death and Reciprocity*. London and New York, Routledge.

Macris, C. 2018. 'Pythagore de Samos', in R. Goulet (ed.), *Dictionnaire des philosophes antiques VII*. Paris, CNRS: 681–850 and Annexe II, 1025–1174.

Malkin, I. 1987. *Religion and Colonization in Ancient Greece*. Leiden, Brill.

———— 2009. 'Foundations', in K. Raaflaub and H. van Wees (eds.), *A Companion to Archaic Greece*. Chichester and Malden, MA, Wiley-Blackwell: 373–94.

Manfrini, I. 1992. 'Femmes à la fontaine: réalité et imaginaire', in Bron and Kassapoglou 1992: 127–48.

Mansfeld, J. 1992. *Heresiography in Context. Hippolytus' Elenchos as a Source of Greek Philosophy*. Leiden, Brill.

Mantis, A. G. 1990. *Problemata tes eikonographias ton iereion kai ton iereon sten archaia Ellenike techne*. Athens, Tameio Archaiologikon Poron kai Apallotrioseon.

March, J. 1987. *The Creative Poet. Studies on the Treatment of Myths in Greek Poetry*. London, University of London, Institute of Classical Studies.

———— 1989. 'Euripides' Bakchai: A Reconsideration in the Light of Vase Paintings', *BICS* 36: 33–66.

Marcos Macedo, J. 2017. 'Noun Apposition in Greek Religious Language: A Linguistic Account', in P. Poccetti and F. Logozzo (eds.), *Ancient Greek Linguistics. New Approaches, Insights, Perspectives*. Berlin and Boston, MA, 2017, De Gruyter: 565–79.

———— 2017. 'Zeus as (Rider of) Thunderbolt: A Brief Remark on Some of His Epithets', *HSCP* 109: 1–30.

Marinatos, N. 1993. *Minoan Religion. Ritual, Image, and Symbol*. Columbia, SC, University of South Carolina Press.

Markschies, C. 2019. *God's Body. Jewish, Christian, and Pagan Images of God*. Translated by A. J. Edmonds. Waco, TX, Baylor University Press.

Martin, G. 2009. *Divine Talk. Religious Argumentation in Demosthenes*. Oxford, Oxford University Press.

Martin, R. 1989. *The Language of Heroes. Speech and Performance in the Iliad*. Ithaca, NY, Cornell University Press.

Martini, W. 1990. *Die archaische Plastik der Griechen*. Darmstadt, Wissenschaftliche Buchgesellschaft.

———— 2013. 'Die visuelle Präsenz der Amazonen in Athen im 6. und 5 Jh. v. Chr.', in C. Schubert and A. Weiss (eds.), *Amazonen zwischen Griechen und Skythen. Gegenbilder in Mythos und Geschichte*. Berlin and Boston, MA, De Gruyter: 171–84.

Massetti, L. 2019. '*Phraseologie und indogermanische Dichtersprache in der Sprache der griechischen Chorlyrik: Pindar und Bakchylides*', PhD thesis, University of Cologne, http://nrs.harvard.edu/urn-3:hul.ebook:CHS_MassettiL.Phraseologie_und_indogermanische_Dichtersprache.2019.

Masson, O. 1990. *Onomastica Graeca selecta*, vol. 2. Paris, Université de Paris X.

Mattern, T. 2007. 'Griechische Kultbildschranken', *Athenische Mitteilungen* 122: 139–59.

Maxmin, J. 1975. 'Meniskoi and the Birds', *JHS* 95: 175–80.

Mazarakis Ainian, A. 2016. 'Early Greek Temples', in M. M. Miles (ed.), *A Companion to Greek Architecture*. Chichester, Wiley-Blackwell: 15–30.

Mazarakis Ainian, A. (ed.) 2017. *Les sanctuaires archaïques des Cyclades.* Rennes, Presses universitaires de Rennes.

McGlashan, V. 2021 (forthcoming). 'The Bacchants are Silent: Using Cognitive Science to Explore Ancient Religious Experience', in E. Eidinow, A. W. Geertz, and J. North (eds.), *Cognitive Approaches to Ancient Religious Experience.* Cambridge, Cambridge University Press.

McInerney, J. 2014. 'Bouphonia: Killing Cattle on the Acropolis', in A. Gardeisen and C. Chandezon (eds.), *Équidés et bovidés de la Méditerranée antique. Rites et combats. Jeux et savoirs.* Lattes, Éditions de l'Association pour le développement de l'archéologie en Languedoc-Roussillon: 113–24.

McLardy, K. R. L. 2015. 'The Megara of the Thesmophoria: Reconciling the Textual and Archaeological Records', *Chronika* 5: 1–8.

McPhee, I. 1992. 'Kallisto', in *LIMC* VI.1: 940–4.

Meert, A. 2017. '*Positive Atheism in Antiquity: A Social and Philosophical Analysis (500 BC–200 AD)*'. PhD thesis, Ghent University.

Mehl, V. 2018. 'Atmosphère olfactive et festive du sanctuaire grec: l'odeur du divin', *Pallas* 106: 85–103.

—— and Brulé, P. eds. 2008. *Le sacrifice antique. Vestiges, procédures et stratégies.* Rennes: Presses universitaires de Rennes.

Meineck, P., Short, W. M., and Devereaux, J. (eds.) 2019. *The Routledge Handbook of Classics and Cognitive Theory.* London and New York, Routledge.

Meissner, T. 2013. Review of Beekes 2010. *Kratylos* 58: 1–32.

Merthen, C. 2014. 'Mädchen als Teil der Totenklage: aus Sicht der griechischen Vasenbilder vom 8. bis zum 5. Jahrhundert v. Chr.', in Moraw and Kieburg 2014: 149–70.

Meuli, K. 1975. *Gesammelte Schriften.* 2 vols, Basel, Schwabe.

Meyer, M. 2007. 'Athena und die Mädchen: zu den Koren auf der Athener Akropolis', in M. Meyer and N. Brüggemann (eds.), *Kore und Kouros. Weihegaben für die Götter.* Vienna, Phoibos: 13–89.

—— 2010. 'Heldinnen in Aktion: zur Problematik weiblicher Vorbilder und Identifikationsfiguren', in M. Meyer and R. von den Hoff (eds.), *Helden wie sie. Übermensch – Vorbild – Kultfigur in der griechischen Antike.* Freiburg, Rombach: 107–35.

—— 2014. 'Was ist ein Mädchen? Der Blick auf die weibliche Jugend im klassischen Athen', in Moraw and Kieburg 2014: 221–36.

—— 2017. *Athena, Göttin von Athen. Kult und Mythos auf der Akropolis bis in klassische Zeit.* Vienna, Phoibos.

—— 2019. 'Friede in der Bilderwelt der Griechen', in G. Althoff, E.-B. Krems, C. Meier, and H.-U. Thamer (eds.), *Frieden. Theorien, Bilder, Strategien von der Antike bis zur Gegenwart.* Dresden, Michel Sandstein: 59–85.

Migeotte, L. 2006. 'L'endettement des cités grecques dans l'antiquité', in J. Andreau, G. Béaur, and J.-Y. Grenier (eds.), *La dette publique dans l'histoire*. Paris, Comité pour l'histoire économique et financière de la France: 115–28.

Miguel, C. 1992. 'Images d'Hermès', in Bron and Kassapoglou 1992: 13–23.

Mikalson, J. D. 1982. 'The *Heorte* of Heortology', *GRBS* 23: 213–21.

––––– 1983. *Athenian Popular Religion*. Chapel Hill, NC, and London, University of North Carolina Press.

––––– 1989. 'Unanswered Prayers in Greek Tragedy', *JHS* 109: 81–98.

––––– 1998. *Religion in Hellenistic Athens*. Berkeley, CA, University of California Press.

––––– 1991. *Honor Thy Gods. Popular Religion in Greek Tragedy*. Chapel Hill, NC, and London, University of North Carolina Press.

Miles, M. M. 2012. 'Entering Demeter's Gateway', in B. Wescoat and R. Ousterhoust (eds.), *Architecture of the Sacred. Space, Ritual and Experience from Classical Greece to Byzantium*. Cambridge, Cambridge University Press: 114–51.

––––– 2016. 'The Interiors of Greek Temples', in M. M. Miles (ed.), *A Companion to Greek Architecture*. Chichester, Wiley-Blackwell: 206–22.

Mili, M. 2015. *Religion and Society in Ancient Thessaly*. Oxford, Oxford University Press.

Miller, M. C. 1992. 'The Parasol: An Oriental Status-Symbol in Late-Archaic and Classical Athens', *JHS* 112: 91–105.

Mirón, D. 2004–5 [2007]. 'The Heraia at Olympia: Gender and Peace', *AJAH* n.s. 3–4: 7–38.

Momigliano, A. 1984. *Settimo contributo alla storia degli studi classici e del mondo antico*. Rome, Edizioni di Storia e Letteratura.

Moraw, S. 1998. *Die Mänade in der attischen Vasenmalerei des 6. und 5. Jahrhunderts v. Chr. Rezeptionsästhetische Analyse eines antiken Weiblichkeitsentwurfs*. Mainz, P. von Zabern.

––––– and A. Kieburg (eds.) 2014. *Mädchen im Altertum / Girls in Antiquity*. Münster and New York, Waxmann.

Moreau, A. 1994. *Le mythe de Jason et Médée. Le va-nu-pied et la sorcière*. Paris, Belles Lettres.

Moret, J.-M. 1991. 'Circé tisseuse sur les vases du Cabirion', *RA* n.s. 2: 227–66.

––––– 1992. 'The Earliest Representations of the Infant Herakles and the Snakes', in B. K. Braswell, *A Commentary on Pindar Nemean One*. Fribourg, University Press Fribourg: 83–90.

Moretti, L. 1991. 'Dagli Heraia all'Aspis di Argo', in *Miscellanea greca e romana 16*. Rome, Istituto italiano per la storia antica: 179–89.

Morgan, C. 1990. *Athletes and Oracles. The Transformation of Olympia and Delphi in the Eighth Century bc*. Cambridge, Cambridge University Press.

Morgan, T. 2015. *Roman Faith and Christian Faith. Pistis and Fides in the Early Roman Empire and Early Churches*. Oxford, Oxford University Press.

Motte, A. 1973. *Prairies et jardins de la Grèce antique*. Brussels, Palais des Académies.

———— 1986. 'L'expression du sacré dans la religion grecque', in J. Ries (ed.), *L'expression du sacré dans les grandes religions, vol. 3: Mazdéisme, cultes isiaques, religion grecque, Manichéisme, Nouveau Testament, vie de l'homo religiosus*. Louvain-la-Neuve, Centre d'histoire des religions: 109–256.

Mulryan, J. and Brown, S. (ed. and trans.) 2006. *Natale Conti's Mythologiae*. 2 vols, Tempe, AZ, Arizona Center for Medieval and Renaissance Studies.

Muth, S. 1998. *Erleben von Raum, Leben im Raum. Zur Funktion mythologischer Mosaikbilder in der römisch-kaiserzeitlichen Wohnarchitektur*. Heidelberg, Verlag Archäologie und Geschichte.

Mylona, D. 2008. *Fish-Eating in Greece from the Fifth Century B.C. to the Seventh Century A.D. A Story of Impoverished Fishermen or Luxurious Fish Banquets?* Oxford, Archaeopress.

———— 2015. 'From Fish Bones to Fishermen: Views from the Sanctuary of Poseidon at Kalaureia', in D. C. Haggis and C. M. Antonaccio (eds.), *Classical Archaeology in Context. Theory and Practice in Excavation in the Greek World*. Berlin and Boston, MA, De Gruyter: 385–417.

Mylonopoulos, J. 2003. *Πελοπόννησος οἰκητήριον Ποσειδῶνος. Heiligtümer und Kulte des Poseidon auf der Peloponnes*. Liège, Centre international d'étude de la religion grecque antique.

———— 2008. '"Fremde" Weihungen in Heiligtümern der Ostägäis im 7. und 6. Jh. v. Chr.', in *Tagung Austausch von Gütern, Ideen und Technologien in der Ägäis und im östlichen Mittelmeer*. Weilheim, Verein zur Förderung der Aufarbeitung der Hellenischen Geschichte: 327–49.

———— 2008. 'Natur als Heiligtum: Natur im Heiligtum', *ARG* 10: 45–76.

———— (ed.) 2010. *Divine Images and Human Imaginations in Ancient Greece and Rome*. Leiden and Boston, MA, Brill.

———— 2011. 'Divine Images "Behind Bars": The Semantics of Barriers in Greek Temples', in M. Haysom and J. Wallensten (eds.), *Current Approaches to Religion in Ancient Greece*. Stockholm, Svenska institutet i Athen: 269–91.

Naerebout, F. G. 1997. *Attractive Performances. Ancient Greek Dance. Three Preliminary Studies.* Amsterdam, J. C. Gieben.

———— 2005. 'Territorialität und griechische Religion: die aufgeteilte Landschaft', in E. Olshausen and V. Sauer (eds.), *Die Landschaft und die Religion.* Stuttgart, Franz Steiner: 191–213.

———— and Beerden, K. 2012. '"Gods cannot tell lies": Riddling and Ancient Greek Divination', in J. Kwapisz, D. Petrain, and M. Szymański (eds.), *The Muse at Play. Riddles and Wordplay in Greek and Latin Poetry.* Berlin and Boston, MA, De Gruyter: 121–47.

Naiden, F. S. 2013. *Smoke Signals for the Gods. Ancient Greek Sacrifice from the Archaic through Roman Periods.* New York, Oxford University Press.

———— 2015. 'Sacrifice', in E. Eidinow and J. Kindt (eds.), *The Oxford Handbook of Ancient Greek Religion.* Oxford, Oxford University Press: 463–75.

———— 2016. 'Contagious Ἀσέβεια', *CQ* 66: 59–74.

Natale Conti 1567. *Mythologiae (sive explicationum fabularum libri X).* Second edition, Venice, repr. New York, Garland, 1976. (First edition 1551.)

Neils, J. 1990. 'Iason', in *LIMC* V.1: 629–38.

———— (ed.) 1992. *Goddess and Polis. The Panathenaic Festival in Ancient Athens.* Hanover, NH, Hood Museum of Art, and Princeton, NJ, Princeton University Press.

———— 2014. '"Bronze-belled braying": The Salpinx in Athenian Art', in P. Valavanis and E. Manakidou (eds.), *Essays on Greek Pottery and Iconography in Honour of Professor Michalis Tiverios.* Thessaloniki, University Studio Press: 257–70.

———— and Oakley, J. H. (eds.) 2003. *Coming of Age in Ancient Greece. Images of Childhood from the Classical Past.* New Haven, CT, Yale University Press.

Nenci, G. 1993. 'I donativi di Creso a Delfi', *ASNP* 3rd ser. 23: 319–31.

Nering, K. 2015. *Schatzhäuser in griechischen Heiligtümern.* Rahden, Verlag Marie Leidorf.

Nesselrath, H.-G. 2013. 'Triptolemos: ein mythischer Kulturheld im Wandel der Zeiten', in A. Zgoll and R. G. Kratz (eds.), *Arbeit am Mythos. Leistung und Grenze des Mythos in Antike und Gegenwart.* Tübingen, Mohr Siebeck: 195–216.

———— 2020. 'Zum Hades und darüber hinaus: mythische griechische Vorstellungen zum Weg des Menschen über den Tod ins Jenseits von Homer bis Platon', in A. Zgoll and C. Zgoll (eds.), *Mythische Sphärenwechsel. Methodisch neue Zugänge zu antiken Mythen in Orient und Okzident.* Berlin and Boston, MA, De Gruyter: 161–212.

Nicgorski, A.M. 2004. 'Interlaced Fingers and Knotted Limbs: The Hostile Posture of Quarrelsome Ares on the Parthenon Frieze', in A. P. Chapin (ed.), *Charis. Essays in Honor of Sara A. Immerwahr*. Princeton, NJ, American School of Classical Studies at Athens: 291–303.

Nilsson, M. P. 1967. *Geschichte der griechischen Religion*, vol. 1: *Die Religion Griechenlands bis auf die griechische Weltherrschaft*. Third edition, Munich, Beck.

Nisoli, A. 2003. 'Defixiones politiche e vittime ilustri: l caso della defixio di Focione', *Acme* 56: 271–86.

Nissinen, M. 2017. *Ancient Prophecy. Near Eastern, Biblical, and Greek Perspectives*. Oxford, Oxford University Press.

Nobili, C. 2014. 'Performances of Girls at the Spartan Festival of the Hyakinthia', in Moraw and Kieburg 2014: 135–48.

Noel, D. 1999. 'Les anthestéries et le vin', *Kernos* 12: 125–52.

Nongbri, B. 2008. 'Dislodging "Embedded" Religion: A Brief Note on a Scholarly Trope', *Numen* 55: 440–60.

North, J. 1992. 'The Development of Religious Pluralism', in J. Lieu, J. North, and T. Rajak (eds.), *The Jews among Pagans and Christians in the Roman Empire*. London, Routledge: 174–93.

Notomi, N. 2010. 'Prodicus in Aristophanes', in S. Giombini and F. Marcacci (eds.), *Il quinto secolo. Studi di filosofia antica in onore di Livio Rossetti*. Perugia, Aguaplano: 655–64.

Nowicka, M. 1990. 'Les portraits votifs peints dans la Grèce antique', *Eos* 78: 133–36.

Nuchelmans, J. 1989. 'A propos de hagios avant l'époque hellénistique', in A. Bastiaensen, A. Hilhorst, and C. H. Kneepens (eds.), *Fructus centesimus. Mélanges offerts à Gerard J. M. Bartelink*. Dordrecht, Kluwer: 239–58.

Oakley, J. H. and Sinos, R. H. 1993. *The Wedding in Ancient Athens*. Madison, WI, University of Wisconsin Press.

Obbink, D. 1994. 'A Quotation of the Derveni Papyrus in Philodemus' *On Piety*', *CErc* 24: 111–35.

Oberhelman, S. M. 2014. 'Anatomical Votive Reliefs as Evidence for Specialization at Healing Sanctuaries in the Ancient Mediterranean World', *Athens Journal of Health* 1: 47–62.

Oesterheld, C. 2008. *Göttliche Botschaften für zweifelnde Menschen. Pragmatik und Orientierungsleistung der Apollon-Orakel von Klaros und Didyma in hellenistisch-römischer Zeit*. Göttingen, Vandenhoeck & Ruprecht.

Oettinger, N. 2008. 'An Indo-European Custom of Sacrifice in Greece and Elsewhere', in A. Lubotsky, J. Schaeken, and J. Wiedenhof (eds.), *Evidence and Counter-Evidence. Essays in Honour of Frederik Kortlandt.* 2 vols, Amsterdam, Rodopi: i.403–14.

—— 2015. 'Apollo: indogermanisch oder nicht-indogermanisch?', *MSS* 69: 123–43.

Ogden, D. (ed.) 2007. *A Companion to Greek Religion.* Oxford, Blackwell.

—— 2008. *Perseus.* Abingdon, Routledge.

—— 2021. *The Werewolf in the Ancient World.* Oxford, Oxford University Press.

Osborne, R. 1994. 'Looking On – Greek Style: Does the Sculptured Girl Speak to Women Too?', in I. Morris (ed.), *Classical Greece. Ancient Histories and Modern Archaeologies.* Cambridge, Cambridge University Press: 81–96.

—— 2000. 'Women and Sacrifice in Classical Greece', in Buxton 2000: 294–313.

—— 2004. 'Hoards, Votives, Offerings: The Archaeology of the Dedicated Object', *World Archaeology* 36: 1–10.

—— 2010a. *Athens and Athenian Democracy.* Cambridge, Cambridge University Press.

—— 2010b. 'Relics and Remains in an Ancient Greek World Full of Anthropomorphic Gods', in A. Walsham (ed.), *Relics and Remains. P&P* suppl. 5: 56–72.

—— 2011. *The History Written on the Classical Greek Body.* Cambridge, Cambridge University Press.

—— and Alcock, S. E. (eds.) 1994. *Placing the Gods. Sanctuaries and Sacred Space in Ancient Greece.* Oxford, Oxford University Press.

Oschema, K. 2015. '"Dass" und "wie": Performanz und performative Qualität als Kategorien historischer Analyse', in K. Oschema, C. Andenna, G. Melville, and J. Peltzer (eds.), *Die Performanz der Mächtigen. Rangordnung und Idoneität in höfischen Gesellschaften des späten Mittelalters.* Ostfildern, Jan Thorbecke: 9–31.

Osek, E. 2018. 'Ritual Imitation during the Thesmophoria at Syracuse: Timaeus of Tauromenium's History of Sicily', in H. L. Reid and J. C. DeLong (eds.), *The Many Faces of Mimesis. Selected Essays from the 2017 Symposium on the Hellenic Heritage of Western Greece.* Sioux City, IA, Parnassos Press: 279–92.

Østby, E. 1993. 'Twenty-Five Years of Research on Greek Sanctuaries: A Bibliography', in N. Marinatos and R. Hägg (eds.), *Greek Sanctuaries. New Approaches.* London, Routledge: 197–227.

Oudemans, T. C. W. and Lardinois, A. 1987. *Tragic Ambiguity. Anthropology, Philosophy and Sophocles' Antigone.* Leiden, Brill.

Padilla, M. (ed.) 1999. *Rites of Passage in Ancient Greece. Bucknell Review* 43.1.

Paliompeis, S. 1996. '*Studien zur Innenausstattung griechischer Tempel: Skulptur und Malerei*'. PhD thesis, University of Mainz.

Pàmias, J. (ed.) 2017. *Apollodoriana. Ancient Myths, New Crossroads*. Berlin and Boston, MA. De Gruyter.

Papakonstantinou, Z. 2014. 'Some Observations on Litigants and Their Supporters in Athenian Judiciary *Defixiones*', in Á. Martínez Fernández, B. Ortega Villaro, H. Velasco López, and H. Zamora Salamanca (eds.), *ÁGALMA. Ofrenda desde la filología clásica a Manuel García Teijeiro*. Valladolid, Ediciones Universidad de Valladolid: 1027–35.

Papasavvas, G. and Fourrier, S. 2012. 'Votives from Cretan and Cypriot Sanctuaries: regional versus island-wide influence', in G. Cadogan, M. Iacovou, K. Kopaka, and J. Whitley (eds.), *Parallel Lives. Ancient Island Societies in Crete and Cyprus*. London, British School at Athens: 289–305.

Papazarkadas, N. 2011. *Sacred and Public Land in Ancient Athens*. Oxford, Oxford University Press.

Pariente, A. 1992. 'Le monument argien des "Sept contra Thèbes"', in M. Piérart (ed.), *Polydipsion Argos. Argos de la fin des palais mycéniens à la constitution del'état classique*. Paris, de Boccard: 195–229.

Parker, R. 1983. *Miasma. Pollution and Purification in Ancient Greek Religion*. Oxford, Clarendon Press.

——— 1986. 'Greek Religion', in J. Boardman, J. Griffin, and O. Murray (eds.), *The Oxford History of the Classical World*. Oxford, Oxford University Press: 254–76.

——— 1988. 'Demeter, Dionysus and the Spartan Pantheon', in Hägg *et al.* 1988: 99–103.

——— 1991. 'The *Hymn of Demeter* and the *Homeric Hymns*', *G&R* 38: 1–17.

——— 1994. 'Athenian Religion Abroad', in R. Osborne and S. Hornblower (eds.), *Ritual, Finance, Politics. Athenian Democratic Accounts Presented to David Lewis*, Oxford, Clarendon Press: 339–46.

——— 1995. 'Early Orphism', in A. Powell (ed.), *The Greek World*. London, Routledge: 483–510.

——— 1996. *Athenian Religion. A History*. Oxford, Clarendon Press.

——— 1997. 'Gods Cruel and Kind: Tragic and Civic Theology', in C. Pelling (ed.), *Greek Tragedy and the Historian*. Oxford, Clarendon Press: 143–60.

——— 1999. 'Apology', *Gnomon* 71 (1999) 383.

——— 2000a. 'Greek States and Greek Oracles', in Buxton 2000: 76–108.

——— 2000b. 'Sacrifice and Battle', in H. van Wees (ed.), *War and Violence in Ancient Greece*. London, Duckworth: 299–314.

———— 2000c. 'Theophoric Names and Greek Religion', in S. Hornblower and E. Matthews (eds.), *Greek Personal Names*. Oxford, Oxford University Press: 53–79.

———— 2004. 'Greek Dedications: Introduction', *ThesCRA* I: 269–80.

———— 2005. *Polytheism and Society at Athens*. Oxford, Oxford University Press.

———— 2011. *On Greek Religion*. Ithaca, NY, and London, Cornell University Press.

———— 2016. 'Seeking Advice from Zeus at Dodona', *G&R* 63: 69–90.

———— 2017a. *Greek Gods Abroad. Names, Natures, and Transformations*. Oakland, CA, University of California Press.

———— 2017b. 'Zeus Plus', in C. Bonnet, N. Belayche, M. Albert Llorca, A. Avdeeff, F. Massa, and I. Slobodzianek (eds.), *Puissances divines à l'épreuve du comparatisme. Constructions, variations et reseaux relationnels*. Turnhout, Brepols: 309–20.

———— 2018a. 'Regionality and Greek Ritual Norms', *Kernos* 31: 73–81.

———— 2018b. 'Religion in the Polis or Polis Religion', *Praktika tes Akademias Athinon*: 20–39.

———— 2020. 'Priapean Problems', in A. Taddei (ed.), *Hierà kai Hosia. Studi per Riccardo do Donato*. Pisa, Edizioni ETS: 143–59.

Partida, E. C. and Schmidt-Dounas, B. (eds.) 2019. *Listening to the Stones. Essays on Architecture and Function in Ancient Greek Sanctuaries*. Oxford, Archaeopress.

Patera, I. 2016. 'Les possessions d'Athéna', *Pallas* 100: 139–54.

———— 2020. 'Identifier Déméter Thesmophoros et son culte en Sicile à partir des données matérielles', in M. De Cesare, N. Sojc, and E. C. Portale (eds.), *The Akragas Dialogue. New Investigations on Sanctuaries in Sicily*. Berlin and Boston, MA, De Gruyter: 27–57.

Pautasso, A. 2020. 'Dedicants, Offerings, and Sacrifice: The Values of the Images', in M. De Cesare, N. Sojc, and E. C. Portale (eds.), *The Akragas Dialogue. New Investigations on Sanctuaries in Sicily*. Berlin and Boston, MA, De Gruyter: 59–78.

Peels, S. 2016. *Hosios. A Semantic Study of Greek Piety*. Leiden and Boston, MA, Brill.

Peirce, S. 1993. 'Death, Revelry, and *Thysia*', *ClAnt* 12: 219–66.

Perrin, B. 1919. *Plutarch. Lives, Volume VII. Demosthenes and Cicero, Alexander and Caesar*. Loeb Classical Library 99. Cambridge, MA, Harvard University Press.

Petridou, G. 2015. *Divine Epiphany in Greek Literature and Culture*. Oxford, Oxford University Press.

———— 2016. 'Speaking Louder with the Eyes: Eye-Shaped Ex-Votos in Context', *Religion in the Roman Empire* 2: 372–90.

Petrovic, A. and Petrovic, I. 2016. *Inner Purity and Pollution in Greek Religion*, vol. 1: *Early Greek Religion*. Oxford, Oxford University Press.

Pfisterer-Haas, S. 2002. 'Mädchen und Frauen am Wasser: Brunnenhaus und Louterion als Orte der Frauengemeinschaft und der möglichen Begegnung mit einem Mann', *JDAI* 117: 1–79.

Piano, V. 2016. *Il papiro di Derveni tra religione e filosofia*. Florence, Leo S. Olschki Editore.

Piccaluga, G. 1974. *Minutal. Saggi di storia delle religioni*. Rome, Edizioni dell'Ateneo.

Piccinini, J. 2017. *The Shrine of Dodona in the Archaic and Classical Ages. A History*. Macerata, Edizioni Università di Macerata.

Piérart, M. 1982. 'Deux notes sur l'itinéraire argien de Pausanias', *BCH* 106: 139–52.

Pilz, O. 2011a. 'Achilleus und Penthesileia auf einem kretischen Tonrelief aus Phanes auf Rhodos', in O. Pilz and M. Vonderstein (eds.), *Keraunia. Beiträge zu Mythos, Kult und Heiligtum in der Antike*. Berlin and Boston, MA, De Gruyter: 195–213.

——— 2011b. 'The Performative Aspect of Greek Ritual: The Case of the Athenian Oschophoria', in M. Haysom and J. Wallensten (eds.), *Current Approaches to Religion in Ancient Greece*. Stockholm, Svenska institutet i Athen: 151–67.

——— 2020. *Kulte und Heiligtümer in Elis und Triphylien. Untersuchungen zur Sakraltopographie der westlichen Peloponnes*. Berlin and Boston, MA, De Gruyter.

Pirenne-Delforge, V. 1994. *L'Aphrodite grecque*. Liège, Presses universitaires de Liège.

——— (ed.) 1998. *Les Panthéons des cités des origines à la 'Périégèse' de Pausanias*. Liège, Presses universitaires de Liège.

——— 2005. 'Prêtres et prêtresses', in *ThesCRA* V: 3–31.

——— 2010. 'Greek Priests and "Cult statues"': How Far Are They Unnecessary?', in Mylonopoulos 2010: 121–41.

——— and Georgoudi, S. 2006. 'Personnel du culte (monde grec)', in *ThesCRA* V: 1–60.

——— and Pironti, G. 2016. *L'Héra de Zeus. Ennemie intime, épouse définitive*. Paris, Les Belles Lettres.

——— and Prescendi, F. (eds.) 2011. *'Nourrir les dieux?' Sacrifice et representation du divin*. Liège, Presses universitaires de Liège.

——— and J. Scheid 2017. 'Vernant, les dieux et les rites: héritages et controverses', in C. Bonnet, N. Belayche, M. Albert Llorca, A. Avdeeff, F. Massa, and I. Slobodzianek (eds.), *Puissances divines à l'épreuve du comparatisme. Constructions, variations et reseaux relationnels*. Turnhout, Brepols: 33–52.

———— and Suárez de la Torre, E. (eds.) 2000. *Héros et héroïnes dans les mythes et les cultes grecs.* Liège, Presses universitaires de Liège.

Pironti, G. 2007. *Entre ciel et guerre. Figures d'Aphrodite en Grèce ancienne.* Liège, Centre international d'étude de la religion grecque antique.

———— and Bonnet, C. (eds.) 2017. *Les dieux d'Homère. Polythéisme et poésie en Grèce ancienne.* Liège, Presses universitaires de Liège.

Planeaux, C. 2000. 'The Date of Bendis' Entry into Attica', *CJ* 96: 165–92.

Platt, V. 2011. *Facing the Gods. Epiphany and Representation in Graeco-Roman Art, Literature and Religion.* Cambridge, Cambridge University Press.

Pleket, H. W. 1981. 'Religious History as the History of Mentality: The "Believer" as Servant of the Deity in the Greek World', *in Versnel 1981: 152–92.*

Polinskaya, I. 2013. *A Local History of Greek Polytheism. Gods, People, and the Land of Aigina, 800–400 BCE.* Leiden, Brill.

Polomé, E. 1987. 'Der indogermanische Wortschatz auf dem Gebiete der Religion', in W. Meid (ed.), *Studien zum indogermanischen Wortschatz.* Innsbruck, Institut für Sprachwissenschaft: 201–17.

Prange, M. 1992. 'Der Raub der Leukippiden auf einer Vase des Achillesmalers', *AK* 35: 3–18.

Prescendi, F. 2010. 'Children and the Transmission of Religious Knowledge', in V. Dasen and T. Spaeth (eds.), *Children, Memory, and Family Identity in Roman Culture.* Oxford, Oxford University Press: 73–93.

Prêtre, C. (ed.) 2009. *Le donateur, l'offrande et la déesse.* Liège, Presses universitaires de Liège.

Pritchett, W. K. 1991. *The Greek State at War, Part 5.* Berkeley, CA, University of California Press.

Pronk, T. 2018. 'Old Church Slavonic *(j)utro,* Vedic *usár:* "daybreak, morning"', in L. van Beek, A. Kloekhorst, G. Kroonen, M. Peyrot, T. Pronk, M. de Vaan, and A. Lubotsky (eds.), *Farnah. Indo-Iranian and Indo-European Studies in Honor of Sasha Lubotsky.* Ann Arbor, MI, and New York, Beech Stave Press: 298–306.

Pugliese Carratelli, G. 1988. (ed.), *Magna Grecia,* vol. 3. Milan, Electa.

Pulleyn, S. 1997. *Prayer in Greek Religion.* Oxford, Oxford University Press.

Purvis, A. 2003. *Singular Dedications. Founders and Innovators of Private Cults in Classical Greece.* London and New York, Routledge.

Race, W. H. (ed. and trans.) 1997. *Pindar. Nemean Odes. Isthmian Odes. Fragments.* Loeb Classical Library 485. Cambridge, MA, Harvard University Press.

Radt, S. (ed.) 1985. *Tragicorum graecorum fragmenta, Volume 3. Aeschylus.* Göttingen: Vandenhoeck & Ruprecht.

Rambach, H. 2011. 'Reflection on Gems Depicting the Contest of Athena and Poseidon', in C. Entwistle and N. Adams (eds.), *'Gems of Heaven'. Recent Research on Engraved Gemstones in Late Antiquity, c. ad 200–600.* London, British Museum: 263–8.

Rask, K. 2016. 'Devotionalism, Material Culture, and the Personal in Greek Religion', *Kernos* 29: 9–40.

Raubitschek, A. 1991. *The School of Hellas. Essays on Greek History, Archaeology, and Literature.* New York, Oxford University Press.

Räuchle, V. 2008. 'Mythische Mörderinnen: Klytaimnestra, Prokne und Eriphyle auf attischen Vasen des 5. Jahrhunderts v. Chr.' Diplomarbeit, Universität Wien, http://othes.univie.ac.at/1975/.

——— 2015. 'The Myth of Mothers as Others', *Cahiers Mondes Anciens* 6, https://doi.org/10.4000/mondesanciens.1422.

Reitzammer, L. 2016. *The Athenian Adonia in Context. The Adonis Festival as Cultural Practice.* Madison, WI, University of Wisconsin Press.

Richardson, N. J. 1983. 'Innovazione poetica e mutamenti religiosi nell'antica Grecia', *SCO* 33: 15–27.

——— (ed.) 1974. *The Homeric Hymn to Demeter.* Oxford, Clarendon Press.

Riedweg, C. 1987. *Mysterienterminologie bei Platon, Philon, und Klemens von Alexandrien.* Berlin and New York, De Gruyter.

——— 1993. *Jüdisch-hellenistische Imitation eines orphischen Hieros Logos. Beobachtungen zu OF 245 und 247 (sog. Testament des Orpheus).* Tübingen, G. Narr.

Riethmüller, J. 2005. *Asklepios. Heiligtümer und Kulte.* 2 vols, Heidelberg, Archäologie und Geschichte.

Robert, J. and Robert, L. 1950. *Hellenica* 9. Paris, Adrien-Maisonneuve.

Robert, L. 1969. *Opera minora selecta*, vol. 2. Amsterdam, Adolf M. Hakkert.

——— 1989. *Opera minora selecta*, vol. 5. Amsterdam, Adolf M. Hakkert.

——— 1990. *Opera minora selecta*, vol. 7. Amsterdam, Adolf M. Hakkert.

Roccos, L. J. 1995. 'The Kanephoros and Her Festival Mantle in Greek Art', *AJA* 99: 641–6.

Roesch, P. 1984. 'L'Amphiaraion d'Oropos', in G. Roux (ed.), *Temples et sanctuaires.* Lyon, GIS–Maison de L'Orient: 173–84.

Romano, A. J. and Marincola, J. (eds.) 2019. *Host or Parasite? Mythographers and Their Contemporaries in the Classical and Hellenistic Periods.* Berlin and Boston, MA, De Gruyter.

Romano, D. G. 2019. 'Mt. Lykaion as the Arcadian Birthplace of Zeus', in Scheer 2019: 219–37.

Rosa, F. 1997. 'À Frazer ce qui est de Frazer', *Archives Européennes de Sociologie* 38: 301–10.

Rosen, R. M. and Sluiter, I. (eds.) 2003. *Andreia. Studies in Manliness and Courage in Classical Antiquity.* Leiden and Boston, MA, Brill.

Rosenbloom, D. 2013. 'Argos/Mycenae in Tragedy', in H. Roisman (ed.), *The Blackwell Encyclopedia of Greek Tragedy.* 3 vols, Oxford, Blackwell: i.27–8.

Rotstein, A. 2012. '*Mousikoi Agones* and the Conceptualization of Genre in Ancient Greece', *ClAnt* 31: 92–127.

Rousset, D. 2013. 'Sacred Property and Public Property in the Greek City', *JHS* 133: 113–33.

Rubarth, S. 2014. 'Competing Constructions of Masculinity in Ancient Greece', *Athens Journal of Humanities & Arts* 1: 21–32.

Rubel, A. 2014. *Fear and Loathing in Ancient Athens. Religion and Politics during the Peloponnesian War.* London, Taylor & Francis.

Rudhardt, J. 1992. *Notions fondamentales de la pensée religieuse et actes constitutifs du culte dans la Grèce classique.* Second edition, Paris, Picard.

Rühfel, H. 1992. 'Ein frühklassisches Knabenköpfchen', in H. Froning, T. Hölscher, and H. Mielsch (eds.), *Kotinos. Festschrift für Erika Simon.* Mainz, P. von Zabern: 175–80.

Rüpke, J. 2011. 'Lived Ancient Religion: Questioning "Cults" and "Polis Religion"', *Mythos* 5: 191–204.

Ruscillo, D. 2013. 'Thesmophoriazousai. Mytilenean Women and Their Secret Rites', in G. Ekroth and J. Wallensten (eds.), *Bones, Behaviour and Belief. The Zooarchaeological Evidence as a Source for Ritual Practice in Ancient Greece and Beyond.* Stockholm, Svenska Institutet i Athen: 181–95.

Rusten, J. S. 1983. '*Geitôn héros*: Pindar's Prayer to Heracles (*N.* 7.86–101) and Greek Popular Religion', *HSCP* 87: 289–97.

Rutherford, I. (ed.) 2001. *Pindar's Paeans. A Reading of the Fragments with a Survey of the Genre.* Oxford, Oxford University Press.

———— 2009. 'Hesiod and the Literary Traditions of the Near East', in F. Montanari, A. Rengakos, and C. Tsagalis (eds.), *Brill's Companion to Hesiod.* Leiden, Brill: 9–35.

———— 2010. 'Canonizing the Pantheon: The Dodekatheon in Greek Religion and Its Origins', in Bremmer and Erskine 2010: 43–54.

———— 2018. 'Kingship in Heaven in Anatolia, Syria and Greece: Patterns of Convergence and Divergence', in Audley-Miller and Dignas 2018: 3–23.

———— 2020. *Hittite Texts and Greek Religion. Contact, Interaction, and Comparison.* Oxford, Oxford University Press.

Saïd, S. 1993. 'Tragic Argos', in A. Sommerstein et al. (eds.), *Tragedy, Comedy and the Polis*. Bari, Lavante Editori: 167–89.

—— 2008. *Approches de la mythologie grecque. Lectures anciennes et modernes*. Second edition, Paris, Les Belles Lettres.

Salapata, G. 2018. 'Tokens of Piety: Inexpensive Dedications as Functional and Symbolic Objects', *Opuscula* 11: 97–109.

Santamaría, M. A. 2013. 'The Term βάκχος and Dionysos Βάκχιος', in Bernabé et al. 2013: 38–57.

—— (ed.) 2019. *The Derveni Papyrus. Unearthing Ancient Mysteries*. Leiden and Boston, MA, Brill.

Sanzo, J. E. 2020. 'Deconstructing the Deconstructionists: A Response to Recent Criticisms of the Rubric "Ancient Magic"', in A. Mastrocinque, J. E. Sanzo, and M. Scapini (eds.), *Ancient Magic. Then and Now*. Stuttgart, Franz Steiner: 25–46.

Sarti, S. 1992. 'Gli strumenti musicali di Apollo', *AION(archeol)* 14: 95–104.

Scarpi, P. 2002. *Le religioni dei misteri*. 2 vols, Milan, Mondadori.

Schachter, A. 1992a. 'Policy, Cult, and the Placing of Greek Sanctuaries', in Schachter 1992b: 1–57.

—— (ed.) 1992b. *Le sanctuaire grec. Entretiens sur l'Antiquité Classique* 37. Geneva, Fondation Hardt.

Scheer, T. S. 1993. *Mythische Vorväter. Zur Bedeutung griechischer Heroenmythen im Selbstverständnis kleinasiatischer Städte*. Munich, Editio Maris.

—— 1996. 'Ein Museum griechischer "Frühgeschichte" im Apollontempel von Sikyon', *Klio* 78: 353–73.

—— 2000. *Die Gottheit und ihr Bild. Untersuchungen zur Funktion griechischer Kultbilder in Religion und Politik*. Munich, C. H. Beck.

—— 2011. *Griechische Geschlechtergeschichte*. Munich, Oldenbourg Wissenschaftsverlag.

—— 2014. 'Heyne und der griechische Mythos', in B. Bäbler and H.-G. Nesselrath (eds.), *Christian Gottlob Heyne. Werk und Leistung nach zweihundert Jahren*. Berlin, De Gruyter: 1–28.

—— (ed.) 2019. *Nature – Myth – Religion in Ancient Greece*. Stuttgart, Franz Steiner.

Scheibler, I. 1987. 'Bild und Gefäss', *JDAI* 102: 57–118.

Scheid, J. (ed.) 1993. *Les bois sacrés*. Naples, Centre Jean Bérard.

Schlatter, E. 2018. *Der Tod auf der Bühne. Jenseitsmächte in der antiken Tragödie*. Berlin and Boston, MA, De Gruyter.

Schlesier, R. 1993. 'Mixtures of Masks; Maenads as Tragic Models' in Carpenter and Faraone 1993: 89–114.

—— (ed.) 2011. *A Different God? Dionysos and Ancient Polytheism*. Berlin and Boston, MA, De Gruyter.

———— and Schwarzmaier, A. (eds.) 2008. *Dionysos. Verwandlung und Ekstase.* Berlin, Staatliche Museen zu Berlin–Stiftung Preussischer Kulturbesitz.

Schmidt, S. 2005. *Rhetorische Bilder auf attischen Vasen. Visuelle Kommunikation im 5. Jahrhundert v. Chr.* Berlin, Reimer.

Scholfield, A. F. (ed. and trans.) 1959. *Aelian. On Animals Books 12–17.* Loeb Classical Library 449. Cambridge, MA: Harvard University Press.

Scholl, A. 2007. 'Hades und Elysion: Bilder des Jenseits in der Grabkunst des klassischen Athens', *JDAI* 122: 51–79.

———— 2018. 'Aigina, Megara, Salamis. Zur Heroisierung des Verstorbenen im frühen attischen Grabrelief der Klassik', *JDAI* 133: 187–239.

Schörner, G. 2015. 'Anatomical ex votos', in R. Raja and J. Rüpke (eds.), *A Companion to the Archaeology of Religion in the Ancient World.* Chichester, Wiley Blackwell: 397–411.

Schröder, J. 2020. *Die Polis als Sieger. Kriegsdenkmäler im archaisch-klassischen Griechenland.* Berlin and Boston, MA, De Gruyter.

Schröder, S. 1999. *Geschichte und Theorie der Gattung Paian. Eine kritische Untersuchung mit einem Ausblick auf Behandlung und Auffassung der lyrischen Gattungen bei den alexandrinischen Philologen.* Stuttgart and Leipzig, Teubner.

Schürr, D. 2014. 'Zur Herkunft des Pegasus', *GLO* 35–36: 113–22.

Schwarz, G. 1997. 'Triptolemos', in *LIMC* VIII.1: 56–68.

Scobie, A. 1979. 'Storytellers, Storytelling, and the Novel in Graeco-Roman Antiquity', *RhM* 122: 239–59.

Scott, M. 2015. *Delphi. A History of the Center of the Ancient World.* Princeton, NJ, and London, Princeton University Press.

Seaford, R. 1993. 'Dionysus as Destroyer of the Household: Homer, Tragedy, and the Polis', in Carpenter and Faraone 1993: 115–46.

———— 2018. *Tragedy, Ritual, and Money in Ancient Greece.* Cambridge, Cambridge University Press.

Seelentag, G. 2015. *Das archaische Kreta. Institutionalisierung im frühen Griechenland.* Berlin and Boston, MA, De Gruyter.

Segal, R. A. 2016. 'Friedrich Max Müller on Religion and Myth', *Publications of the English Goethe Society* 85: 135–44.

Serwint, N. 1993. 'The Female Athletic Costume at the Heraia and Prenuptial Initiation Rites', *AJA* 97: 403–22.

Sfameni Gasparro, G. 1987. 'Critica del sacrificio cruento e antropologia in Grecia. Da Pitagora a Porfirio I: la tradizione pitagorica, Empedocle e l'orfismo', in F. Vattioni (ed.), *Sangue e antropologia nella liturgia.* Rome, Pia Unione Preziosissimo Sangue: 107–55.

Shapiro, H. 1990. 'Old and New Heroes: Narrative, Composition, and Subject in Attic Black-Figure', *ClAnt* 9: 114–48.

—— 1991. 'The Iconography of Mourning in Athenian Art', *AJA* 95: 629–56.

—— 1992. '*Mousikoi Agones*: Music and Poetry at the Panathenaia', in Neils 1992: 53–75.

—— 1993. *Personifications in Greek Art. The Representation of Abstract Concepts, 600–400 B.C.* Zurich, Akanthus.

—— 1994a. 'From Athena's Owl to the Owl of Athens', in R. Rosen and J. Farrell (eds.), *Nomodeiktes. Greek Studies in Honor of Martin Ostwald.* Ann Arbor, MI, University of Michigan Press: 213–24.

—— 1994b. *Myth into Art. Poet and Painter in Classical Greece.* London, Routledge.

Shaya, J. L. 2005. 'The Greek Temple as Museum: The Case of the Legendary Treasure of Athena from Lindos', *AJA* 109: 432–42.

Siebert, G. 1990. 'Hermes', in *LIMC* V.1: 285–387.

Simkin, O. B. 2011. 'Greek Etymology', *CR* n.s. 61: 1–3.

Simon, E. 2009. 'Bellerophon', in *LIMC*, suppl. 1: 127–30.

Sinn, U. 1991. 'Die Stellung der Wettkämpfe im Kult des Zeus Olympios', *Nikephoros* 4: 31–54.

—— 2000. 'Greek Sanctuaries as Places of Refuge', in Buxton 2000: 155–79.

Sissa, G. and Detienne, M. 2000. *The Daily Life of the Greek Gods.* Translated by J. Lloyd. Stanford, CA, Stanford University Press. (First published in French 1989.)

Smarczyk, B. 1990. *Untersuchungen zur Religionspolitik und politischen Propaganda Athens im Delisch-Attischen Seebund,* Munich, Tuduv.

Smith, N. D. 1989. 'Diviners and Divination in Aristophanic Comedy', *ClAnt* 8: 140–58.

Smith, R. S. and Trzaskoma, S. (eds.). Forthcoming. *The Oxford Handbook of Greek and Latin Mythography.* Oxford, Oxford University Press.

Smith, T. J. 2016. 'The Art of Ancient Greek Sacrifice: Spectacle, Gaze and Performance', in C. Murray (ed.), *Diversity of Sacrifice. Form and Function of Sacrificial Practices in the Ancient World and Beyond.* Albany, State University of New York Press: 127–43.

—— 2021. *Religion in the Art of Archaic and Classical Greece.* Philadelphia, PA, University of Pennsylvania Press.

Snodgrass, A. 1989–90. 'The Economics of Dedication at Greek Sanctuaries', *Scienze dell'Antichità* 3–4: 287–94.

Söding, T. 1992. 'Das Wortfeld der Liebe im paganen und biblischen Griechisch', *EThL* 68: 284–330.

Sofroniew, A. 2012. 'Women's Work: The Dedication of Loom Weights', *Pallas* 86: 191–209.

Sonnino, M. 2010. *Euripidis Erecthei quae exstant*. Florence, Felice le Monnier.

Sourvinou-Inwood, C. 1988. *Studies in Girls' Transitions. Aspects of the Arkteia and Age Representation in Attic Iconography*. Athens, Kardamitsa.

———— 1990. 'Sophocles' Antigone as a "Bad Woman"', in F. Dieteren and E. Kloek (eds.), *Writing Women into History*. Amsterdam, Historisch Seminarium van de Universiteit van Amsterdam: 11–38.

———— 1991. *'Reading' Greek Culture. Texts and Images, Rituals and Myths*. Oxford, Oxford University Press.

———— 1993. 'Early Sanctuaries, the Eighth Century and Ritual Space', in N. Marinatos and R. Hägg (eds.), *Greek Sanctuaries. New Approaches*. London, Routledge: 1–17.

———— 1995. *'Reading' Greek Death to the End of the Classical Period*. Oxford, Clarendon Press.

———— 2000. 'What is *Polis* Religion?' and 'Further Aspects of *Polis* Religion', in Buxton 2000: 13–55.

———— 2011. *Athenian Myths & Festivals. Aglauros, Erechtheus, Plynteria, Panathenaia, Dionysia*. Oxford, Oxford University Press.

Speyer, W. 1989. *Frühes Christentum im antiken Strahlungsfeld*. Tübingen, Mohr Siebeck.

Sporn, K. 2002. *Heiligtümer und Kulte Kretas in klassischer und hellenistischer Zeit*. Heidelberg, Verlag Archäologie und Geschichte.

———— 2013a. '"Der göttliche Helikon": Bergkulte oder Kulte auf den Bergen in Griechenland?', in R. Breitwieser, M. Frass, and G. Nightingale (eds.), *Calamus. Festschrift für Herbert Graßl zum 65. Geburtstag*. Wiesbaden, Harrassowitz: 465–75.

———— 2013b. 'Mapping Greek Sacred Caves: Sources, Features, Cults', in F. Mavridis and J. T. Jensen (eds.), *Stable Places and Changing Perceptions. Cave Archaeology in Greece*. Oxford, Archaeopress: 202–16.

———— 2014. 'Individuum und Gott: Privatbildnisse in griechischen Tempeln', in J. Griesbach (ed.), *Polis und Porträt. Standbilder als Medien der öffentlichen Repräsentation im hellenistischen Osten*. Wiesbaden, Reichert: 119–29.

———— 2015. 'Rituale im griechischen Tempel: Überlegungen zur Funktion von Tempelrampen', in D. Panagiotopoulos, I. Kaiser, and O. Kouka (eds.), *Ein Minoer im Exil. Festschrift für Wolf-Dietrich Niemeier*. Bonn, Habelt: 349–74.

Stafford, E. J. 2000. *Worshipping Virtues. Personification and the Divine in Ancient Greece*. London, Duckworth.

Stansbury-O'Donnell, M. 2009. 'The Structural Differentiation of Pursuit Scenes', in D. Yatromanolakis (ed.), *An Archaeology of Representations*.

Ancient Greek Vase-Painting and Contemporary Methodologies. Athens, Institut du Livre: 342–73.

Starobinski, J. 1989. *Le remède dans le mal. Critique et légitimation de l' artifice à l'âge des Lumières*. Paris, Gallimard.

Stausberg, M. et al. 2006. "'Ritual": A Lexicographic Survey of Some Related Terms from an Emic Perspective', in J. Kreinath, J. Snoek, and M. Stausberg (eds.), *Theorizing Rituals. Issues, Topics, Approaches, Concepts*. Leiden, Brill: 51–98.

Steiner, D. T. 2001. *Images in Mind. Statues in Archaic and Classical Greek Literature and Thought*. Princeton, NJ, and Oxford, Princeton University Press.

——— 2013. 'The Priority of Pots: Pandora's *Pithos* Re-Viewed', *Mètis* n.s. 11: 211–38.

Stephenson, B. 2019. 'Ritualization and Ritual Invention', in R. Uro, J. J. Day, R. Roitto, and R. E. DeMaris (eds.), *The Oxford Handbook of Early Christian Ritual*. Oxford, Oxford University Press: 18–54.

Steuernagel, D. 2009. 'Wozu brauchen Griechen Tempel? Fragen und Perspektiven', in H. Cancik and J. Rüpke (eds.), *Die Religion des Imperium Romanum. Koine und Konfrontationen*. Tübingen, Mohr Siebeck: 115–38.

Stewart, Z. 1977. 'La religione', in R. Bianchi Bandinelli (ed.), *Storia e civiltà dei Greci* 8. Milan, Bompiani: 503–616.

Stibbe, C. 1993. 'Das Eleusinion am Fusse des Taygetos in Lakonien', *BABesch* 68: 71–105.

Stocking, G. W., Jr. 1987. *Victorian Anthropology*. New York, Free Press, and Oxford, Maxwell Macmillan.

——— 2001. *Delimiting Anthropology. Occasional Essays and Reflections*. Madison, WI, University of Wisconsin Press.

Strauss, B. 1985. 'Ritual, Social Drama and Politics in Classical Athens', *AJAH* 10: 67–83.

Tanner, J. 2006. *The Invention of Art History. Religion, Society and Artistic Differentiation in Ancient Greece*. Cambridge, Cambridge University Press.

Tantillo, I. 2015. 'Sanctuaires pèripheriquès de Dèmetèr dans la Sicile archaïque', in H. Ménard and R. Plana-Mallart (eds.), *Espaces urbains et pèriurbains dans le monde méditerranéen antique*. Montpellier, Presses universitaires de la Mediterranée: 113–28.

Tassignon, I. 2005. '*Naturalia et curiosa* dans les sanctuaires grecs', in V. Dasen and M. Piérart (eds.), Ἰδίᾳ καὶ δημοσίᾳ. *Les cadres 'privés' et 'publics' de la religion grecque antique*. Liège, Presses universitaires de Liège: 289–303.

Taylor, A. E. (ed. and trans.) 1960. *The Laws of Plato*. London: Dent & Sons.

ThesCRA (*Thesaurus cultus et rituum antiquorum*) 2004–12. 8 vols., Los Angeles, CA, J. Paul Getty Museum.

Thomas, R. 1989. *Oral Tradition and Written Record in Classical Athens*. Cambridge, Cambridge University Press.

Thomassen, E. 2016. 'What Is a "God" Actually? Some Comparative Reflections', in P. Antes, A. W. Geertz, and M. Rothstein (eds.), *Contemporary Views on Comparative Religion*. Sheffield, Equinox Publishing: 365–74.

Thonemann, P. 2020. 'Lysimache and Lysistrata', *JHS* 140: 128–42.

Todd, S. C. 2004. 'Revisiting the Herms and the Mysteries', in D. L. Cairns and R. A. Knox (eds.), *Law, Rhetoric, and Comedy in Classical Athens*. Swansea, Classical Press of Wales: 87–102.

Toillon, V. 2017. 'Danse et gestuelle des ménades: textes et images aux ve–ive s. av. J.-C.', *Théologiques* 25: 55–86.

Topper, K. 2010. 'Maidens, Fillies and the Death of Medusa on a Seventh-Century Pithos', *JHS* 130: 109–19.

Tor, S. 2017. *Mortal and Divine in Early Greek Epistemology. A Study of Hesiod, Xenophanes, and Parmenides*. Cambridge, Cambridge University Press.

Trampedach, K. 2005. 'Hierosylia. Gewalt in Heiligtümern', in G. Fischer and S. Moraw (eds.), *Die andere Seite der Klassik. Gewalt im 5. und 4. Jahrhundert v. Chr.* Stuttgart, Franz Steiner: 143–65.

———— 2015. *Politische Mantik. Die Kommunikation über Götterzeichen und Orakel im klassischen Griechenland*. Heidelberg, Verlag Antike.

Trépanier, S. 2010. 'Early Greek Theology: God as Nature and Natural Gods', in Bremmer and Erskine 2010: 273–317.

Trinkl, E. 2009. 'Sacrificial and Profane Use of Greek Hydriai', in A. Tsingarida (ed.), *Shapes and Uses of Greek Vases (7th–4th Centuries b. c.)*. Brussels, CReA-Patrimoine: 153–71.

Trümpy, C. 1997. *Untersuchungen zu den altgriechischen Monatsnamen und Monatsfolgen*. Heidelberg, C. Winter.

Trzaskoma, S. M. and Smith, R. S. (eds.) 2013. *Writing Myth. Mythography in the Ancient World*. Leuven, Peeters.

Trzcionkowski, L. 2018. 'Hieroi Logoi in 24 Rhapsodies: The Orphic Codex?', in M. Edwards and E. Pachoumi (eds.), *Praying and Contemplating in Late Antiquity. Religious and Philosophical Interactions*. Tübingen, Mohr Siebeck: 181–94.

Tsantsanoglou, K. and Parássoglou, G. M. 1987. 'Two Gold Lamellae from Thessaly', *Hellenika* 38: 3–16.

Tsiafakis, D. 2019. *Corpus Vasorum Antiquorum 10. Athenian Red-Figure Column and Volute-Kraters*. Los Angeles, CA, Getty Publications.

Tsoukala, V. 2009. 'Honorary Shares of Sacrificial Meat in Attic Vase Painting: Visual Signs of Distinction and Civic Identity', *Hesperia* 78: 1–40.

Tuck, A. 2009. 'Stories at the Loom: Patterned Textiles and the Recitation of Myth in Euripides', *Arethusa* 42: 151–9.

Tuplin, C. 1999. Review of Smarczyk 1990, *Gnomon* 71: 420–4.

Vajda, L. 2008. 'Die Adonisgärtchen und das Wunder der Keimung', *Münchner Beiträge zur Völkerkunde* 12: 7–23.

Valdés Guía, M. 2015. 'Antesterias y basileia en Atenas', *Mythos* 9: 125–48.

van den Bosch, L. P. 2002. *Friedrich Max Müller. A Life Devoted to Humanities*. Leiden, Brill.

van den Eijnde, F. 2010–11. 'The Forgotten Sanctuary of Zeus on Mount Parnes', *Talanta* 42–3: 113–28.

van den Toorn, K., Becking, B. and van der Horst, P. W. (eds.) 1999. *Dictionary of Deities and Demons in the Bible*. Second edition, Leiden, Brill.

van der Horst, P. W. 1994. *Hellenism–Judaism–Christianity. Essays on Their Interaction*. Kampen, Kok Pharos.

Van Hove, R. 2019. 'A Dream on Trial: The Contest of Oracular Interpretations and Authorities in Hyperides' In Defence of Euxenippus', *Mnemosyne* 4th ser. 72: 405–36.

Van Nortwick, T. 2008. *Imagining Men. Ideals of Masculinity in Ancient Greek Culture*. Westport, CT, Praeger.

van Rossum-Steenbeek, M. 1997. *Greek Reader's Digests? Studies on a Selection of Subliterary Papyri*. Leiden, Brill.

van Straten, F. T. 1974. 'Did the Greeks Kneel before Their Gods?', *BABesch* 49: 159–89.

——— 1976. 'Daikrates' Dream', *BABesch* 51: 1–38.

——— 1981. 'Gifts for the Gods', in Versnel 1981: 65–151.

——— 1992. Review of Alroth 1989, *Opuscula Atheniensia* 19: 194–5.

——— 1995. *Hierà kalá. Images of Animal Sacrifice in Archaic and Classical Greece*. Leiden, Brill.

——— 2000. 'Votives and Votaries in Greek Sanctuaries', in Buxton 2000: 191–223.

van Wees, H. 1992. *Status Warriors. War, Violence, and Society in Homer and History*. Amsterdam, J. C. Gieben.

Vérilhac, A.-M. and Vial, C. 1998. *Le mariage grec du VIe siècle av. J.-C. à l'époque d'Auguste*. Athens, École française d'Athènes.

Vernant, J.-P. 1974. *Mythe et société en Grèce ancienne*. Paris, Maspero.

——— 1981. 'Théorie générale du sacrifice et de la mise à mort dans la thusia grecque'. In *Le sacrifice dans l'Antiquité*. Entretiens sur l'Antiquité Classique 27. Geneva: Fondation Hardt: 1–39.

———— 1985. *La mort dans les yeux. Figures de l'autre en Grèce ancienne.* Paris, Hachette.

———— 1990. *Figures, idoles, masques.* Paris, Julliard.

———— 1991. *Mortals and Immortals. Collected Essays.* Edited by F. Zeitlin. Princeton, NJ, Princeton University Press.

———— 2007. *Oeuvres. Religions, rationalités, politique.* Paris, Seuil.

Versnel, H. S. (ed.) 1981a. *Faith, Hope, and Worship. Aspects of Religious Mentality in the Ancient World.* Leiden, Brill.

———— 1981b. 'Religious Mentality in Ancient Prayer', in Versnel 1981a: 1–64.

———— 1990. *Ter unus. Isis, Dionysos, Hermes. Three Studies in Henotheism.* Leiden, Brill.

———— 1993. *Transition and Reversal in Myth and Ritual.* Leiden, Brill.

———— 1995. 'Religion and Democracy', in W. Eder (ed.), *Die athenische Demokratie im 4. Jahrhundert v. Chr.* Stuttgart, Franz Steiner: 367–87.

———— 2011. *Coping with the Gods.* Leiden, Brill.

Vicente Sánchez, A. 2015. 'La conducta ἀσεβής, y sus vínculos (θέμις, Ἐρινύς y otros) en la obra de Esquilo', *CFC(G)* 25: 125–55.

Vidal-Naquet, P. 1983. *Le chasseur noir. Formes de pensées et formes de société dans le monde grec.* Second edition, Paris, Maspero.

———— 1992. 'Retour au chasseur noir', in J.-P. Vernant and P. Vidal-Naquet, *La Grèce ancienne,* vol. 3: *Rites de passage et transgressions.* Paris, Seuil: 215–51.

Villagra, N. 2012. 'Commenting on Asclepiades of Tragilos: Methodological Considerations on a Fragmentary Mythographer', in A. Castro Correa et al. (eds.), *Learning from the Past. Methodological Considerations on Studies of Antiquity and Middle Ages.* Oxford, British Archaeological Reports: 286–96.

———— 2018. 'Female Group Violence in Greek Myth: A Case Study on the Lemnian Androctony and the Crime of the Danaids', in M. C. Pimentel and N. Simoes Rodrigues (eds.), *Violence in the Ancient and Medieval Worlds.* Leuven, Peeters: 405–16.

Villanueva Puig, M.-C. 2009. *Ménades. Recherches sur la genèse iconographique du thiase féminin de Dionysos. Des origines à la fin de la période archaïque.* Paris, Les Belles Lettres.

Villing, A. 1998. 'Athena as Erganê and Promachos: The Iconography of Athena in East-Greece', in N. Fisher and H. van Wees (eds.), *Archaic Greece. New Approaches and New Evidence.* London, Duckworth: 147–68.

———— 2017. 'Don't Kill the Goose that Lays the Golden Egg? Some Thoughts on Bird Sacrifices in Ancient Greece', in Hitch and Rutherford 2017: 63–101.

Viscardi, G. P. 2015. *Munichia. La dea, il mare, la polis. Configurazioni di uno spazio artemideo*. Ariccia, Aracne.

———— 2020. 'The Wilderness Experience: Liminality and Cosmogony in Ancient Greece Kingship Narratives', *Historia religionum* 12: 87–112.

Viti, C. 2017. 'Mehrfache Benennungen bei den Indogermanen', in H. Bichlmeier and A. Opfermann (eds.), *Das Menschenbild bei den Indogermanen*. Hamburg, Baar: 151–72.

von Mangoldt, B. 2013. *Griechische Heroenkultstätten in klassischer und hellenistischer Zeit. Untersuchungen zu ihrer äusseren Gestaltung, Ausstattung und Funktion*. Tübingen, Wasmuth.

von Staden, H. 1992a. 'Spiderwoman and the Chaste Tree: The Semantics of Matter', *Configurations* 1: 23–56.

———— 1992b. 'Women and Dirt', *Helios* 19: 7–30.

Waldner, K. 2009. 'Zwischen Kreta und Rom: Ovids Bearbeitung eines aitiologischen Mythos aus Nikanders Heteroiumena (Ant. Lib. 17) in den Metamorphosen (666–797)', in A. Bendlin and J. Rüpke (eds.), *Römische Religion im historischen Wandel. Diskursentwicklung von Plautus bis Ovid*. Stuttgart, Franz Steiner: 171–86.

Walter, H., Clemente, A., and Niemeier, W.-D. (eds.) 2019. *Ursprung und Frühzeit des Heraion von Samos*. Wiesbaden, Reichert.

Wathelet, P. 1988. *Dictionnaire des Troyens de l'Iliade*. 2 vols, Liège, Université de Liège.

———— 1992. 'Arès le mal aimé', *LEC* 60: 113–28.

Watkins, C. 1995. *How to Kill a Dragon. Aspects of Indo-European Poetics*. New York, Oxford University Press.

Watson, P. 1995. *Ancient Stepmothers. Myth, Misogyny and Reality*. Leiden, Brill.

Weber, G. 1992. 'Poesie und Poeten an den Höfen vorhellenistischer Monarchen', *Klio* 74: 25–77.

Weiler, I. 1974. *Der Agon im Mythos. Sur Einstellung der Griechen zum. Wettkampf*. Darmstadt, Wissenschaftliche Buchgesellschaft.

West, M. L. 1983. *The Orphic Poems*. Oxford, Clarendon Press.

———— 1990. *Studies in Aeschylus*. Stuttgart, Teubner.

———— 2007. *Indo-European Poetry and Myth*. Oxford, Oxford University Press.

———— 2011. *Hellenica, Volume 1*. Epic. Oxford, Oxford University Press.

———— 2013. *The Epic Cycle. A Commentary on the Lost Troy Epics*. Oxford, Oxford University Press.

West, S. 2003. 'Kerkidos paramythia? For Whom Did Chariton Write?', *ZPE* 143: 63–9.

Whitmarsh, T. 2015. *Battling the Gods. Atheism in the Ancient World*. New York, Alfred A. Knopf.

Wickkiser, B. L. 2008. *Asklepios, Medicine, and the Politics of Healing in Fifth-Century Greece. Between Craft and Cult.* Baltimore, MD, Johns Hopkins University Press.

Wifstrand Schiebe, M. 2020. *Das anthropomorphe Gottesbild. Berechtigung und Ursprung aus der Sicht antiker Denker.* Stuttgart, Franz Steiner.

Wijma, S. 2014. *Embracing the Immigrant. The Participation of Metics in Athenian Polis Religion (5th–4th Century bc).* Stuttgart, Franz Steiner.

Willi, A. 2009. *Sikelismos. Sprache, Literatur und Gesellschaft im griechischen Sizilien (8.–5. Jh. v. Chr.).* Basel, Schwabe.

Wilson, P. 2018. 'The Theatres and Dionysia of Attica', in A. Kavoulaki (ed.), Πλειών. *Papers in Memory of Christiane Sourvinou-Inwood.* Rethymnon, School of Philosophy, University of Crete: 97–144.

Winiarczyk, M. 2016. *Diagoras of Melos. A Contribution to the History of Ancient Atheism.* Berlin and Boston, MA, De Gruyter.

Winkler, J. 1990. *The Constraints of Desire. The Anthropology of Sex and Gender in Ancient Greece.* London, Routledge.

Woodard, R. (ed.) 2007. *The Cambridge Companion to Greek Mythology.* Cambridge, Cambridge University Press.

Woodford, S. et al.., 1992. 'Meleagros', in *LIMC* VI.1: 414–35.

Wünsche, R. 2008. (ed.), *Starke Frauen.* Munich, Staatliche Antikensammlungen und Glyptothek München.

Yakubovich, I. 2017. Review of Bachvarova 2016, *JNES* 76: 365–8.

Yalouris, N. 1990. 'Io I', in *LIMC* V.1: 665–9.

Yates, D. C. 2019. *States of Memory. The Polis, Panhellenism, and the Persian War.* New York, Oxford University Press.

Yunis, H. 1988. *A New Creed. Fundamental Religious Beliefs in the Athenian Polis and Euripidean Drama.* Göttingen, Vandenhoeck & Ruprecht.

Zeitlin, F. 1990. 'Thebes: Theatre of Self and Society in Athenian Drama', in J. Winkler and F. Zeitlin (eds.), *Nothing to Do with Dionysos? Athenian Drama in Its Social Context.* Princeton, NJ, Princeton University Press: 63–96.

——— 1996. *Playing the Other. Gender and Society in Classical Greek Literature.* Chicago, IL, and London, University of Chicago Press.

Zimmer, S. 2009. '"Sacrifice" in Proto-Indo-European', *JIES* 37: 178–90.

Zimmermann, B. 1992. *Dithyrambos. Geschichte einer Gattung.* Göttingen, Vandenhoeck & Ruprecht.

Zingg, E. 2016. *Die Schöpfung der pseudohistorischen westpeloponnesischen Frühgeschichte.* Munich, C. H. Beck.

Zoumbaki, S. 2019. 'Monetization of Piety and Personalization of Religious Experience: The Role of Thesauroi in the Greek Mainland and the Cyclades', in S. Krmnicek and J. Chameroy (eds.), *Money Matters. Coin Finds and Ancient Coin Use*. Bonn, Habelt: 189–208.

Zucker, A., Fabre-Serris, J., Tilliette, J.-Y., and Besson, G. (eds.) 2016. *Lire les mythes. formes, usages et visées des pratiques mythographiques de l'antiquité à la Renaissance*. Villeneuve d'Asq, Presses universitaires du Septentrion.

Zuntz, G. 1971. *Persephone. Three Essays on Religion and Thought in Magna Graecia*. Oxford, Clarendon Press.

General Index

For authors and works cited, see also the index of passages (p. 178). Works named in this index are discussed in general terms. Page numbers in italic indicate illustrations.

Index of passages

Locations in ancient texts are given in bold, page numbers in this volume in italics.

NEW SURVEYS IN THE CLASSICS

Regular subscribers to the journal *Greece & Rome* receive a volume in the New Surveys in the Classics series as part of their subscription. The following volumes are also available to purchase as books.

Volume 45 *The Sophists* (ISBN 9781108706216)
Volume 44 *Sophocles* (ISBN 9781108706094)
Volume 43 *Early Greek Hexameter Poetry* (ISBN 9781316608883)
Volume 42 *Horace*, (ISBN 9781107444447)
Volume 41 *Homer,* Second Edition (ISBN 9781107670167)
Volume 40 *Greek Art,* Second Edition (ISBN 9781107601505)
Volume 39 *Roman Landscape: Culture and Identity* (ISBN 9781107400245)
Volume 38 *Epigram* (ISBN 9780521145701)
Volume 37 *Comedy* (ISBN 9780521706094)
Volume 36 *Roman Oratory* (ISBN 0521687225)
Volume 35 *The Second Sophistic* (ISBN 0198568819)
Volume 34 *Roman Art* (ISBN 9780198520818)
Volume 33 *Reception Studies* (ISBN 0198528655)
Volume 32 *The Invention of Prose* (ISBN 0198525234)
Volume 31 *Greek Historians* (ISBN 019922501X)
Volume 30 *Roman Religion* (ISBN 0199224331)
Volume 29 *Greek Science* (ISBN 0199223955)
Volume 28 *Virgil* (ISBN 0199223424)
Volume 27 *Latin Historians* (ISBN 0199222932)
Volume 26 *Homer* (ISBN 0199222096)
Volume 25 *Greek Thought* (ISBN 0199220743)

For books purchases please contact customer_service@cambridge.org and orders@cambridge.org. For journal subscriptions outside North America, call +44 (0) 1223 326070, or email journals@cambridge.org. In North America, call customer services at +1 845 348 4550 or email subscriptions_newyork@cambridge.org.

THE CLASSICAL ASSOCIATION

The Classical Association has a worldwide membership and is open to all who value the study of the history, civilisations, languages, art, material culture and legacy of ancient Greece and Rome and the broader ancient Mediterranean. It creates opportunities for friendly exchange and co-operation among classicists, encourages scholarship through its journals and other publications, and supports Classics in schools and universities. Every year it holds an annual conference, and it sponsors branches all over the country which put on programmes of lectures and other activities.

The Classical Association publishes three journals, *Classical Quarterly*, *Classical Review* and *Greece & Rome*. Members may subscribe at substantially reduced cost. Non-members and institutions can subscribe via Cambridge University Press (email journals@cambridge.org).

For more information about membership please see the Classical Association's website: https://classicalassociation.org/ or contact the Secretary, The Classical Association, Cardinal Point, Park Road, Rickmansworth, WD3 1RE, UK, e-mail: office@classicalassociation.org, Tel: +44 (0) 7926 632598. The Secretary can also give information about the reduced journal subscription rates, and about the Association's other occasional publications.

Cover illustration: Sacrificing Nike. Tondo of Attic red-figure cup, Sabouroff Painter, c. 460 bc. © Allard Pierson Museum, Amsterdam.

Greece & Rome is a journal which delivers scholarly research to a wider audience. It showcases original and informative articles on ancient history, literature, art, archaeology, religion, philosophy, and reception of the ancient world. Although its content reflects current research and its contributors include leading figures in the field, undergraduates and general readers who wish to be kept informed of current thinking will also find it engaging and accessible, as well as professional scholars in Classics and in other disciplines. With the wider audience in mind all Greek and Latin quotations are translated.

A subscription to *Greece & Rome* includes an annual supplement of *New Surveys in the Classics*.

For information on subscribing or submitting to the journal, please visit journals.cambridge.org/gar

CPSIA information can be obtained
at www.ICGtesting.com
Printed in the USA
LVHW080438150822
725948LV00004B/80